SCIENCE AND RELIGION

SCIENCE AND RELIGION

A Revised and Expanded Edition of
The Interface of Science and Religion

Rodinmawia Ralte

Christian World Imprints

First Published in 2017
Revised and Expanded Edition Published in January 2022
Reprint in July 2022
Reprint in September 2023 by

Christian World Imprints
Christian Publishing & Books from India
A-71 Group, Wazirpur Industrial Area
Delhi-110052
cwidelhi2017@gmail.com
www.ChristianWorldImprints.com
Phone: +91 11 41526079

ISBN: 978-93-5148-615-2 (HB)
ISBN: 978-93-5148-616-9 (PB)

Printed in India.

Contents

Preface to the Revised and Enlarged Edition

The Interface of Science and Religion: An Introductory Studies was published in 2017. I am happy to know that it was used as one of the primary textbooks for Science and Religion subject by the Bachelor of Divinity students of the Senate of Serampore College (University). The syllabus for Science and Religion was revised, and I was also part of that revision team. We have made substantial changes, and the previous book no longer covers the whole syllabus on Science and Religion. Several people asked me to revise it to cover the BD syllabus on Science and Religion so that it may be more relevant for the students in particular and the other readers in general. I spent nearly a year revising the book thoroughly, where a few new chapters are added, and several new sections are added to some chapters.

I thank my friend Mr Sudhanshu Kanda of the Christian World Imprints, who encouraged me and pushed me to revise the book. Several reminders sent by him to finish the work were really helpful. I also appreciate the Christian World Imprints for their interest in publishing the book. I thank my wife and children for their help and encouragement to go the extra mile in doing the revision. Above all, I thank God for giving me the strength to finish the revision of this book for the benefit of especially the students who are studying Science and Religion at Bachelor of Divinity level.

Date: 21.10.2021

Rodinmawia Ralte
SCEPTRE
74B AJC Bose Road
Kolkata – 700016
West Bengal

Foreword to the first Edition

It is my privilege and joy to write a Foreword to *The Interface of Science and Religion: An Introductory Study*, written by my good friend, the Revd. Dr. Rodinmawia Ralte.

There is much confusion, especially among Christians, about the relation between Science and Religious Faith, with many choosing to keep them in separate compartments. Further, some Christians feel so threatened by scientific discoveries and theories that they close their mind to any reason and become fundamentalists and religious fanatics.

Having gone through the contents of the book, I find it to be a very systematic work and one that can be easily understood by those who do not have a background in the physical sciences. It will certainly be of help to those Christians who, knowing that God is a God of reason, seek to accommodate the best in Scientific knowledge within the framework of their understanding of who God is and what God's purposes in this universe are. It will also be of immense value to students of theology who want to learn more about how Religion and Science have interacted down the centuries. The book also deals comprehensively with the question of the ethical side of how science is applied in everyday life and has a good discussion of the biases that are so often present within the scientific community.

I warmly recommend the book to all who want to learn more about the wonders of God's creation and who try to make sense of the latest scientific discoveries within the framework of belief in the Creator God.

7th April, 2017

The Revd. Dr. Sunil M. Caleb
Principal & Professor of Christian
Theology and Ethics
Bishop's College, Kolkata

Preface to the first Edition

Science and Religion was introduced into B.D. syllabus of the Senate of Serampore College (University) as one of the integrated papers recently. I have heard, from many theological colleges and seminaries under Senate, of the struggles students and teachers are going through due to unavailability of enough sources to study this subject and also lack of competent teachers in this area. This is because most of us who teach in the department of religions and other theological teachers as well, did not do any course on Science and Religion during our secular or theological education. Having been a student of science in my secular education and now being a teacher of religions in general and Science and Religion in particular, I took upon myself the responsibility to provide resource for students and teachers, though in a small and limited way, to study the interface of Science and Religion. This book, therefore, is written with a view to help B.D. students of various theological colleges and seminaries in India and neighbouring countries affiliated to the Senate of Serampore College (University) in particular, and also the general readers who want to study science and religion interface.

I spent a month in the Chinese University of Hong Kong where I did my research on Science and Religion using the University Library and the Library of Chung Chi College. I thank both the Libraries and also the United Board which enabled me to do research in this particular field. I have worked on this book for the past one year and I thank God that it comes out now, though much later than I had anticipated.

I want to express my gratitude to a number of persons who helped me in the publication of this book. I express my heartfelt thanks to Rev. Dr. Sunil M. Caleb, the Principal of Bishop's College for granting me one month leave that enabled me to do research work in Hong Kong. He also took the pain of reading the whole manuscript and gave me useful suggestions for improvement. He was kind enough to write a Forward to this book. I am greatly indebted to him for many things. I also thank Dr. V. J. John, the Professor of New Testament at Bishop's college and NIIPGTS for having read some part of the manuscript and giving me useful suggestions for improvement. I also want to record my sincere thanks to my wife, C. Laltanpuii and our children for their constant support and encouragement throughout the writing of this book. I am grateful to Mr. Sudhanshu Kanda of Christian World Imprints for his interest in the publication of my humble work.

This book is not a critical study on the relationship between Science and Religion as such, but an introduction to the interactions between Science and Religion. I started with the survey of scientific explanations of the universe starting from the Greeks and coming up to Newton, and discussed the conflict with the church, and then moved on to explain some of the important scientific discoveries in the nineteenth and twentieth centuries. I also discussed the various theories, both scientific and religious of the origin of the universe. Introductory explanation is also given to Philosophy and Sociology of science with the highlights of the contributions of some of the philosophers and sociologists of science. The historical survey of the relationship between science and religion was made and some of the prominent models of science-religion relations were discussed. I have also presented a brief explanation of the ethical issues in Genetic Sciences and also the negative impacts of modern scientific developments. The most recent development in the study of science is the Social Studies of Science. I have briefly discussed this with special reference to feminist critique of science and postcolonial studies of science. The book is closed with a discussion on the theological responses to science and religion dialogue where I discussed in brief four theologies – Natural Theology, Theology of Nature, Process Theology and Hefner's Theology of created co-creators.

It is my hope and prayer that the readers of this book will be enlightened with the mysteries of Science and Religion and would pay homage to the author of both – the Almighty God, and realize that Science and Religion are partners rather than enemies. Let's join Albert Einstein in asserting that:

"Science without religion is lame and religion without science is blind."

7th April, 2017

Rodinmawia Ralte
Associate Professor of Religions
and Philosophy
Bishop's College, Kolkata

Chapter 1

Science and Religion Interface A Historical Survey

It has been generally conceived that there are fundamental differences between Science and Religion and between scientific research and theological - philosophical formulation, making it almost impossible to relate the two with any measure of harmony. Conflict is the most appropriate 'word' to explain the relationship between Science and Religion, and so on. The history of science is full of a history of conflict between Science and Religion. Such expressions colonise the mind of the people who are thinking about the relationship between Science and Religion. In this chapter, I will show that these ideas are wrong!

I will briefly discuss the natures of Science, technology and religion, and give a brief historical survey of science and religion interface. Then, I will highlight the ways and means in which Science and Religion relate with one another and the possibility of having dialogical engagement between them.

1. The Nature of Science, Technology and Religion

There has been a wrong and misleading idea concerning the reality of science that has been taught to students from generation to generation – Science is facts, scientific laws are ultimate facts that have been established beyond doubt, science only speaks in terms of facts, and there is no room for falsehood in it. Scientific research is always objective and produces an objective truth. So, science is reliable through and through. These and many more like ideas have been imparted to students worldwide for hundreds of years. However, most of these ideas are wrong and incredibly deceptive. In order to put ourselves in the right position, we need to know about the nature of science, technology and religion. Thus, I try to discuss the nature of Science, Technology and Religion before discussing the interface between Science and Religion in history. I hope this discussion will help us dive deeper into understanding the relationship between Science and Religion.

1.1. The Nature of Science

There are many ways to define science, and many definitions have been put forward before us. It is a branch of knowledge or study dealing with a body of facts or truths systematically arranged and showing the operation of general laws. Science is also defined as a systematic knowledge of the physical or material world gained through observation and experimentation. Still, it may also be defined as "the intellectual and practical activity encompassing the systematic study of the structure and behaviour of the physical and natural world through observation and experiment."[1] It is the intellectual endeavour to know the nature, workings and reality of the physical world through a set of methods called the 'scientific method.'

There are several underlying presuppositions and conditions with which science works. Some of these may be pointed out here – *Firstly*, the primary purpose of science is to acquire knowledge of the physical and natural world. It has more or less no concern for the outcome and implication of that knowledge. *Secondly*, there is an underlying order in the world that science seeks to describe in a maximally comprehensive and straightforward manner. *Thirdly*, there is no one single scientific method which is universally applicable.[2] There is no such thing as 'the Scientific Method.' Scientists in different fields often approach their scientific testing in different ways.[3] Rather than working to a standard research plan, scientists use multiple ways to obtain and organise knowledge, including intuition and chance. Newer texts are adopting the approach of discussing science methods rather than any particular scientific method alone.[4]

The *Fourth* presumption is that the physical world is understandable. Science presumes that the things and events in the universe occur in consistent patterns that are comprehensible through careful and systematic study. Scientists believe that through the use of the intellect with the aid of instruments, people

1 Denny Casey, "The Nature of Science," Virgina Science Standard Institute, 2012, in *https://docplayer.net/14447685-The-nature-of-science-2012-virginia-science-standards-institute-denny-casey-ph-d.html* (17.12.2020).

2 See Juli T. Eflin, Stuart Glennan and George Reisch, "The Nature of Science: A Perspective from the Philosophy of Science" in *Journal of Research in Science Teaching*, (Vol. 36, No. 1, 1999), pp. 108-109.

3 Christine V. McLelland, *The Nature of Science and Scientific Method*, in *https://www.geosociety.org/documents/gsa/geoteachers/NatureScience.pdf* (23.11.2020), p. 7.

4 Peter Eastwell, "The Nature of Science," in *The Science Education Review*, (Vol. 1, No. 2, 2002), p. 46.

can discover patterns in all of nature.[5] This reflects the famous words of Albert Einstein, "The most incomprehensible thing about the world is that it is comprehensible." Scientists believe that with the help of an apt instrument and intellectual analytical and observational skills, people can discover the hidden things in the physical world. *Lastly*, science assumes that the world is real, and it exists apart from our sensory perception of it. Humans can accurately perceive and attempt to understand the physical universe. It also assumes that natural processes are sufficient to explain or account for natural phenomena or events accurately.[6]

A clear understanding of science's nature is essential for all of us in general and science students in particular. The "Standards for Science Teacher Preparation 2003" produced by the National Science Teacher Association, USA acknowledges the value of the knowledge of the nature of science as, "Knowledge of the nature of science can enable individuals to make more informed decisions with respect to scientifically based issues; promote students' in-depth understandings of 'traditional' science subject matter, and help them distinguish science from other ways of knowing." However, the nature of science is so complex that it is more or less impossible to give a simple definition or explanation. It encompasses the whole range of history, philosophy, sociology and the entire development of science. There is no consensus among scientists, philosophers and sociologists of science about the meaning and characteristics of the nature of science. There may be some points where these people agree together. Still, there are several contention areas where scientists and philosophers of science would disagree on science and its varied natures and characters.

Now, let me turn to discuss the nature of science more comprehensively and systematically as follows.

1.1.1. Science Demands Empirical Evidence

Scientific knowledge demands empirical evidence, that is to say, science is derived from and guided by observation or experiment. Logic, imagination, curiosity, and luck contribute to scientific exploration. Again, scientific tests or observations are repeatable. Sometimes such repeated tests may give a different result.[7]

1.1.2. Testable and Falsifiable

Scientific claims are testable and falsifiable. One of the greatest philosophers of science, Karl Popper suggested that only potentially falsifiable ideas are scientific ideas. For example, the notion that fully-formed species were placed on earth by

5 *Exploring the Nature of Science*, The American Association for the Advancement of Science (AAAS), Project 2061, 2010), in *https://www.aaas.org/sites/default/files/reports/p2061-guide-science.pdf* (05.112.2010), p. 5.

6 Christine V. McLelland, *The Nature of Science and Scientific Method*, p. 1.

7 Peter Eastwell, "The Nature of Science", pp. 44-45.

some supernatural force is a religious belief and not part of the scientific paradigm because it cannot be tested or falsified.[8]

1.1.3. Scientific Ideas are Inconstant and Tentative

Science is a process for producing knowledge. The knowledge gained is also variable. No matter how well one theory explains a set of observations, it is possible that another theory may fit just as well or better or may fit a still wider range of observations.[9] Again scientific explanations are limited. Scientific knowledge is necessarily contingent knowledge rather than absolute, and therefore must be evaluated and assessed and is subject to modification in the light of new evidence.[10] These imply that science is not always speaking in terms of truth.

Scientific knowledge is tentative and developmental and hence fallible. There are different degrees of tentativeness associated with different types of scientific knowledge. While we are sure about certain things, such as Boyle's law, that copper is a good conductor of electricity, and that the earth is round rather than flat, we are far less certain about the exact time of the origins of human beings, the reason for the mass extinction of the dinosaurs, etc. So, science provides the truth that can hardly be falsified in some areas, but scientific knowledge is tentative in other areas.[11]

1.1.4. Durability of Scientific Knowledge

Although scientific knowledge cannot be considered absolute and unchangeable, most scientific knowledge is durable. There may be some changes and modifications, but there are always specific scientific knowledge that is lasting. Rather than outright rejection, the modification of ideas is the norm in science, as powerful constructs tend to survive and grow more precise and become widely accepted. Though there is a general notion that Einstein's theory of relativity replaced Newton's laws of motion, in reality, Einstein never totally discarded Newtonian mechanics, "but rather showed them to be only an approximation of limited application within a more general concept."[12] However, we know that there were many scientific knowledge held as truth for hundreds of years but were falsified and replaced by new knowledge. For instance, the geocentric idea of the universe, where the earth was considered as static and at the centre of the solar system where the sun and other planets revolve around it, was replaced by the heliocentric cosmology – it is the sun which is at the centre and all planets, including our earth, are revolving around it.

---

8 *Ibid.*, p. 44.

9 *Exploring the Nature of Science*, The American Association for the Advancement of Science (AAAS), Project 2061, 2010) p. 5.

10 Christine V. McLelland, *The Nature of Science and Scientific Method*, p. 1.

11 Peter Eastwell, "The Nature of Science," p. 44.

12 *Exploring the Nature of Science*, p. 5.

1.1.5. Limitations of Science

Science is a human product and endeavour, which is based on observation, experimentation, etc. As imperfect human beings are doing science, science and scientific theories and laws cannot be perfect through and through. It implies that all the 'scientific truths' should not be taken as absolute truth. Science is limited. "Science cannot be used, by definition, to study events or phenomena that cannot be perceived by natural or empirical senses and do not follow any natural rules or regularities."[13] There are many matters that cannot be examined scientifically. There are many things in the universe that scientists are trying to explain but in vain. Realities like supernatural power, miracles and other such phenomena, the causes and remedies of numbers of diseases, the question of good and evil, the mystery of life, etc., cannot be explained scientifically. Peter Eastwell rightly states that although science cannot answer moral, ethical, aesthetic, social, and metaphysical questions, it may only provide some useful insights. For example, it is inappropriate to ask science an ethical question to determine whether or not abortion is acceptable.[14] Therefore, we should honestly accept that though science provides answers to many things, it cannot provide a complete answer to all questions.

1.1.6. Self Correcting

Science is self-correcting. If any scientific theory is found to be wrong after repeated testing, science itself makes corrections by providing alternative theory.

1.1.7. Science as a Social Activity

Over against the claim that science and scientific research are purely objective devoid of any outside influence, philosophers and sociologists of science had established beyond doubt that science, like any other discipline, is socially constructed, and scientific research is not purely objective but a fair amount of subjectivity is always involved in any scientific research. Peter Eastwell maintains that Science is a social activity, influencing society and being influenced by people's values and opinions. Personalities, funding, social movements, public opinion, the media, politicians, and others drive science.[15] The social condition of a scientist, the belief system – whether he or she believes in God or not, the scientific theories he or she inherited and his or her mental disposition – all are actively involved in his or her research. As many factors condition a scientific investigation, it may not always be reliable as Christine V. McLelland puts it:

---

13 Christine V. McLelland, *The Nature of Science and Scientific Method*, p. 7.

14 Peter Eastwell, "The Nature of Science," in *The Science Education Review*, (Vol. 1, No. 2, 2002), p. 45.

15 *Ibid.*

"By the nature of human mental processing, rooted in previous experiences, our perceptions may be inaccurate or biased."[16]

1.1.8. Probabilistic Nature of Scientific Explanations

Scientific explanations are not always final. "A scientific theory is a well-substantiated explanation for a set of natural phenomena that has been tested and verified but is still subject to falsification. Theories are supported, modified, or replaced as new evidence appears and are central to scientific thinking," notes Christine V. McLelland.[17] The *National Science Education Standards*, a body responsible for giving guidelines for science education in primary and secondary school in the USA, states as follows for the *Nature of Science*:

> Scientists formulate and test their explanations of nature using observation, experiments, and theoretical and mathematical models. Although, all scientific ideas are tentative and subject to change and improvement in principle, for most major ideas in science, there is much experimental and observational confirmation. Those ideas are not likely to change greatly in the future. Scientists do and have changed their ideas about nature when they encounter new experimental evidence that does not match their existing explanations (NSES, 1996, p. 171).[18]

1.1.9. Non-dogmatic Nature of Science

One of the essential natures of science is that science is non-dogmatic. "Science never requires ideas to be accepted on belief or faith alone," notes McLelland.[19] Science is built upon the non-dogmatic principle, it is open to new ideas, and scientific theories and laws are always subject to scrutiny, debate, rejection and acceptance depending on the evidence. People accept scientific laws and theories only after they are convinced by shreds of evidence, logical argument and mathematical proof. The new development we see today - making science almost as a religion, the so-called Scientology is against the very nature of science.

1.1.10. Science is Not a Moral Judge

Science cannot give moral judgments. For example, science provides skill and knowledge to clone a sheep, but whether cloning is morally right or wrong cannot be judged. McLelland observes, "Science does not prove nor disprove religious or spiritual beliefs, nor does it replace either. Science provides a method of understanding the natural world only."[20]

16 Christine V. McLelland, *The Nature of Science and Scientific Method*, p. 1.

17 *Ibid.*, p. 7.

18 Quoted in *Ibid.*, p. 1.

19 *Ibid.*, p. 7.

20 Christine V. McLelland, *The Nature of Science and Scientific Method*, p. 7.

1.2. Nature of Technology

The word 'technology' is derived from two Greek words – *techne* and *logos* where the term '*techne*' refers to the use of a tool, or the implementation of a craft or skill, and '*logos*' refers to a word or conversation about a particular topic, or the concept of reason or logic. Dictionaries define technology as the application of scientific knowledge for practical purposes, especially in industry. It is also defined as the branch of knowledge dealing with engineering or applied sciences. Technology may also be defined as the application of scientific knowledge to the practical aims of human life to the change and manipulation of the human environment. Thus, "Technology is a combination of a kind of knowing and a kind of making, and technology happens at the crossroads of tool use and human communication."[21]

Brian Arthur, in his book – *The Nature of Technology: What It Is and How It Evolves,* brings forth three definitions of technology: The *first* and the most basic, according to him, is that technology is a means to fulfil a human purpose. As a means, technology may be a method or process or device, such as a particular speech recognition algorithm, a filtration process in chemical engineering, or a diesel engine. Technology may be as simple as a roller bearing or as complicated as a wavelength division multiplexer. Technology may be material, such as an electrical generator, or it may be nonmaterial, like, a digital compression algorithm. Whichever it is, it is always a means to carry out a human purpose.[22]

The *second* definition, which Arthur proposes, explains technology as an assemblage of practices and components. This includes technologies like electronics or biotechnology that are collections or toolboxes of individual technologies and practices. The *third* definition renders technology as the entire collection of devices and engineering practices available to a culture. For instance, we have Oxford's collection of mechanical arts. Arthur says, "We use this collective meaning when we blame 'technology' for speeding up our lives, or talk of 'technology' as hope for mankind. Sometimes this meaning shades off into technology as a collective activity as in 'technology is what Silicon Valley is all about.'"[23]

The American Association for the Advancement of Science brings out a significant book for science students entitled: *Science for all Americans* in 1990. Chapter 3 of this book talks about the Nature of Technology. Explaining the range of technology, the author stresses the relationship of technology with human existence. It maintains:

> On the whole, technology has been a powerful force in the development of civilisation, all the more so as its link with science has been forged.

---

21 Maxwell Kennel, "Technology in the Life of Faith: A Call for Critical Engagement," in *Vision* (Fall 2015), p. 6.

22 W. Brian Arthur, *The Nature of Technology: What It Is and How It Evolves*, (London: Allen Lane, an Imprint of Penguin Books, 2009), p. 11.

23 *Ibid.*,

> Technology - like language, ritual, values, commerce, and the arts - is an intrinsic part of a cultural system and it both shapes and reflects the system's values. In today's world, technology is a complex social enterprise that includes not only research, design, and crafts but also finance, manufacturing, management, labour, marketing, and maintenance.[24]

The author continues to explore the use of technology, saying that technology extends our abilities to change the world: to cut, shape, or put together materials; to move things from one place to another; to reach farther with our hands, voices, and senses. We use technology to try to change the world to suit us better to provide us with survival needs such as food, shelter, or defence, or they may relate to human aspirations such as knowledge, art, or control.[25]

Science for all Americans highlights the nature of technology as follows:

1.2.1. The Inter-dependence of Science and Technology

Science provides essential knowledge and guidance for technology to develop. Science often suggests new kinds of behaviour that had not been imagined before, leading to new technologies. On its part, technology provides the tools and instruments for science. For example, an electronic computer has led to substantial progress in the study of weather systems, demographic patterns, gene structure, and other complex systems that would not have been possible otherwise. Again, technology is essential to science for measurement, data collection, treatment of samples, computation, transportation to research sites, sample collection, protection from hazardous materials, and communication. New instruments and techniques are being developed through technology that makes it possible to advance various lines of scientific research.[26]

1.2.2. The Side Effects of Technology

We all know that technology is vital for our lives, and we cannot imagine life without it. However, as useful as it might be, technology is not without drawbacks. A simple example can be given – sitting in front of a computer may strain the users' eyes, causing problems. Bigger and more complicated technologies, such as nuclear reactors, could cause great disaster, technology for a green revolution in agriculture had an adverse effect on the soil, etc. The cooling system used in refrigerators may have a substantial adverse impact on the earth's atmosphere.[27]

---

24 *Science for All Americans: Project 2061*, American Association for the Advancement of Science, (New York: Oxford University Press, 1990), p. 25.

25 *Ibid.*

26 *Ibid.*, p. 26.

27 *Ibid.*, pp. 30-31.

For example, hydroelectricity production is another example where technology becomes tremendously useful for human beings, but it adversely impacts humans, animals, and the environment.

1.2.3. Control of Technology

Technology does not work by itself; it needs human effort to make it work properly. All technologies, from the simplest to the most complex, require control to keep them operating correctly. This means that all technological systems include human as well as mechanical or electronic components. Even the most automatic system requires human control at some point, such as to programme the built-in control elements, monitor them, take over from them when they malfunction and change them when the purposes of the system change.[28]

1.2.4. Limitation of Technology

We all know the importance and usefulness of technology; we practically depend on various technological systems in our everyday lives. These technical systems we use are mostly reliable and function accurately. But, technology has its limitation in the sense that it is not a perfect entity. We have experienced the failure of technological systems several times in which we depend, though such failures are rare. A system or device may fail for different reasons: some part fails, some part is not well matched to some other, or because the design of the system is not adequate for all the conditions under which it is used.[29]

1.2.5. Relationship between Technology and Social System

There is a strong relationship between technology and the social system. We may say that social and economic forces strongly influence what technologies will be undertaken, paid attention to, invested in, and used. These decisions directly control government policy and also depend on the values of a society at any particular time. Again, technology has strongly influenced the course of history and the nature of human society, and it continues to do so. For instance, the great revolutions in agricultural technology have probably had more influence on how people live than political revolutions; changes in sanitation and preventive medicine have contributed to the population explosion; likewise, the weapon technology in a particular context determines the scale of war. Thus, technology is largely responsible for such large-scale changes as the increased urbanisation of society and the dramatically growing economic interdependence of communities worldwide. It is safe to conclude that technological change causes social change and social change leads to technological change.[30]

---

28 *Ibid.*, pp. 29-30.

29 *Ibid.*, p. 31.

30 *Ibid.*, p. 34.

1.3. Nature of Religion

Religion is a complex and multi-faceted phenomenon that cannot be explained in one way. During the past 200 years, a variety of definitions of religion have come down to us, along with diverse explanations of what religion really is. A brief discussion may help us grasp the nature of religion though we may confess that religion cannot be fully explained and understood.

1.3.1. Defining Religion

A number of scholars have put forward several definitions of religion from different fields, and some of these may be reproduced here. For Max Muller, the famous philologist and Orientalist, religion is a mental faculty or deposition that enables humans to apprehend the Infinite under different names and varying guises. Emil Durkheim, a French sociologist, defines religion as a unified system of beliefs and practices relative to sacred things - that is to say, things set apart and forbidden - beliefs and practices which unite into one single moral community all those who adhere to them. According to E. B. Tylor, an English anthropologist, the founder of cultural anthropology, religion is a belief in a supernatural being. Immanuel Kant, a German philosopher and one of the most celebrated Enlightenment thinkers, defines religion as the recognition of all duties as divine commands. For William James, a noted Philosopher and Psychologist, religion means the feeling, acts and experience of individual humans in their solitude so far as they apprehend themselves, to stand in relation to whatever they may consider the divine.

Another definition of religion seems to be the most encompassing of all, advanced by Eric Lott, a professor of religion. He defines religion as "the way humans experience and relate to some sacred Focus (or foci). It is an experience transmitted with sacred symbols, places, times, people, and sometimes scripture; it is expressed in rituals, myths, doctrines, and ethical-cultural values; by participating in this constantly adapting tradition, perceived human limitations and threats to existence are experienced as overcome or transcended."[31]

From Lott's definition, there are three important things to note: (a) *A sacred focus* is central to any religion but may be different in different religions. For instance, in Islam, the sacred focus is Allah. In Theravada Buddhism, which is basically atheistic religion, it is Nirvana. In Advaita Vedanta, the sacred focus is Brahman and so on. It is our focus towards which all our worships and rituals are addressed. (b) *Human limitations* – Human existence is always perceived as limited or even threatened by various problems like sin, karmic bondage, attacked by spirits, the demonic powers of darkness, sickness, death, etc. For most Indian religions, karmic bondage is the problem that limits and threatens humanity. For Christian, sin is their main problem. But for the Tribal community, demonic

31 Eric J. Lott, "Approching a Religious Tradition," in *Religious Traditions of India*, edited by P. S. Daniel, David C. Scott and G. R. Singh, (Delhi: ISPCK, 2002), p. 2.

powers, malevolent spirits are limiting and threatening their life. Doing away with these problems or limitations is the primary goal of religion. (c) *Adaptation* – Religion is a dynamic entity. It is continually adapting to the changes in human history. It drops some practices and develops new practices, plays down some beliefs and draws on the beliefs of surrounding cultures to meet the challenges in its changing environment.[32]

As we observed above, the general understanding of religion, including those advanced by the classical religionists and the contemporary Western scholars in religion, is deeply flawed due to what I may call 'anthropological bias.' For the classical psychologists, sociologists and anthropologists of religion and philosophers, religion is through and through humans – created by humans, for human's needs and of human's socio-psychological experiences. The contemporary Western scholars in religion define religion inadequately as 'human response to…', assuming religion as a purely humans' activity. But religion is more than that.

Religion is the combination of humans' activities - physical, mental and spiritual, and divine intervention. Even atheistic religions, such as Theravada Buddhism and Jainism, acknowledge something 'beyond human.' For example, *Nirvana*, the religious end of the Buddhist spiritual journey, is 'beyond human', and it is deeply involved in the religiosity and spirituality of the Buddhists as a driving force of their religious activities. Therefore, religion is a combination of humans' activities and divine or 'supra-human' works. In other words, religion is the interplay between humans and supra-human or divine, having both humanness and supra-human elements. Outwards visible and measurable aspects of religion or what W. C. Smith called 'cumulative traditions' are the humanness of religion. In contrast, the inner invisible and immeasurable aspect of religion, the spiritual reality, is the supra-humanness of religion. These two aspects of religion should always be considered when we talk about the Science and Religion interface.

1.3.2. Dimensions of Religion

In order to understand the nature of religion, we need to understand what Ninan Smart (1927-2001), a well-known professor of religion, called 'dimensions of religion.'[33] According to Smart, there are six dimensions of Religion: *Ritual* – there is no religion without ritual. The very fact that we built churches or temples shows that religion has a ritual dimension as these are used for ritual practices like worship, prayers, offering and the like. Smart says that even the simplest form of religious service involves rituals like closing eyes during prayer. Ritual has both an inner and an outer aspect. Although the outer tend to dominate the inner,

32 *Ibid.*, pp. 2-4.

33 See Ninian Smart, *The Religious Experience of Mankind*, Second Edition, (New York: Charles Scribner's Sons, 1973), pp. 3-23.

it does not mean that religion is too ritualistic and degenerated. Ritual plays an important part in all religions.

The second dimension of religion is a *mythological dimension,* but the term 'myth' should not be understood as 'false.' In relation to the study of religion, 'myth' should be understood as a created story with a purpose to convey the truth. So, myths are essential as they enshrine the truth. While the mythical story itself is not important, the truth it attempts to convey is important. The third dimension is the *Doctrinal dimension* which, according to Smart, is an attempt to give system, clarity, and intellectual power to what is revealed through the mythological and symbolic language of religious faith and ritual. There is another dimension called the *Ethical dimension.* Smart maintains that throughout history, we find that religions usually incorporate a code of ethics. Ethics concern the individual's behaviour and, to some extent, the principle of ethics of the dominant religion controls the community. Religions have been influential in moulding the ethical attitudes of the societies they are part of it.

The fifth dimension of religion, according to Ninan Smart, is the *Social dimension.* Religions are not just systems of belief: they are also organisations or parts of organisations. They have communal and social significance. This social shape of religion is, of course, to some extent, determined by the religious and ethical ideas and practices that it harbours. In turn, people's social lives profoundly influenced religion, and that is why several sociologists of religion consider religion a socially conditioned phenomenon. Religious worldviews of each religion are created by the community concerned. What we believe is also primarily determined by the structure that already existed in society.[34] Or, in other words, our ideas, according to Emil Durkheim, a well-known sociologist of religion, of the sacred originate from the community itself; they are nothing but symbols of society.[35] So, the sociological approach focuses "on the interaction between religion and society" where religion is understood as "one form of social construction."[36]

The last one is the *Experiential dimension* – Smart opines that those dimensions mentioned before would be hard to account for were it not for the last dimension, experience. For Smart experiential dimension is the most important one among all those dimensions. This nature of religion reveals that religion cannot be measured and marked out from the visible aspect alone because there is an inner personal experience that cannot be measured empirically. This is where religion differs from science.

---

34 Eric J. Lott, "Approching a Religious Tradition," pp. 16-17.

35 K. P. Aleaz, *Dimensions of Indian Religion: Study, Experience and Interaction*, (Calcutta: Punthi Pustak, 1995), p. 20.

36 Michael S. Northcott, "Sociological Approaches" in *Approaches to the Study of Religion*, Edited by Peter Connolly, (New York: Continuum, 2001), p. 193.

The discussion on religion provided above shows the complexities and intricacies of religion and its encompassing nature. Religion is not to be understood as something which deals with the spiritual life of an individual only; it is rather wholistic, touching all aspects of human existence, including the social, economic and political life of a person. In that sense, religion even touches what many of us would consider as the arena of science. Therefore, it is not practical to completely separate religion from science.

2. Historical Survey of Science and Religion Interaction

What we know now as 'modern science' was born in the middle of the sixteenth century with the works of Copernicus, Kepler, Galileo, and of course, Newton, etc. The word 'science' was used only since the eighteenth century when it replaced the term 'natural philosophy.' We may say that there was no antagonism between Science and Religion till the middle of the sixteenth century. There could be no clear cut distinction between science, philosophy and religion as scientists were also philosophers, theologians and clergy. Till the sixteenth century, in the Western world, science was under the control of the Church. The Church dictated what to write, read and believe, and under such conditions, there could be no visible conflict between Science and Religion.

With the publication of Copernicus' *De Revolutionibus* in 1543, the atmosphere was set to turn in a new direction. The general notion prevalent among the masses in the Western world - that God acts in history and in nature, that God is the creator of the world, that God's providence sustains life and guides destiny which were the foundations for the understanding of the world and beyond – were all in question with the rise of modern science and its interpretation by the Enlightenment philosophies of reductionism, materialism and naturalism. With Copernicus, our universe was inverted, the earth no longer at the centre. With Newton, this living universe became an unthinking machine whose entirely predictable, deterministic, clock-work regularity seemed to leave no room for us to act, let alone for God. The 'age of reason' began to question the authority of revelation and the Church as a surer guide to knowledge and behaviour. By the nineteenth century, the age of the earth had been multiplied from mere thousands of years to countless millions of years. The intricacies of organic life, which had once seemed the product of a loving God, were being explained by Darwin as the product of natural selection and 'blind chance.'[37] It appears that the stage had been set for science-religion warfare.

However, amid such a critical situation where religion was challenged and cornered by the upsurge of several enlightenment thinkers, atheists and agnostics alike who use science and scientific 'discoveries' as their weapon, astonishing new discoveries in the natural sciences and equally impressive changes in

37 CTNS Team, "Bridging the Gap between Science and Religion - The Center for Theology and the Natural Sciences," *Revista Portuguesa de Filosofia*, (T. 57, Fasc. 3, Jul. - Sep., 2001), p. 603.

Western philosophy re-opened the grounds for dialogue between Science and Religion. Relativity theory, quantum mechanics, Big Bang cosmology, chaos and complexity, human genetic engineering, etc. are challenging, even tearing down, the rigid and simplistic Enlightenment assumption that the world is a closed network of cause and effect, an autonomous machine made entirely of tiny bits of matter in motion. In its place, the visions of nature suggested by the discoveries of Einstein, Heisenberg, Hubble, Hawking, etc., point in concert to nature more open, subtle, numinous, interconnected than we have known for centuries.[38] Moreover, in and through the work of philosophers of science, such as Popper, Kuhn, Polanyi, Holton, Feyerabend, Lakatos, etc., we know that scientific knowledge, scientific theories and discoveries are also subject to their socio-cultural and religious context. These scientist-philosophers help us witness the fading out of the negative distinction between Science and Religion - that science is objective, universal, rational, and based on concrete observational evidence, whereas religion is subjective, parochial, emotional, and based on faith. This discovery opens wide a door for science-religion dialogue.

2.1. Harmony Under the Rule of Religion

The controversy between Science and Religion was of recent origin. During ancient, medieval and some centuries of the modern periods, there was more or less no conflict between them. Right from the time of the Greeks, not only in Europe but also in Asia among the Muslims, Buddhists and Hindus, science was always under the control of religion. This was mainly because scientific learning was not an independent discipline but part of religious undertakings. In the middle ages, Christians in Europe were under the influence of the Two Book theory – the book of nature (Science) reveals God as creator and sustainers of the universe, the book of Scripture (Religion) reveals God as the redeemer. Science and religion enjoyed perfect harmony because scientists and theologians were normally the same people. Both Muslims, who were deeply influenced by medieval Islamic theologians and philosophers, such as al-Kindi (after 870 AD), al-Farabi (875-950 AD), Abū 'Ali ibn-Sinā ((980-1037 AD), better known as Avicenna, Al-Ghazali (1058-1111) and ibn-Rushd known as Averroes (1126–1198) who worked under the influence of Aristotle and other Greek philosophers, and the whole of Western Christians simply adhered to Aristotle-Ptolemy's geocentric cosmology. Harmony prevailed as science was under the control of religion, where till the sixteenth century, most scientists in Europe were theologians and church leaders.

2.2. The Conflict Thesis

After the scientific revolution in the middle of the sixteenth century, the history of science and religion has been marked with conflicts and disagreements, basically due to some atheists who used science to fight against religions; and also because

38 *Ibid.*, p. 604.

of some scientific discoveries that actually went against the traditional belief of the Church. The cases of Galileo and Darwin were the most prominent among these conflicts. Discord between Science and Religion was brought about not only by the new scientific theories, which were inconsistent with the then Church's position, but also by the emergence of philosophical movements like Positivism of Auguste Comte (1798-1857), and Scientism. These philosophical schools proclaimed science as the only source of valid knowledge, scientific knowledge as almost flawless as it is based on observational data and well-performed experimentation. So, it is claimed that scientific laws were definite, determinate and reliable. Job Kohzhamthadam, a prominent Indian philosopher of science, notes, "Hence there was no room for doubt and no reason to call its reliability into question. Science was strictly governed by the canons of rationality, and no irrationality element had any place in it. Its knowledge was characterised by objectivity and hence was independent of person, place or time."[39] On the other hand, religion was considered irrational, unreliable, subjective and stood on the shaky ground of faith. There could be no proper dialogue and no mutual understanding between Science and Religion in such a situation.

Some books that came out in the nineteenth century emphasised the conflict between Science and Religion. Three books are noteworthy – William Draper's *History of the Conflict between Religion and Science*, published in 1874, and *Welfare of Science*, published in 1876, and *A History of the Warfare of Science with Theology in Christendom* that came out in 1896, both of which were written by Andrew Dickson White. He suggested that Giordano Bruno was burned alive by the Church authority, Galileo was subjected to indignity, imprisonment, and threats equivalent to torture. On the other hand, the Church gave promotion to the Dominican Father Caccini, who insisted that geometry is of the devil and mathematicians should be banished as the author of all heresies.[40] But, these claims made by White are considered as myths without real historical evidential proof.[41] According to White, the conflict is not science and religion conflict as such, but the expansive force of human intellect in conflict with the mistaken conception of rigid Scriptural interpretation. White views that "whenever such religion sought to constrain Science, Science eventually won but with harm to both Religion and Science in the process. Science and 'true religion', however, were not at odds."[42]

---

39 Job Kohzhamthadam, "Science and Religion; Contenders or Collaborators?" in *Vidyajoyti Journal of Theological Reflection*, (Vol. 52, No. 8, August, 1988), p. 366.

40 Andrew Dickson White, *A History of the Warfare of Science with Theology in Christendom Vol. I.* (New York: Cambridge University Press, This edition first published 1896; digitally printed version 2009), pp. 15, 133,142.

41 See Ronald L. Numbers (ed.), *Galileo Goes to Jail and Other Myths about Science and Religion* (Cambridge: Harvard University Press, 2009).

42 David B. Wilson, "The Historiography of Science and Religion," in Cary B. Ferngren (ed), *Science and Religion: A Historical Introduction*, (Baltimore: The Johns Hopkins University Press, 2002), p. 16.

There were stern opposition to the above works then and now. Let me cite one such resistance to the book - *History of the Conflict between Religion and Science* by William Draper. The American theologian and writer Orestes Brownson described the book as "a tissue of lies from beginning to end" and went to the extent of saying, "A thousand highway- robberies or a thousand cold-blooded murders would be but a light social offence in comparison with the publication of one such book as this before us."[43] White's works also received the same kind of opposition. Still, these books encouraged many people to oppose the possibility of science and religion dialogue.

Colin Russell gave four issues that account for the conflict.[44] The *first* issue was in the area of epistemology – Could what we know about the world through science be integrated with what we learn about it from religion? If not, conflict seems to be unavoidable. Copernicus-Galileo's conflict with the Roman Catholic Church was of this type. The *second* area of contention has been in the methodology vividly depicted in the age-old polarisation between science understood as based on facts and theology understood as based on faith. The *third* potential for conflict has been in the field of ethics. This type of conflict is of recent origin – ethical questions about genetic engineering, nuclear power, and the proliferation of insecticides confront today's scientific and theological communities. The *last* issue is social power, where the conflict was more of a fight to improve the position of science and make it occupy the central position in people's lives.

2.2.1. Atheists' Use of Science against Faith

Since the middle of the sixteenth century C.E., atheists used science and scientific discoveries as a weapon to attack religions and religious teachings, creating the impression in the minds of many people that Science and Religion are incompatible. Atheists projected science as a 'counterproof' against religion where scientific knowledge is used to show that religious claims are wrong. "Focusing on the Bible and the Quran, the New Atheists put forward numerous examples that ought to show that religious accounts of biological or geographical facts are faulty. Because of this, the New Atheism declares religion, in general, to be groundless and dispensable," notes Kaden and Lux.[45]

---

43 Cited in Ronald L. Numbers, "Introduction" in *Galileo Goes to Jail and Other Myths about Science and Religion*, (Cambridge: Harvard University Press, 2009), p. 3.

44 See Colin A. Russell, *The Conflict of Science and Religion*, in Cary B. Ferngren (ed), *Science and Religion: A Historical Introduction*, (Baltimore: The Johns Hopkins University Press, 2002), pp. 4-7.

45 Tom Kaden and Thomas Schmidt-Lux, "Scientism and Atheism then and Now: The Role of Science in the Monist and New Atheist Writings" in *https://www.researchgate.net/publication/299520211* (30.12.2020).

According to Sam Harris, a well-established atheist and the author of the *New York Times* best-selling, "Science, in the broadest sense, includes all reasonable claims to knowledge about ourselves and the world. If there were good reasons to believe that Jesus was born of a virgin, or that Muhammad flew to heaven on a winged horse, these beliefs would necessarily form part of our rational description of the universe."[46] Thus, anything which cannot be rationally described is dumped as untrue. According to him, religion is fast growing incompatible with the emergence of a global, civil society. While science is genuinely open to the fruits of human inquiry in the twenty-first century, religion is closed to such openness. He maintains that the beliefs about God, the soul, sin, free will, etc., continue to impede medical research and distort public policy. He concludes that when human beings do away with their religious connection, only then will we stand a chance of healing the deepest and most dangerous fractures in our world.[47]

The atheists intend to show that the religious texts are full of mistakes and false knowledge, which, in return, proves science's superiority. One of the most frequently used topics to demonstrate the insufficiency and outdated worldview of all religions is the evolution theory. According to them, only the theory of evolution can sufficiently explain all biological variations and all existing and extinct forms of human and other life on earth. Richard Dawkins, a famous British evolutionary biologist who confesses that he lives his life on the assumption that God is not there, considers natural selection as a solution of stunning elegance and power. He opines that every form of design would be as improbable as the emergence by chance because the design hypothesis raises the larger problem of designing the designer.[48]

2.2.2. Scientism

The movement that eventually culminates in the emergence of scientism could be traced back as early as the sixteenth century. The advancement of the "new Science" accelerated the movement. According to Eric Voegelin, this movement resulted in a *scientistic creed* which is characterised by three principal dogmas: (i) the assumption that the mathematised science of natural phenomena is a model science to which all other sciences ought to conform; (ii) that all realms of being are accessible to the methods of the sciences of phenomena; and (iii) that all reality which is not accessible to sciences of phenomena is either irrelevant or, in

---

46 Sam Harris, "Science Must Destroy Religion," in *https://samharris.org/science-must-destroy-religion/* (30.12.2020).

47 *Ibid.*

48 Tom Kaden and Thomas Schmidt-Lux, "Scientism and Atheism then and Now: The Role of Science in the Monist and New Atheist Writings," pp. 7-8.

the more radical form of the dogma, illusionary.[49] This *scientistic creed* is what we call '*scientism*'.

Scientism is the idea that "there are no real limits to the competence of science, no limits to what can be achieved in the name of science... There is nothing outside the domain of science, nor is there any area of human life to which science cannot successfully be applied."[50] It is also known as *scientific materialism* or sometimes called *scientific naturalism*. This way of overrating science is popular not only among scientists but also among non-scientists as well. Our India first Prime Minister, Jawaharlal Nehru, is reported to have said this, which is nothing but scientism: "It is science alone that can solve the problems of hunger and poverty, of insanitation and illiteracy, of superstition and deadening custom and tradition, of vast resources running to waste, of a rich country inhabited by starving people. ... Who indeed could afford to ignore science today? At every turn, we seek its aid... The future belongs to science and to those who make friends with science."[51]

Mikael Stenmark classifies scientism into various categories; I shall briefly reproduce here:[52]

Scientism has been used to refer to programmes or strategies within science. Thus, this version is called ***academic-internal scientism***. It attempts to reduce an academic discipline that has not previously been understood as a natural science into natural science or, if that is not attainable, to deny its scientific status or significance. One way of interpreting academic-internal scientism is to understand it as an attempt to extend the use of natural science methods to other academic disciplines. It may be called *methodological scientism*.

Another level of understanding scientism is to understand it within a broader society. It is called ***academic external scientism*** which may be defined as "the view that all or, at least, some of the essential non-academic areas of life can be reduced to (or translated into) science." There are several layers within this academic external scientism. The *first* version of academic external scientism is called *Epistemic Scientism,* which believes that 'all genuine knowledge must either be scientific or at least be able to be reduced to scientific knowledge. In other words, it is the idea that the scientific method is the only reliable path to knowledge, or science is our only mean to access a reality. The idea is that what lies beyond the reach of scientists cannot be counted as knowledge.[53] This view asserts that science alone gives authentic, reliable knowledge, and any knowledge that science cannot or does not provide is not real knowledge.

49 Eric Voegelin, "The Origins of Scientism," *Social Research*, (Vol. 15, No. 4, December 1948), p. 462.

50 Mikael Stenmark, "What Is Scientism?" in *Religious Studies*, (Vol. 33, No. 1, 1997), p. 15.

51 Tom Sorell, *Scientism*, (London: Routledge, 199I), p. 2, quoted in *Ibid.* Footnote No. 2.

52 Ref. Mikael Stenmark, "What Is Scientism?" p. 15-32.

53 *Ibid.*, pp. 16-19.

According to Stenmark, there can be a stronger epistemological version of scientism than epistemic scientism. He called this type of scientism *rationalistic scientism,* which he defines as: "The view that we are rationally entitled to believe only what can be scientifically proved or what is scientifically knowable."[54] Bertrand Russell, who was a British philosopher, scientist and politician and Nobel Laureate, can be put in this category as it is cleared from what he said:

> God and immortality, the central dogmas of the Christian, find no support in science. ... No doubt people will continue to entertain these beliefs because they are pleasant, just as it is pleasant to think ourselves virtuous and our enemies wicked. But for my part, I cannot see any ground for either. I cannot pretend to be able to prove that there is no God. I equally cannot prove that Satan is fiction. Christian God may exist; so may the Gods of Olympus, or of ancient Egypt or of Babylon. But no one of these hypotheses is more probable than the other; they lie outside the region of even probable knowledge, and therefore there is no reason to consider any of them.[55]

The *third* layer, which is a more extreme form of scientism, is *Ontological Scientism* – it does not merely state that the only reality that we can know or can really believe anything is the one science has to excess to, but further maintains that only the reality that science can discover exists.[56] This shows that if anything is beyond scientific explanation or that existence is not scientifically proven; it is simply non-existent. For instance, God's existence cannot be verified by science, so God does not exist!

The *fourth* type of scientism, according to Stenmark, is *Axiological Scientism* which may be defined as a belief that science, especially natural science, is much the most valuable part of human learning. Sorell writes, "What is crucial to scientism is not the identification of something as scientific or un-scientific but the thought that the scientific is much more valuable thought than the non-scientific or the thought that the on-scientific is of negligible value."[57]

The *fifth* type of scientism under ***academic external scientism*** is known as *Redemptive Scientism,* which believes, as the name indicates, that science is the answer to all human questions and problems. Richard Dawkins, who holds this idea, maintains that human beings no longer have to resort to superstition when faced with great problematic questions, such as, what is human? Is there a meaning to life? What is the purpose of our life? Because science is capable of dealing with all these questions and is the only alternative to superstition.

54 *Ibid.*, p. 21.

55 Bertrand Russell, *Why I Am Not a Christian* (London: Unwin Paperbacks, 1957), p. 44 quoted in *Ibid.*, p. 21.

56 Mikael Stenmark, "What Is Scientism?" p. 22.

57 Tom Sorell, *Scientism*, p. 1 cited in Mikael Stenmark, "What Is Scientism?" pp. 24-25.

Similarly, Stephen Hawking maintains that scientific cosmological theory will help us answer questions like why we are here and where we came from. The goal is nothing less than a complete description of the universe we live in. In the end, with the help of science, we will be able to understand the mind of God.[58]

The *sixth* one is called *Comprehensive Scientism,* which may be defined as science alone can and will eventually solve all, or almost all, of our genuine problems.[59] The idea given by Radnitzky may fall into this category. He says, "Scientism is roughly the view that science has no boundaries, i.e., that eventually it will answer all theoretical questions and provide solutions for all our practical problems."[60] Arthur Peacocke, who was a British theologian, biochemist, and the Anglican priest, a well-known figure in the field of Science and Religion, writes: "The tendency of science to imperiousness in our intellectual and cultural life has been dubbed 'scientism' - the attitude that the only kind of reliable knowledge is that provided by science, coupled with a conviction that all our personal and social problems are 'soluble' by enough science."[61]

The various types of scientism explicated above reveal how scientism became one of the most significant forces working against the relationship between Science and Religion since the time of enlightenment in the seventeenth and eighteenth centuries. Even now, the worldview that scientism imparted to many people becomes the main hurdle in bringing Science and Religion into mutual relations. Thus, we may say that it is not science *per se* that is against religion or *vice versa,* but the atheists and agnostics who adopt scientism as their primary worldview are the greatest hurdles to science and religion relations.

3. Possibility of Positive Interaction

For nearly a century, the conflict theory initiated by Draper and White occupied the content of popular-science writings by the media and a few older histories of science. Only in the last thirty years of the twentieth century did historians of science attack the conflict thesis and eventually convinced the people that there are severe deficiencies in this theory and that there are possibilities of relating Science and Religion.[62] According to Russell, the shortcomings of conflict thesis arise from a multiplicity of reasons which he summarises as follows:-[63]

Firstly, the conflict thesis hinders the recognition of a relationship between Science and Religion. At different phases of their history, Science and Religion were

58 Mikael Stenmark, "What Is Scientism?" p. 27.

59 *Ibid.*, p. 30.

60 Quoted in *Ibid.*, p. 29.

61 Arthur Peacocke, *Theology for a Scientific Age*, (Minneapolis: Fortress Press, 1993), pp. 7-8 cited in *Ibid.*, p. 29.

62 Colin A. Russell, *The Conflict of Science and Religion*, in Cary B. Ferngren (ed), *Science and Religion: A Historical Introduction*, (Baltimore: The Johns Hopkins University Press, 2002), p. 4.

63 *Ibid.*, pp. 7-9.

not so much at war but mostly independent, sometimes mutually encouraging or even symbiotic. *Secondly*, the conflict thesis ignores the many documented examples of Science and Religion operating in close alliance. Scientists in the seventeenth and eighteenth centuries like Boyle, Newton, Blaise Paschal, etc. and nineteenth-century scientists, such as Michael Faraday, James Joule, James Clark Maxwell, etc., were continually making efforts to integrate their Science and Religion. This testifies to the poverty of a conflict thesis. *Thirdly*, the conflict thesis enshrines a flawed view of history in which victory has been portrayed as inevitable. Why should there be a situation where one is winning, and the other is losing? Can we not have mutual winning, mutual growth and progress? *Fourthly*, the conflict model failed to see the rich diversity of ideas in both Science and Religion. Science is not one, so also religion. Galileo's controversy was mainly with Roman Catholics, not with Protestant churches. *Fifthly*, the conflict thesis engenders a distorted view of disputes resulting from causes other than religion versus Science. *Lastly*, the conflict thesis exalts minor arguments or even differences of opinion to the status of war.

In short, we may say that Colin Russell presents before us quite an acceptable argument that, though there was a definite conflict between Science and Religion like that of the cases of Galileo and Darwin, the issue of conflict is blown out of proportion. From the middle of the twentieth century, several works have come out opposing the Draper-White conflict thesis. Herbert Butterfield's *Origins of Modern Science,* published in 1949, was one of the first books of such a kind. Three other books published in the 1950s, namely, Alexandre Koyre's *From the Closed World of the Infinite Universe* (1957), Thomas Kuhn's *Copernican Revolution* (1957), and Richard Westfall's *Science and Religion in Seventeenth-Century England*, were all united in their fight against the conflict theory. These authors affirm the existence of cooperation between Science and Religion rather than conflict. Koyte argued that the working together of philosophy, Religion and Science brought about the scientific revolution, whereas Westfall noted that in general, scientists of that time regarded their discovery as the confirmation of their religious views. For Kuhn, astronomers' philosophical and religious views are equally fundamental to their scientific ones.[64] This trend continues till today, and people realise now that fruitful interaction between Science and Religion is not only possible but also necessary for the continued existence of the whole creation.

Let me quote the Team of CTNS (Center for Theology and the Natural Sciences) to show positive dialogue between Science and Religion:[65]

> Within the past three decades, philosophers of religion have noticed the similarities now showing up between their field and science.

64 See David B. Wilson, "The Historiography of Science and Religion", pp. 17-18.

65 CTNS Team, "Bridging the Gap between Science and Religion - The Center for Theology and the Natural Sciences", p. 605.

> Particularly because of the pioneering work of such scholars as Ian Barbour and Arthur Peacocke, and more recently by philosophers, scientists, and theologians such as Nancy Murphy, Holmes Rolston, Tom Torrance, John Polkinghorne, Nicholas Wolterstorf, and many more, we now realise that Science and Religion are not at opposite poles of objectivity and subjectivity. Instead, they form a continuum in which the insights, methods and discoveries of each can be shared fruitfully with the other, without threatening their separate foundations and central beliefs about the world. Similarly, the theological community per se is moving out of the shadow of a 'two worlds' approach to Religion and Science. Furthermore, the global problems of today urge us to reshape our thinking in interdisciplinary terms. The problems of today's world do not respect our disciplinary categories. We will need the cooperation of Science and Religion, among other disciplines, to meet these challenges.

Concluding Remark

"The greatest myth in the history of science and religion holds that they have been in a state of constant conflict," boldly states Ronald L. Numbers, the editor of a famous book, *Galileo Goes to Jail and Other Myths about Science and Religion.*[66] Many people perceive science as the enemy of religion. It can be safely said that this idea was not there before the Enlightenment period. Science and religion do not fight each other, but they rather complement each other. Thus, the conflict theory – that Science and Religion are in constant conflict and war - that had been popularised during and after the Enlightenment period does not give us an accurate picture of the relationship between Science and Religion. Let me conclude the present discussion on science and religion interface with the words of Peter Harrison, a well-known scholar in religion and science:[67]

> Those who argue for the incompatibility of Science and Religion will draw little comfort from history. ... The myth of a perennial conflict between Science and Religion is one to which no historian of science would subscribe. ...This is not to deny that there have been those in the past who have opposed certain scientific views on religious grounds... Most important of all, perhaps, religious considerations provided vital sanctions for the pursuit of scientific knowledge and, arguably, it is these that account for the positive attitudes to science which have led to the high status of science in the modern West.

---

66 Ronald L. Numbers, (Ed.) *Galileo Goes to jail and Other Myths about Science and Religion*, (Cambridge: Harvard University Press, 2009), p. 1.

67 Peter Harrison, "Christianity and the Rise of Western Science," in *https://www.abc.net.au/religion/christianity-and-the-rise-of-western-science/10100570* (16.12.2020).

Chapter 2

Christianity and Modern Science

Many people have a wrong impression that Science and Religion, especially Christianity in our context now, are two separate entities that have no connection, let alone relations. They were originated from different locations and are heading towards different ends. Scientists and theologians have nothing in common. A truly religious person cannot be a genuine scientist. Such and many like assumptions are in circulation among the people. This chapter will prove wrong such ideas by producing how science and Christianity are not only connected but also deeply and inseparably related; and how Christianity is responsible for the emergence of modern science and how a genuine Christian, deeply committed to Christian faith and strongly believed in God can be a leading scientist. Thus, this chapter is, in a way, a demonstration that modern science cannot be divorced from its religious root and foundation. I will also present brief accounts of several contemporary scientists deeply committed to God and the Christian faith to show that one can be a good Christian and a good scientist simultaneously.

1. Christian Roots of Modern Science

There is a book, well-received by the academic community worldwide, named *Galileo Goes to Jail and Other Myths About Science and Religion,* published in 2009 by the Harvard University Press. It is a collection of 25 essays written by eminent scholars and professors in science and religion. Chapter 9 of this book is entitled: "Myth 9: That Christianity Gave Birth to Modern Science" and is written by Noah J Efron, who chairs the Program in Science, Technology and Society at Bar-Ilan University in Israel and serves as the President of the Israeli Society for History and Philosophy of Science. This Essay primarily denounces the idea that it is Christianity *alone* that gave birth to modern science. Although, the Essay is an attempt to prove wrong that Christianity is *exclusively* responsible for the birth of modern science, the author Noah J. Efron never misses to point out Christianity's role in the genesis, growth and development of modern science as we shall see in the following discussion.

Pierre Duhem(1861-1916), a distinguished physicist and mathematician, may be the first scientist who maintained that Christianity had played a vital role in the emergence of Modern Science. His ten volumes books, five of which were published several decades after his death, narrated the history of science and depicted Christianity's contribution to the birth of modern science. Stanley Jaki, a prominent figure in the philosophy of science and the author of *The Road of Science and the Ways to God,* praises Duhem in the following lines: "What Duhem unearthed among other things from long-buried manuscripts was that supernatural revelation played a crucial liberating role in putting scientific speculation on the right track."[1] Peter E. Hodgson, a professor of Nuclear Physics at Oxford University, also mentions the contribution of Duhem as follows: "The work of Duhem is of great relevance today, for it shows clearly the Christian roots of modern science, thus decisively refuting the alleged incompatibility of Science and Christianity still propagated by the secularist establishment. Science is an integral part of Christian culture, a lesson to be learned even within the Christian Church."[2]

Alfred North Whitehead, a famous mathematician, co-author with Bertrand Russell of *Mathematica Principia*, strongly supports the idea that modern science owes much from Christianity. He says in his celebrated book: *Science and the Modern World*, "the faith in the possibility of science, generated antecedently to the development of modern scientific theory, is an unconscious derivation from medieval theology."[3] Although, Noah J. Efron tries to argue that modern science alone has not birthed by Christianity, he admits that Christianity played a crucial role in the development of modern science. Here is what he says,

> To be fair, the claim that Christianity led to modern science captures something true and important. Generations of historians and sociologists have discovered many ways in which Christians, Christian beliefs, and Christian institutions played crucial roles in fashioning the tenets, methods, and institutions of what in time became modern science. They found that some forms of Christianity provided the *motivation* to study nature systematically.[4]

1 Donald DeMarco, "The Christian Roots of Modern Science" in *http://www.churchinhistory.org/pages/science/roots-of-science.htm* (12.12.2020), p. 2.

2 *Ibid.*

3 Quoted in Noah J. Efron, "Myth 9: That Christianity Gave Birth to Modern Science," in *Galileo Goes to Jail and Other Myths about Science and Religion*, edited by Ronald L. Numbers, (Cambridge: Harvard University Press, 2009), 79.

4 *Ibid.*, p. 80.

He continues to point out that several pioneers of modern science, such as René Descartes (1596–1650), Isaac Newton (1642–1727), etc. credited their faith in the Christian religion as a driving force in their scientific endeavour. He quotes Descartes as saying that his physics "is in much better agreement with all the truth of faith than that of Aristotle." He also maintains that Newton believed that his system restored the original divine wisdom God had provided to Moses and had no doubt that his Christianity bolstered his physics and that his physics bolstered his Christianity.[5] Thus he concludes, "one cannot recount the history of modern science without acknowledging the crucial importance of Christianity," but maintains his original thesis that "this does not mean that Christianity and Christianity alone produced modern science."[6]

Peter Harrison, the Andreas Idreos Professor of Science and Religion at the University of Oxford, claims that despite the widespread view of the conflict between science and religion, "historians of science have long known that religious factors played a significantly positive role in the emergence and persistence of modern science in the West. Not only were many of the key figures in the rise of science individuals with sincere religious commitments, but the new approaches to nature that they pioneered were underpinned in various ways by religious assumptions."[7]

To claim that Christianity alone produces modern science may be presumptuous but to ignore Christianity's contribution to the genesis, growth and development of modern science is equally arrogant. The following discussion will throw more lights on this issue.

1.1. Church Supported Scientific Research

False Impression was created among the people that Church and scientific development were enemies and that Church was against many scientific truths. However, as of now, we know that many of these claims evaporated in the light of new findings in the history of science. James Hannam, who has a Ph.D in the History and Philosophy of Science from the University of Cambridge and is the author of *The Genesis of Science: How the Christian Middle Ages Launched the Scientific Revolution,* makes a vivid comment on this issue:[8]

> The ongoing clash of creationism with evolution obscures the fact that Christianity has actually had a far more positive role to play in the history of science than commonly believed. Indeed, many of the

---

5 *Ibid.*, p. 81.

6 *Ibid.*, p. 82.

7 Peter Harrison, "Christianity and the Rise of Western Science" in *https://www.abc.net.au/religion/christianity-and-the-rise-of-western-science/10100570* (6.11.2020).

8 James Hannam, "Science Owes Much to Both Christianity and the Middle Ages" in *http://blogs.nature.com/soapboxscience/2011/05/18/science-owes-much-to-both-christianity-and-the-middle-ages.*

> alleged examples of religion holding back scientific progress turn out to be bogus. For instance, the Church has never taught that the earth is flat and, in the Middle Ages, no one thought so anyway. Popes haven't tried to ban zero, human dissection or lightning rods, let alone excommunicate Halley's Comet. No one, I am pleased to say, was ever burnt at stake for scientific ideas. Yet, all these stories are still regularly trotted out as examples of clerical intransigence in the face of scientific progress.

The Catholic Church was at the forefront of sponsoring scientific research in the Middle age. The Church supported priest, monks and friars to study the cosmos. John Heilbron writes in his book - *The Sun in the Church*: "The Roman Catholic Church gave more financial and social support to the study of astronomy for over six centuries, from the recovery of ancient learning during the late Middle Ages into the Enlightenment, than any other, and probably all, other institutions."[9] Hannam notes that the Church even insisted that science and mathematics be a compulsory subject in the syllabus. "By the seventeenth century, the Jesuit order had become the leading scientific organisation in Europe, publishing thousands of papers and spreading new discoveries around the world. The cathedrals themselves were designed to double up as astronomical observatories to allow ever more accurate determination of the calendar. And of course, modern genetics was founded by a future abbot growing peas in the monastic garden."[10]

1.2. Christian Faith Encouraged People to Study Science

During the sixteenth and seventeenth centuries, peoples wanted to study the natural world because of their Christian conviction. A strong faith in God and his works prompted many people to study science to discover the works of God. Their curiosity to know more about God's hidden work was the main driving force of several scientific discoveries. We may go along with Hannam to state that faith led Copernicus to reject the Ptolemaic geocentric universe. It was his Christian conviction that drove Johannes Kepler to discover the constitution of the solar system, and it was his faith in God that convinced James Clerk Maxwell that he could reduce electromagnetism to a set of equations so elegant they take the breath away.[11]

In his celebrated book – *Bible, Protestantism and the Rise of Natural Science*, Peter Harrison writes how the Christian faith inspires the study of science. As a response to a question as to why science arose in the West and why in the seventeenth century, he says,

9 Cited in Michael H. Shank, "Myth 2: That the Medieval Christian Church Supressed the Growth of Science," *Galileo Goes to jail and Other Myths about Science and Religion*, edited by Ronald L. Numbers, (Ed.) (Cambridge: Harvard University Press, 2009), p. 21.

10 James Hannam, "Science Owes Much to Both Christianity and the Middle Ages."

11 *Ibid.*

> The Christian doctrine of creation assumes an intelligible world, created to be understood by its human inhabitants, and to serve their needs. Throughout the patristic and medieval periods, the book of God's works was interpreted, like scripture, and served both spiritual and physical needs. A change took place in the sixteenth century which challenged the assumption that the purpose of the material world lay in its referential or symbolic functions. Henceforth the quest for the divinely-instituted purpose of nature is diverted solely into the search for its practical utilities. The literal approach to texts precipitated this change of attitude towards the world, while the literal content of key passages of the Bible further motivated natural philosophers in their quest to master nature.[12]

1.3. Science Progressed Under Medieval Christianity

That the growth of science is galvanised by religion or, to be specific, Christianity is self-evident from the facts that the era most dominated by Christianity in the history of the world, the medieval period, interestingly, witnessed intense scientific activities and inventions. Had it not for the positive attitude and contribution of the Church, such scientific progress would not have been possible. Michael H. Shank has the following words in connection with the Church's support to the studies of science during the medieval period, "Put succinctly, the medieval period gave birth to the university, which developed with the active support of the papacy. This unusual institution sprang up rather spontaneously around famous masters in towns like Bologna, Paris, and Oxford before 1200... About 30 per cent of the medieval university curriculum covered subjects and texts concerned with the natural world."[13]

Lael Weinberger, a lawyer and historian who is currently the Olin-Searle-Smith Fellow in Law at Harvard Law School, writes how Christians in the medieval period devoted themselves to the study of science:

> The Platonic tendency to divorce the biblical narrative from the physical and the natural was mitigated somewhat in the Middle Ages. Theologians were willing to pay more attention to the physical. Human relations were now seen as a subject of symbolic communication, a move toward legitimizing "this-worldly" inquiry. The universities fostered philosophical discussions about nature, and helped produce

12 Peter Harrison, *The Bible, Protestantism, and the Rise of Natural Science*, (Cambridge: Cambridge University Press), 1998, p. 629.

13 Michael H. Shank, "Myth 2: That the Medieval Christian Church Supressed the Growth of Science," *Galileo Goes to jail and Other Myths about Science and Religion*, edited by Ronald L. Numbers, (Cambridge: Harvard University Press, 2009), p. 21.

> natural theology that explored God's communication to man (*sic*) through His creation.[14]

Weinberger maintains that it is no wonder that Christianity inspires the development of science because it is God who is the truth wants the truth of nature to be revealed: "That Christianity would inspire and foster the development of science is a logical consequence of a religion that proclaims its adherence to the Redeemer who is the Truth and who revealed truth to mankind."[15] Therefore, we may maintain that the significant scientific developments in the Middle Age in Europe are because of Christianity, which fostered scientific development.

1.4. Bible Played an Important Role in Scientific Development

Several scholars in the history of science and religion maintain that the Bible played a positive and constructive role in the development of modern science. After the Reformation, when the literal interpretation of the Bible became widespread, many scientists became aroused and encouraged by the new form of biblical interpretation and made them turn to the study of nature in a drastically different form. A well-known scholar in this field, Peter Harrison, explains this new development as follows:

> Strange as it may seem, the Bible played a positive role in the development of science...
>
> Had it not been for the rise of the literal interpretation of the Bible and the subsequent appropriation of biblical narratives by early modern scientists, modern science may not have arisen at all. In sum, the Bible and its literal interpretation have played a vital role in the development of Western Science."[16]

He continues to say that the new literal reading of the Bible, especially the creation narratives in Genesis, provided the seventeenth-century thinkers with powerful motivating images for pursuing the natural sciences. He says,

> Adam was thought to have possessed a perfect knowledge of all sciences, a knowledge lost to posterity when he fell from grace and was expelled from the Garden of Eden. The goal of 17th-century scientists such as Francis Bacon and his successors in the Royal Society of London was to regain the scientific knowledge of the first man. Indeed, for these individuals, the whole scientific enterprise was an

---

14 Lael Weinberger, "Reading the Bible and Understanding Nature," in *Journal of Creation*, Vol. 23, No. 3, 2009, p. 21.

15 *Ibid.*, p. 23.

16 Peter Harrison, "The Bible and Science," *Australasian* Vol. 23, No. 3, quoted in Jonathan Sarfati, "The Biblical Roots of Modern Science" in *https://creation.com/biblical-roots-of-modern-science* (13.11.202).

> integral part of a redemptive enterprise that, along with the Christian religion, was to help restore the original race to its original perfection. The biblical account of the creation thus provided these scientists with an important source of motivation, and in an age still thoroughly committed to traditional Christianity, the new science was to gain social legitimacy on account of these religious associations."[17]

After discussing the Christian roots of modern science, Jonathan Sarfati makes the following conclusion:

> Science requires certain presuppositions to work at all, and these are found in the Bible. Europe in the Middle Ages, with its general Christian world view, advanced greatly in science and technology. The Reformation, with its emphasis on the authority of Scripture and a historical-grammatical understanding, led to a great leap forward in science as such methods were carried over into the study of nature. Belief in a literal first man Adam and his Fall inspired science as a means to rediscover knowledge Adam had before the Fall. It is futile to expect continued fruits of the scientific enterprise while undermining the roots in biblical Christianity.[18]

The argument is loud and clear and even convincing that not only Christianity but also the Bible itself inspired and encouraged people to turn to the natural order and study meticulously to unveil things hidden by God. Thus, we may say that the Bible is one of the roots of modern science.

1.5. Mathematical God

There was a pertinent question with which the medieval people were wrestling– whether mathematical truths are human construction or are eternal reality embedded in God? The Mediaeval scholarship holds that mathematical principles, though useful in many senses, could not accurately describe the natural world. However, it was considered that mathematics provides a valuable tool for a correct prediction of reality. Peter Harrison notes, "Hence, mathematical astronomy, while regarded as falling short of offering a true account of the nature of heavenly bodies and the causes of their motions, was regarded as useful because it made it possible to predict their positions. Mathematical models were thus thought of as useful fictions."[19] There was a significant shift of idea about mathematics. Galileo initiated this change – for him, the heliocentric cosmology (the idea that the sun, not the earth, is at

17 *Ibid.*

18 Jonathan Sarfati, "The Biblical Roots of Modern Science" in *https://creation.com/biblical-roots-of-modern-science* (13.11.2002).

19 Peter Harrison, "Christianity and the Rise of Western Science," in *https://www.abc.net.au/religion/christianity-and-the-rise-of-western-science/10100570* (16.12.2020).

the centre) propounded by Copernicus was not only a mathematical truth, a fictitious truth as was held by scientists of his time, but it was an accurate description of the physical world. Over against the Aristotelian world view that nature acts according to its internal properties, which dominated the medieval period's philosophical thinking, the seventeenth-century scientists asserted that it was God who controls the activities, internal and external, of nature.

Thus, Galileo and many other scientists of modern time, including Johannes Kepler, Rene Descartes, Isaac Newton, etc., held that "mathematical truths were not the product of human minds, but of the divine mind. God was the source of mathematical relations that were evident in the new laws of the universe. Like the Bible, the 'book of nature' had also been written by God and, as Galileo was to insist, this book was 'written in the language of mathematics.'"[20] The idea that it was God who is the source of all activities made scientists of this period believe in the truth of mathematical calculation. Over against the Aristotelian world view that nature acts according to its internal properties, which dominated the philosophical thinking of the medieval period, the seventeenth-century scientists came forward in asserting that it was God who controls the activities, internal and external, of nature. For examples, Johannes Kepler, who discovered the laws of planetary motion, argued that God had used mathematical archetypes in his creation of the cosmos. Rejecting the Aristotelian view of mathematics as a human product, he says, "the reason why the mathematical is the cause of natural things (a theory which Aristotle carped at in so many places) is that God the Creator had mathematicals with him as archetypes from eternity in their simplest divine state of abstraction."[21]

Thus, the Christian idea of God as the author of everything, including mathematics, influences how scientists perceive the natural world and their approach to it. In the same line, Descartes also maintained that God had created the laws of logic and mathematics. Equation 2 + 2 = 4 was correct only because God had so willed it. Descartes even took the help of the Bible to support his position that mathematical truth was in God: "Thou hast ordered all things in measure and number and weight" (*Wisdom of Solomon* 11.20). Isaac Newton also described the cosmos as inhabited by an 'infinite and omnipresent spirit' in which matter was moved by 'mathematical laws.'[22]

Observing these great Christian scientists' position of a mathematical God, Peter Harrison concludes:

> Identifying God as the author of mathematics was thus a crucial step in asserting the reality of mathematical relations, and it was this development which enabled the subsequent application of

20 *Ibid.*

21 *Ibid.*

22 *Ibid.*

mathematics to the subject matter of physics. Combined with the idea of a divine legislator, this insight produced the modern view that nature is governed by mathematical laws.[23]

1.6. Nature Operates According to God's Law

It is to be noted here that the scientific idea that became prevalent in and after the seventeenth century that nature operates in a fixed law is the consequence of God's legislative moral power to the physical world. Rene Descartes was one of the pioneers of this new understanding of natural laws, and he said that "God alone is the author of all the motions in the world."[24] The scientific idea that became popular in the modern period was that there are orderliness and constancy in nature because of God's law.

The famous scientist and a deeply committed Christian, Robert Boyle, who is considered the father of modern chemistry, opined that creation operates according to the fixed law that God alone established. In the same vein, Rene Descartes approved that there is fix law under which nature operates and maintained that as these laws had their source in an eternal and unchanging God, the laws of nature are also eternal and unchanging. Again, the famous mathematician Isaac Barrow, whom Isaac Newton succeeded as the Lucasian Chair of Mathematics at Cambridge, maintained that the only reason for having confidence that repeated experiments will yield general principles is because we can be assured that the laws of nature that God has instituted are constant. We have no reason to believe that nature is inconstant, for that would imply that "the great Author of the universe is unlike himself."[25]

Thus, the Christian principle that nature is governed by constant and unchangeable principles appointed by God became an important precondition for experimental science since the seventeenth century. It depicts the compatibility of science and religion on the one hand and the influence of Christianity on modern science explicitly, on the other hand.

2. Some Prominent Christian Scientists of Modern Time

Today there is a visible demarcating line between science and religion, and many people even think that they are always at war. But we have already established in our discussion that the conflict between science and religion existed only in the minds of a few people who were influenced by enlightenment scepticism and atheistic philosophy. In reality, there was no such deep real conflict between science and religion by and large. In the light of such a wrong idea of science and religion conflict, it is almost impossible to think of a religious scientist – a scientist who is deeply committed both to God and religion. But, when we look back a few

23 *Ibid.*

24 *Ibid.*

25 *Ibid.*

hundred years, we will notice that such dichotomy between science and religion or scientist and theologian was simply absent. Ian H. Hutchinson lucidly put this development in the following words:

> The strict separation we commonly observe between a researcher's scientific ideas and his or her "personal beliefs" is a modern, and even recent norm. From antiquity through the Scientific Revolution, Science was viewed as a form of philosophy, and many of the thinkers we have retroactively dubbed "scientists" freely intermingled their speculation about the natural world with theological, philosophical, and mathematical writings, often expending a great deal of their scholarly time and energy on religious study. Kepler's seventeenth-century laws of planetary motion, for example, seem to his modern readers like needles of scientific inspiration buried in a haystack of theological speculation. Newton and Boyle likewise intermingled physics and philosophical theology without apparent hesitation.... By the nineteenth century, however, natural philosophy had become more natural and less philosophy. Theology and natural science were substantially separated.[26]

There could be a long list of well-known scientists who are deeply committed to Christian faith. To name a few – Francis Bacon (1561 –1626), an English philosopher and scientist who is credited with developing the scientific method that became popular through the scientific revolution. Johannes Kepler (1571-1630), who was famous for his laws of planetary motion, discovered, among others, that the planets move around the sun in elliptical orbits. Robert Boyle (1627-1691), who was regarded as the father of modern Chemistry, is known for his law called Boyle's law which describes the inversely proportional relationship between the absolute pressure and volume of a gas under constant temperature. John Ray (1627-1705) an English naturalist and botanist who contributed significantly to taxonomy classification - the classification of living and extinct organism. Michael Faraday (1791-1867) is considered one of the greatest scientists of the 19th century; his scientific contribution mainly lies in electromagnetism. Arthur Compton (1892-1962), an American physicist, who was awarded the Nobel Prize in Physics in 1927 for his discovery of what is called 'the Compton effect', which demonstrated the particle nature of electromagnetic radiation. James Clerk Maxwell (1831-1879) is a Scottish physicist famous for his contribution to the formulation of electromagnetic theory. He is regarded as one of the greatest and most influential scientists of the 19th century who is ranked with Sir Isaac Newton and Albert Einstein for his contributions. George

26 Ian H. Hutchinson, "The Genius and Faith of Faraday and Maxwell," *The New Atlantis*, Winter 2014, No. 41, Winter 2014, p. 81.

Lemaitre (1894-1966), a Belgian priest, astronomer and cosmologist, formulated the famous Big-bang theory and the expansion of the universe.

There are still many Christian famous scientists whose contributions to the scientific world are tremendous: Sir Isaac Newton (1643-1727), who is one of the greatest scientists of all time and also a theologian – he wrote more about theology than science! He is famous for his three laws of motion which became the basic principles of modern physics. These three laws resulted in the formulation of his famous law of universal gravitation. Our next important Christian scientist is John Dalton (1766-1844), who is a pioneer in the development of modern atomic theory and famous for his atomic theory known as 'Dalton's atomic theory.' Sir Joseph John Thomson (1856-1940), a British physicist who discovered the electron, the first subatomic particle to be discovered, is another famous Christian scientist. He received a Nobel Prize in Physics in 1906 and knighted in 1908. Pierre Teilhard de Chardin (1881-1955), who was a French Jesuit priest, scientist, philosopher and theologian best known for his theory that human, is evolving mentally and socially, toward a final spiritual stage. Another Christian scientist on our list is Sir John Houghton (1931-2020), a Welsh atmospheric physicist who helps Britain become a global climate science leader. He led the United Nations panel on global warming that won a Nobel Peace Prize in 2007 with Al Gore, the former President of the USA. Houghton was also knighted in 1991. At the age of 88, he passed away on 15th April 2020 due to complications caused by Covid-19.

There are several living scientists who contributed tremendously in the various fields of science and are strongly committed to Christian faiths. A few of them may be pointed out here: Don Knuth (b. 1938), an American Computer scientist who is called the 'father of the analysis of algorithms.' William D Phillips (b. 1948) is another important person in our list of Christian scientists. He is an American physicist and a Nobel Laureate who developed methods of laser cooling and atom trapping, which earned him a Nobel Prize in 1997 with Steven Chu and Claude Cohen-Tannoudji. Francis Collins (b. 1950), who is an American physician and geneticist, becomes famous as the head of the Human Genome Project. Rosalind Wright Picard (b. 1962), who is an American inventor and a professor of Media Arts and Sciences. She is the founder and director of the Affective Computing Research Group. She is also the co-founder of *Affective, Inc.* and *Empatica, Inc.*

The list of scientists who are deeply committed to the Christian faith can go on and on as there are many others who are no less important, but I could not mention them here. This very brief discussion affirms that science and religion are not enemies but are companions, in dialogue with one another, complementing each other in the service to God and humanity. From the above list of Christian scientists, I am going to discuss further some of these.

Chapter 3 will discuss the lives and contributions of two great scientists who are devout Christians, viz. Johannes Kepler and Sir Isaac Newton. Now, I will consider some modern and contemporary scientists who are deeply committed to the Christian faith.

2.1. Francis Bacon (1561-1626)

Francis Bacon was born on 22nd January 1561 in London to a noble and well-to-do family. His father was Sir Nicholas Bacon, who was a keeper of the great seal for Elizabeth I, and his mother was Lady Anne Cooke Bacon.[27] He studied at Trinity College, Cambridge and Gray's Inn, London and became a lawyer and also involved in politics and became a Parliamentarian for thirty-seven years starting from 1548. When James-I became the king of England in 1603, Bacon's career began to prosper. He was knighted that year. He was appointed to a succession of posts culminating, like his father, with a keeper of the great seal. In 1618 he was appointed Lord Chancellor, the most powerful position in England, and in 1621 he was created Viscount St Albans. After this, he was charged with accepting a bribe and became imprisoned. The king pardoned him later, but he retired from public life to his home in Hertfordshire, where he continued his writings. He died on 9th April, 1626, in London.[28]

His main contribution in science and religion is in the area of the scientific method, and he is considered the pioneer of the modern scientific method. Up to his time, the influence of Aristotle on how scientific knowledge is to be gained was prevalent among the people. It was held that scientific truth could be reached by way of authoritative argument – if sufficient knowledgeable men and women discussed a subject long enough, the truth would be eventually discovered. Bacon challenged this, saying that truth required evidence from the real world. He published his idea of the correct method of acquiring natural knowledge initially in *Novum Organum* in 1620.[29] The central idea of Bacon's philosophy of science is *inductive reasoning*, which is explained in Book II of *Novum Organum.* According to him, the defect of all previous systems of beliefs about nature lay in the inadequate treatment of the general propositions from which the deductions were made.[30] The inductive method he proposed which is central to his though, became popular among philosophers of science and scientists themselves.

He is a devout Anglican. He divided knowledge into two – natural knowledge or scientific knowledge which is gained by experimenting and inductive method, and divinity or inspired revelation, which cannot be acquired by experimenting or inductive reasoning. Though he insisted that philosophy and the natural world

27 For details about Francis Bacon's life ref. J. E. G. de Montmorency, "Francis Bacon," *Journal of the Society of Comparative Legislation* , 1905, Vol. 6, No. 2, 1905, pp. 263-283.

28 "Francis Bacon (1561-1626)" in *http://www.bbc.co.uk/history/historic_figures/bacon_francis.shtml* (26.12.2020).

29 *http://www.bbc.co.uk/history/historic_figures/bacon_francis.shtml* (27.01.2021).

30 *https://www.britannica.com/biography/Francis-Bacon-Viscount-Saint-Alban/Thought-and-writings* (27.01.2021).

must be studied inductively, he argued that where religion is concerned, we can only study arguments for the existence of God. Knowledge of God's nature, action, and purposes can only come from special revelation. According to him, a proper study will ultimately help human beings get knowledge which is the rich storehouse for the glory of the Creator. He wrote: "A little philosophy inclineth man's mind to atheism, but depth in philosophy bringeth men's minds about to religion" (exclusive language in the text).[31]

2.2. John Ray (1627-1705)

John Ray was an English naturalist, a theologian and philosopher (until 1670, he wrote his name as John Wray). He was born in 1627 at Black Notley in Essex, England. His father was a blacksmith and his mother a herbal healer; perhaps he inherited the interest in nature from his mother. His father could not afford to send him to Cambridge University, but with Samuel Collins's help, the neighbouring Vicar of Braintree, he could get to Cambridge with financial help in 1644. At Cambridge, he became a Fellow in 1649, a Lecturer in 1651 and a junior Dean in 1658. He was ordained to be a Priest in 1660. However, in 1662 he refused to subscribe to the "Bartholomew Act" (Act of Uniformity), which denied the validity of the oath of the "solemn league and covenant," he was forced to resign from his Fellowship.[32]

The rest of his life was passed as a private scholar, contributing to the proceedings of the newly founded Royal Society of which he was elected a member, travelling considerably, researching industriously, and compiling the voluminous works on which his fame now rests.[33] According to Ian P. Stevenson, Ray's career in biology extended over fifty-five years, during which books never ceased to come from his pen. He polished and revised his works to his death, but he bemoaned the fact that he could not do research for the last edition of his Methodus as his legs did not permit him to walk in the fields. He died amid such academic activity at the age of 77 in 1705 at Black Notley.[34]

Ray was a great researcher and writer. From 1660 he started publishing his research works of plants and animals with the first publication – *Catalogus Plantarum Circa Cantabrigiam Nascentium*, a catalogue of plants growing around Cambridge. Since then, he continued publication till his death. Ray published

31 *https://www.christianitytoday.com/history/people/scholarsandscientists/francis-bacon.html* (27.01.2021).

32 Cf. Ian P. Stevenson, "John Ray and his Contributions to Plant and Animal Classification," *Journal of the History of Medicine and Allied Sciences*, (Vol. 2, No. 2, Spring 1947), pp. 251-252; Frank N. Egerton, "A History of the Ecological Sciences, Part 18: John Ray and His associates Francis Willughby and William Derham," in *Bulletin of the Ecological Society of America*, (Vol. 86, No. 4, October 2005), p. 301. and also *https://ucmp.berkeley.edu/history/ray.html* (01.01.2021).

33 Ian P. Stevenson, "John Ray and his Contributions to Plant and Animal Classification," p. 552.

34 *Ibid.*

about 23 works; the biological works were usually in Latin, the rest in English. His publications were in the fields of botany, zoology, theology and literature.[35] His main contribution in science was in *taxonomy* - the science of classification or the classification of living and extinct organisms – His enduring legacy to botany was the establishment of species as the ultimate unit of taxonomy.[36]

One of Ray's significant contributions, which was also one of his greatest ambitions, was the unification of all living things under one system. Due to this, it is difficult to separate his zoological work from his botanical studies. Likewise, it is difficult to isolate even his theological writings, for his intense love of natural history pervaded all. His reverential attitude toward life in all its manifestations is, itself, awe-inspiring.[37]

Ray was a devout Christian and a great theologian. He published several theological books. *The Wisdom of God Manifested in the Works of the Creation* published in 1691 became his most popular and influential book. It argued that the correlation of form and function in organic nature demonstrates the necessity of an omniscient creator. This argument from design, common to most of the leading scientists of the 17th century, implied a static view of nature that was distinctly different from the evolutionary ideas of the early and mid-nineteenth century.[38] Another important theological book he published was *Three Physico-Theological Discourses,* published in 1692. Both of these books were based on sermons Ray had delivered at Cambridge. Such deep religious feeling may seem out of place in scientific writing today, but his work represented a harmony between science and religion. While several people had the idea of conflict between the study of the natural world and theology, "Ray affirmed powerfully that Nature was a worthy subject for study and reason, and that such activity was pleasing to God."[39]

2.3. Michael Faraday (1791-1867)

Michael Faraday, a British chemist and physicist who was one of the greatest scientists of the nineteenth century, contributed significantly to the study of electromagnetism and electrochemistry. He was born on 22nd September 1791 in South London to a poor blacksmith family. As his family was so poor, he could not afford to get a proper formal education. It is said that there was a time when he has to depend on one loaf of bread for the whole week! However, he was firm in his spiritual life right from his childhood. "The family belonged to a small Christian sect, called *Sandemanians,* that provided spiritual sustenance to Faraday

35 *https://www.britannica.com/biography/John-Ray-English-naturalist* (01.01.2021).

36 *Ibid.*

37 Ian P. Stevenson, "John Ray and his Contributions to Plant and Animal Classification," pp. 258-259.

38 *https://www.britannica.com/biography/John-Ray-English-naturalist* (01.01.2021).

39 *https://ucmp.berkeley.edu/history/ray.html* (01.01.2021).

throughout his life. It was the single most important influence upon him and strongly affected how he approached and interpreted nature."[40]

From the various sources available to us, we know that he was apprenticed to a bookbinder when he was thirteen or fourteen years old. This allowed him to be in touch with various books. He spent his apprenticeship's leisure in reading and studying all the books on natural philosophy and chemistry that were accessible to him. In the spring of 1812, Faraday was invited to the Royal Institution to listen to lectures delivered by Sir Humphrey Davy on scientific subjects. He attended four classes delivered by Davy. He took down notes on these lectures, which he afterwards sent to Davy. Along with the notes, he also sent a letter to Davy asking for a job as his assistant. Davy, who was then at the zenith of his popularity, helped him get a job as a chemical assistant in the Royal Institution laboratory in 1813. His days of bookbinding thus came to an end, and he became himself the maker of books for other people to bind, read, study and cherish.[41]

Faraday accompanied Davy and his wife on an 18 months European tour, visiting France, Switzerland, Italy and Belgium and meeting many influential scientists. On their return in 1815, Faraday continued working at the Royal Institution, helping Davy and other scientists in their experiments.[42] In 1820 he described two new compounds of chlorine and carbon, which filled up the gap in the history of Chemistry. Again in 1825, Faraday discovered benzole, which was again an important landmark in the history of Chemistry.[43] In 1821 he published his work on electromagnetic rotation. In 1826, he founded the *Royal Institution's Friday Evening Discourses* and, in the same year the *Christmas Lectures*, both of which continue to this day. He himself gave many lectures, establishing his reputation as the outstanding scientific lecturer of his time.[44]

In 1831, Faraday discovered electromagnetic induction, the principle behind the electric transformer and generator. This discovery transformed electricity from a curiosity into a powerful new technology. During the remainder of the decade, he worked on developing his ideas about electricity. He was partly responsible for coining many familiar words, including 'electrode', 'cathode' and 'ion.[45]

During the 1840s, his health deteriorated, and he could not do much research. He died on 25th August, 1867 at Hampton Court, where he had been

---

40 *https://www.britannica.com/biography/Michael-Faraday* (01.01..2021).

41 "Michael Faraday" *Scientific American*, (Vol. 17, No. 11, September 14, 1867), p. 169; Joseph Lovering, "Michael Faraday," *Scientific American*, (Vol. 22, No. 4, January 22, 1870), pp. 65-66; "Michael Faraday" *Scientific American*, (Vol. 22, No. 15, April 9, 1870), p. 240; *http://www.bbc.co.uk/history/historic_figures/faraday_michael.shtml*, (01.01.2021).

42 *http://www.bbc.co.uk/history/historic_figures/faraday_michael.shtml*, (01.01.2021).

43 Joseph Lovering, "Michael Faraday," p. 65.

44 *http://www.bbc.co.uk/history/historic_figures/faraday_michael.shtml*, (01.01.2021).

45 *Ibid.*

given official lodgings in recognition of his contribution to science.[46] Joseph Lovering writes, "For fifty years Davy and Faraday together had sustained the glory of the Royal Institution as with the brightness of a whole Academy; each of them of unchallenged greatness, not only as discoverers of physical truths but as expositors also."[47] The greatness of Michael Faraday is revealed from the fact that there are many laws, phenomena and experimental instruments that bear his name – the Faraday cage, the Faraday constant, Faraday's law of induction, the Faraday (rotation) effect, the *farad* (a unit of electrical capacitance), and so on.

Faraday was made a Fellow of the Royal Society of London in 1824, a Corresponding Member of the French Academy of Sciences in 1823, a Foreign Associate of the American Academy in 1844. He received from the Royal Society of London the Rumford, Copley, and Royal medals. He lived a simple life and drew a pension of £ 300 only, conferred upon him in 1835. Napoleon the Emperor was so much interested to hear his lecture, and he acknowledged the obligation by naming him Commander of the Legion of Honour.[48]

Michael Faraday was a strong and committed Christian, and his Church was unorthodox and tried to follow the New Testament precisely as it is. In his 1854 lecture entitled –"Observations on Mental Education" he confessed that he was reading the book of nature written by the finger of God in his scientific research. He maintained that God had been pleased to work in his material creation by laws and the Creator governs his material works by definite laws resulting from the forces impressed on the matter.[49] He argued that science and religion are compatible, saying, "I have never seen anything incompatible between those things of man which can be known by the spirit of man which is within him, and those higher things concerning his future, which he cannot know" (*exclusive language in the text*).[50]

It is said that Faraday had two rooms in his house, which he constantly used: a laboratory and a prayer room. This reflects the harmony between science and religion in the life of Michael Faraday. Gabriel Daly notes:

> Plainly, Faraday saw no inconsistency in moving from one room to the other. It was the same person who used both rooms, though what he did in one room was radically different from what he did in the other. No doubt when praying, he occasionally recalled some phenomenon revealed by his scientific studies and praised God for the glories of creation. When he was in his laboratory, however, he did not appeal

46 *http://www.bbc.co.uk/history/historic_figures/faraday_michael.shtml*, (01.01.2021).

47 Joseph Lovering, "Michael Faraday," p. 65.

48 *Ibid.*

49 Ian H. Hutchinson, "The Genius and Faith of Faraday and Maxwell," p. 86.

50 Quoted in *Ibid.*, p. 87.

to God as an element in, for example, his studies on the relationship between electricity and magnetism."[51]

Let me conclude my brief account on the great scientist and devout Christian, Michael Faraday with the words of Joseph Lovering:

> It is much to say of him that he declined all honours and rewards which were foreign to his scientific character; that, when he might have amassed a fortune of £150,000 by applying old discoveries to commercial uses, he preferred to concentrate his whole mind on the discovery of new truth, dying poor and leaving a widow dependent on a small pension, which, in noble imitation of his example, she refused to have increased... that he was as much exalted above others in modesty as in intellectual greatness; that he made science honourable and attractive ... and that his final departure from the laboratory in the Royal Institution of Great Britain on 20th June, 1862, was followed by one universal pang of grief throughout the world of science.[52]

2.4. George Lemaitre (1894-1966)

Georges Lemaître was a Belgian priest, astronomer and cosmologist who formulated the modern big-bang theory, which holds that the universe began in an explosion of an infinitely small and infinitely dense primaeval super-atom. Lemaître was born in 1894 in Charleroi, Belgium. As a young man, he was attracted to both science and theology. During World War I, he became a civil engineer and served as an artillery officer in the Belgian Army. After the war, he entered a seminary and, in 1923, was ordained a Catholic priest. He continued studying at the University of Cambridge and Massachusetts Institute of Technology, where he received his Ph.D degree. He returned to Belgium to teach relativity to graduates and classical mechanics to undergraduates at the University of Louvain.[53]

Lemaitre had developed the idea that the universe is dynamic against the static theory of Einstein. He was the first scientist who connected an initial singularity idea of an expanding Universe. Although, Einstein and Eddington opposed the idea of an initial singularity, Lemaître proposed that the universe started its expansion from a certain distinguishable moment in the finite past. He thought such a model described the real universe the best, and he was right.[54] He

51 Gabriel Daly, "Science, Religion and Scientism," *The Irish Review* (Summer, 2001, No. 27), p. 50.

52 Joseph Lovering, "Michael Faraday," p. 65-66.

53 Ref. *https://www.britannica.com/biography/Georges-Lemaitre* (02.01.2021) and also "Georges Lemaître, Father of the Big Bang" https://www.amnh.org/learn-teach/curriculum-collections/cosmic-horizons-book/georges-lemaitre-big-bang (02.01.2021); Joseph McCann, "Georges Lemaître: The Priest Who Proposed the 'Big Bang,'" *Studies: An Irish Quarterly Review*, (Vol. 105, No. 418, Summer 2016), p. 216-217.

54 *Ibid.*, p. 69.

opined that if the universe was getting bigger, it had once been much smaller. If the universe were projected back into the long distant past, it would eventually reduce to a very compact, very hot dense mass, 'a primaeval atom' as he called from which the whole universe expanded.[55] Such an "atom," he reasoned, would have exploded into fragments that cooled and became the galaxies, stars and atoms that we know today. He did not coin the term "Big Bang," the phrase seems to have been coined in 1950 by Fred Hoyle, who, being himself an exponent of the rival "steady state" theory then in vogue, used the phrase pejoratively.[56]

He published his idea of a dynamic universe in 1927 in a local Belgian journal, but many people did not read it. Later on, he published its English translation in the better known astronomical journal – the *Monthly Notices of the Royal Astronomical Society*.[57] After this, his idea of a dynamic and expanding universe leading to a Big Bang theory became well known and appreciated.

Lemaitre's theory was eventually supported by the two young American radio astronomers, Arno Penzias and Robert Wilson. They detected in 1965, just before the death of Lemaitre, the primaeval radiation predicted by him, travelling in all directions since the first explosion. In the minds of scientists and many others, this proved beyond doubt that Lemaitre's theory was correct. In the middle of June 1966, he was in hospital in Louvain and heard the news that the Penzias and Wilson discovery was indeed the left-over radiation remaining from the primaeval atom. The Big Bang had indeed happened, as he said. Georges Lemaître died a few days later, on 20th June 1966, at the age of 72.[58] Christopher Dwyer notes:

> This discovery of the "echo of creation" ranks as one of the most momentous in the history of science. Had Lemaitre lived a little longer, he might well have gained a Nobel Prize. But that prize is never awarded posthumously, and after years of hesitation it went to Penzias and Wilson for a discovery they had not sought, and did not recognize when they made it, but which confirmed the insight achieved by Lemaitre over thirty years earlier.[59]

Lemaitre's work was well accepted by the Church also. He was honoured by King Leopold in 1934. He was made a member of the Pontifical Academy of

55 Joseph McCann, "Georges Lemaître: The Priest Who Proposed the 'Big Bang,'" *Studies: An Irish Quarterly Review*, (Vol. 105, No. 418, Summer 2016), p. 218.

56 Christopher Dwyer, "Two Paths to Truth: A Tribute to Georges Lemaitre" *New Blackfriars* (Vol. 75, No. 886, October 1994), pp. 473.

57 Józef Turek "Georges Lemaître's Contribution to the Formation of the Dynamic View of the Universe," *Roczniki Filozoficzne / Annales de Philosophie / Annals of Philosophy*, (Vol. 33, No. 3, 1985), p. 65.

58 Joseph McCann, "Georges Lemaître: The Priest Who Proposed the 'Big Bang,'" p. 222.

59 Christopher Dwyer, "Two Paths to Truth: A Tribute to Georges Lemaitre," p. 474.

Sciences by Pope Pius XI in 1936. He continued his priestly work as well as his university lecturing and research. For 46 years, he was a member of a society of Malines diocesan priests devoted to prayer and spirituality. Apart from taking care of his aged mother until her death, he served as chaplain to the Chinese students.[60]

Georges Lemaître was a scientist as well as a Catholic priest. He was committed and faithful to both of these – scientific research and pastoral ministry. For him, there is no conflict between science and religion as both are of God having different purposes. His attitude to the relationship between science and religion is perhaps best explained by his response to the question: What would you ask God if you had the chance?

> If I had to ask a question of the infallible oracle... I think I should choose this: "Has the universe ever been at rest, or did the expansion start from the beginning?" But, I think, I would ask the oracle not to give the answer in order that a subsequent generation would not be deprived of the pleasure of searching for and of finding the solution.[61]

His letter to Albert Einstein was marvellous as it explicates his stand on the harmony between science and religion. He writes,

> Should a priest reject relativity because it contains no authoritative exposition on the doctrine of the Trinity? Once you realise that the Bible does not purport to be a textbook of science, the old controversy between religion and science vanishes... The doctrine of the Trinity is much more abstruse than anything in relativity or quantum mechanics; but, being necessary for salvation, the doctrine is stated in the Bible. If the theory of relativity had also been necessary for salvation, it would have been revealed to Saint Paul or to Moses... As a matter of fact neither Saint Paul nor Moses had the slightest idea of relativity.[62]

As for the theological implications of his theory of the beginning of the universe, he says,

> As far as I can see, such a theory remains entirely outside any metaphysical or religious question. It leaves the materialist free to deny any transcendental Being... For the believer, it removes any attempt at familiarity with God... It is consonant with Isaiah speaking of the hidden God, hidden even in the beginning of the universe.[63]

60 Joseph McCann, "Georges Lemaître: The Priest Who Proposed the 'Big Bang,'" p. 220.

61 Quoted in *Ibid.*, p. 221.

62 *Ibid.*, pp. 221-222.

63 *Ibid.*, p. 222.

2.5. Sir John Houghton (1931-2020)

John Theodore Houghton is one of the most distinguished climate scientists of our time. He is a persistent campaigner for climate justice. He was born in Dyserth, Wales, the United Kingdom, on 30th December 1931 to a couple named Sidney and Miriam. He has two brothers. He studied at Rhyl Grammar School and Jesus College, Oxford, UK, and received his BA in 1951 and D.Phil in 1955. He was knighted in 1991.

He received so many honours and awards and held many important posts. He was a Fellow of the Royal Society of London; Member of Academia Europea; Honorary Member of the Royal Meteorological Society; Honorary Member of the American Meteorological Society; Honorary Fellow of the Royal Institute of British Architects; Fellow of the Optical Society of America and Fellow of the Institute of Physics. He was the leading figure in the formation and running of the IPCC (Intergovernmental Panel on Climate Change) – a unique relationship between political policy and scientific rigour. He co-chairs the Science Working Group of IPCC from 1988 until 2002. Under his leadership, IPCC received a Nobel Prize for Peace in 2007. He was also the Honorary Scientist, Hadley Centre for Climate Prediction and Research, Meteorological Office, Bracknell from 2002; Honorary Scientist, Rutherford Appleton Laboratory, from 1991; Trustee, Shell Foundation from 2000 and Chairman of the John Ray Initiative from 1997.[64] He was also a Chief Executive of the British Meteorological Office from 1983 to 1991 and Chairman of the Royal Commission on Environmental Pollution. He received many awards, including the prestigious Japan Prize for his lifetime work on climatology in 2006.[65]

He married Dr Margaret Broughton in 1962, and they had two children. After she died in 1986, he set up the Margaret Houghton memorial fund, a medical nursing research unit. He married again to Sheila Thompson in 1988. In 2013 he retired to Aberdovey in west Wales. He died in 15th April 2020 due to Covid-19. He was survived by his second wife, Sheila, his two children and seven grandchildren.

Houghton was a former professor of atmospheric physics at Oxford University. He devoted much of his career to researching the effects of global climate change on the environment and urging the international community to examine and address problems, such as ozone depletion and global warming, in a comprehensive and meaningful way. Human-induced climate change, Houghton has argued, kills more people than terrorism.[66]

Sir John Houghton was a devout Christian, brought up in a highly spiritual family atmosphere. He belonged to evangelical Christianity, which he inherited

---

64 Cf. *https://web.archive.org/web/20131029233107/http://www.consejoculturalmundial.org/winners-science-sirjohnhoughton.php* (03.01.2021).

65 *https://www.pbs.org/moyers/faithandreason/portraits_houghton.html* (03.01.2021).

66 *https://www.pbs.org/moyers/faithandreason/portraits_houghton.html* (03.01.2021).

from his parents. He was also a church elder at Aberdovey Presbyterian Church. He is well known for his view that science and religion could fruitfully coexist, strengthening each other. He even publishes a book entitled *The Search for God: Can Science Help?* Here, he makes his intention clear, saying our search is not so much for a logical proof of God's existence as a meaningful perspective on the universe. Perspective is what an artist puts into a picture to convey depth and meaning. We are looking for views of the universe that convey depth and meaning, and that gives us insight into the God who made it. He tries to show that science and faith can enrich each other as both searches for reality and truth. Their methods are also similar to a great extent, and their area of concern overlap. He says that our thinking in science and religion can be stretched and our understanding deepened by widening their purview and by putting them together.[67]

As a committed evangelical Christian and a serious scientist, he tries to relate science with his faith – evangelical Christianity. Apart from - *The Search for God: Can Science Help?* – he published another book – *Does God play Dice?: A look at the Story of the Universe* in 1988. These books are attempts to relate Science with Christian faith as he believes that science and religion, rather than opposing each other, actually complement one another. He maintains, "There is widespread suspicion of science, fostered by the feeling that science goes against the Bible, this is very unfortunate; it takes a very small view of God, and a very inadequate view of science."[68]

2.6. Donald Knuth (b. 1938)

Donald Ervin Knuth is an American computer scientist who is recognised as "the Father of Computer Science" or widely regarded as "the father of the analysis of algorithms." He was born on the 10th January 1938 in Milwaukee, Wesconsin, the USA, to a devout Lutheran Christian family. His father was a Lutheran school teacher, part-time piano teacher and Church organist. He is proud to be a Lutheran:

> I'm a Lutheran because my parents and grandparents, and indeed all my known ancestors back to the 1600s, were Lutheran. Furthermore, like theologian Joseph Sittler, I'm especially pleased to have been raised in the Lutheran tradition because it taught me that I didn't need a "cerebral bypass operation" in order to approach God. Lutherans use their God-given intelligence to dig deeply into spiritual questions.

67 Cf. *The Search for God: Can Science Help?* Written by John Houghton and reviewed by Ernest Lucas in *https://www.thegospelcoalition.org/themelios/review/the-search-for-god-can-science-help/* (03.01.2021).

68 *https://www.pbs.org/moyers/faithandreason/portraits_houghton.html* (03.01.2021).

> Martin Luther was a great scholar—a man who used his head and his heart simultaneously.[69]

He is a professor emeritus at Stanford University. He has received a very prestigious award – the *ACM Turning Award,* which is the highest distinction in computer science and is often referred to as "the Nobel Prize of computer science." His multi-volume works, which was first published in 1997 and is still adding even today, *The Art of Computer Programming,* is considered a landmark in the development of computer science. He also publishes many other books, including *3:16 Bible Text Illuminated* (1990) and *Things a Computer Scientist Rarely Talks About* (2001).

Knuth is not only one of the finest computer scientists but also a devout Christian. In 1999 Knuth was invited to give a series of lectures at the Massachusetts Institute of Technology (MIT) on the relationship between science and religion. He delivered six lectures, and it was broadcast live on the internet, and many thousands of youths watched regularly. It was published as *Things a Computer Scientist Rarely Talks About.* This lecture and the subsequent publication in the form of a book are good sources for relating science and religion. In these lectures, he talked about the interaction of randomization and religion, the questions of language translation, where he analysed several biblical verses. He also gave his idea of the "3:16 project" – this is his unconventional and innovative method of studying the Bible. Instead of studying the Bible book by book, verse by verse or thematically, he studied chapter 3, verse 16 of every book in the Bible. On the last day of the lecture, he talked about his favourite subject – God and computer science.[70]

He shares the benefit of his methodological approach to the Bible as follows:

> Thus, I decided one day to learn more about the Bible by finding out everything I could about 3:16, starting at Genesis and going through revelation. To my astonishment, each of those verses proved to be extremely interesting and thought-provoking. The Bible was much richer than I'd expected; my Sunday school knowledge had given me a misleading impression. I learned there's plenty of good stuff there for adults to chew on - more than a lifetime's worth.[71]

Unlike many scientists who are satisfied with their scientific works, Knuth urges for things beyond science as he firmly believes that there are many things

69 Megan Brandsrud, "Living Lutheran: I'm a Lutheran: Don Knuth" in *https://www.livinglutheran.org/2018/12/im-a-lutheran-don-knuth/* (04.01.2021).

70 See "Things a Computer Scientist Rarely Talks About" in *https://www-cs-faculty.stanford.edu/~knuth/things.html* (04.01.2021), and also; *https://physicstoday.scitation.org/doi/full/10.1063/1.1480790* (04.01.2021).

71 Megan Brandsrud, "Living Lutheran: I'm a Lutheran: Don Knuth" in *https://www.livinglutheran.org/2018/12/im-a-lutheran-don-knuth/* (04.01.2021).

that science cannot reach and comprehend. He confesses, “My life would not be complete if it was all about cut and dried things. The mystical things I don't understand give me humility. There are things beyond my understanding.”[72] His idea of harmony between science and religion is evident when he says, “My faith has been a source of inspiration because I believe God is pleased when people create innovations that make our world ever better.”[73] For him, science and religion are not only compatible but also his very scientific undertakings are inspired and catalyzed by his faith in God. I may say without hesitation that Knuth's life and contribution is a living example of a mutually enriching relationship between science and religion.

2.7. William D. Phillips (b. 1948)

William Daniel Phillips is an American physicist and a Nobel Laureate. He was born on 5th November 1948 in Wilkes-Barre, Pennsylvania, USA. His father was William Cornelius Phillips, and his mother, Mary Catherine Savino. He graduated from Juniata College in Huntingdon, Pennsylvania and received a doctorate in physics from the famous Massachusetts Institute of Technology (MIT) in 1976. He also completed his post-doctoral research at MIT. In 1978 he joined the National Institute of Standards and Technology as a staff, formerly known as the National Bureau of Standard in Gaithersburg, Maryland. It was here that he conducted an award-winning experiment. He received Nobel Prize in physics in 1997 for his work in laser cooling, where he developed a method to cool and trap atoms using laser light. Before joining MIT, he married his high school sweetheart, Jane Van Wynen, and the couple moved to Boston. They have two daughters – Caitlin Phillips and Christine Phillips.[74]

He confessed in his autobiography written for the Nobel Prize that he believed in the power of prayer right from his childhood and that he and his sister prayed for a sibling though their parents decided already to have only two children. He said that their prayers were apparently effective, resulting in the birth of a brother, Tom, in 1957.[75]

His contribution to science and religion dialogue is tremendrous though it may not be as great as his contribution to physics. Till 1976 William Phillips and his wife were not regular at church service. But after they joined the Fairhaven

72 Susan D'Agostino, “The Computer Scientist Who Can't Stop Telling Stories” in *https://www.quantamagazine.org/computer-scientist-donald-knuth-cant-stop-telling-stories-20200416/* (3.01.2021).

73 Megan Brandsrud, “Living Lutheran: I'm a Lutheran: Don Knuth” in *https://www.livinglutheran.org/2018/12/im-a-lutheran-don-knuth/*.

74 For more on his life cf.https://www.nobelprize.org/prizes/physics/1997/phillips/biographical/ (11.01.2021); *https://www.mediatheque.lindau-nobel.org/laureates/phillips* (04.01.2021); *https://www.britannica.com/biography/William-D-Phillips* (04.01.2021).

75 *https://www.nobelprize.org/prizes/physics/1997/phillips/biographical/* (11.01.2021).

United Methodist Church in Gaithersburg in 1976, they became much involved in the Church's activities. He is a devout Methodist laity and the founding member of the *International Society for Science and Religion*, who firmly believes in the compatibility of science and religion.

2.8. Francis Collins (b. 1950)

Francis Sellers Collins, an American geneticist, was born on 14th April 1950. He is famous for discovering genes causing genetic diseases and is well known for being the Director of the U.S. National Institutes of Health and the head of the Human Genome Project (HGP). He earned a bachelor degree from the University of Virginia in 1970, a Master and Ph.D degrees from Yale University and a Doctor of Medicine in 1977 at the University of North Carolina. He joined the staff of the University of Michigan as an assistant professor in 1984. It was here that in 1989 he discovered the gene that causes cystic fibrosis, and in the following year, Collins and his team found the gene that causes neurofibromatosis, a genetic disorder that generates the growth of tumours. In 1993 Prof. Collins left the University and became the head of the National Human Genome Research Institute.[76]

The human genome project went on successfully under Collins' leadership, and on the 26th June 2000, the then USA President, Bill Clinton, announced in the presence of Collins that the rough draft sequence of the DNA in the human genetic map had been completed. In April 2003, following further analysis of the sequence, the Human Genome Project was closed with great success. The project's success was hailed as the first step toward helping doctors diagnose, treat, and even prevent thousands of illnesses caused by genetic disorders and the contribution of Francis Collins was paramount.[77]

Collins was appointed in 2009 as the head of National Institutes of Health by the then US President, Barack Obama, and on 6th June 2017, US President Donald Trump announced his selection of Collins to continue to serve as the NIH Director. Pope Benedict XVI also appointed Collins to the Pontifical Academy of Sciences. This organization promotes advancement in the fundamental understanding of scientific questions and investigating ethical and philosophical issues associated with science. As a devout Christian, Collins is always sensitive towards the misuse of science and scientific discoveries. He advises the government to set guidelines on how individuals' genetic information could be handled, saying that the success of HGP brings the potential for great mischief.[78]

Francis Collins is not only a highly respected scientist of our time, but he is also the epitome of the relationship between science and religion. His commitment to God and the Christian faith is as great as his commitment to genetic studies.

76 Cf. *https://www.britannica.com/biography/Francis-Collins* (11.01.2021).

77 *Ibid.*

78 *Ibid.*

His contribution towards relating science and religion earned him a prestigious Templeton Prize in 2020. In his 2006 best-selling book -*The Language of God: A Scientist Presents Evidence for Belief*, Collins argues that scientific inquiry and Christianity are not incompatible, but rather, religious faith can inspire scientific discovery.[79]

No one knows better than Francis Collins, who heads the HGP successfully, how easy it might be for scientists to play God. But, for him, the ability to read and understand 'our instruction book' is no obstacle to faith in God. He started as a practising Christian in childhood, became agnostic or almost atheist in his youth, and became a faithful Christian at the age of 27 after reading C. S. Lews' *Mere Christianity* presented to him by "this wonderful minister" as he puts it, a Methodist pastor.[80] In an interview with him, he confesses that as a scientist, he believes in miracles:

> If God is who God claims to be, and who I believe he is, then he is not explainable in natural terms. He is outside the natural world; outside of space and time. So if God chose to intervene from time to time in the natural world by allowing the occurrence of miraculous events, I don't see why that is an illogical possibility. Once one accepts that idea that there could be something outside the natural, then miracles also become possible.[81]

On the relationship between science and religion, Collins maintains that as God is beyond the natural, it is impossible to have scientific proof of God's existence as science operates on the natural level only. He sees the solution to the seeming conflict between science and religion. He says,

> Many people get hung up on the whole evolution versus creation argument - one of the great tragedies of the last 100 years is the way in which this has been polarized. On the one hand, we have scientists who basically adopt evolution as their faith, and think there's no need for God to explain why life exists. On the other hand, we have people who are believers who are so completely sold on the literal interpretation of the first book of the Bible that they are rejecting very compelling scientific data about the age of the earth and the relatedness of living beings. It's unnecessary. I think God gave us an opportunity through the use of science to understand the natural world. The idea that some

79 *https://www.sciencemag.org/news/2020/05/francis-collins-honored-work-bridge-science-and-Religion* (11.01.2021). For details about Collins' religious position, ref. Francis S. Collins, *The Language of God: A Scientist Presents Evidence for Belief*, (New York: Free Press, 2006).

80 Francis S. Collins, *The Language of God: A Scientist Presents Evidence for Belief*, (New York: Free Press, 2006), p. 21.

81 *https://www.pbs.org/wgbh/questionofgod/voices/collins.html* (11.01.2021); also Francis S. Collins, *The language of God: A Scientist Presents Evidence for Belief*, p. 53.

> are asking people to disbelieve our scientific data in order to prove that they believe in God is so unnecessary.[82]

He affirms the compatibility of science and religion, saying, "In me, they both exist. They both exist at the same moment in the day. They're not compartmentalized. They are entirely compatible. And they're part of who I am."[83] I think that is the testimony of a scientist who truly believes in the wonders of science and the manifold blessings it has brought to humanity and also in the mysteries of religion, which has changed his life altogether. After hearing such a strong living testimony and assertion, it is difficult to sustain the conflict theory.

2.9. Rosalind Wright Picard (b. 1962)

The last one in our survey of Christian scientists is an American inventor and scholar, a female scientist named Rosalind Wright Picard. She was born on 17th May 1962. She finished her bachelor degree in electronic engineering from Georgia Institute of Technology in 1984, master degree in 1986 and doctorate in 1991, both from Massachusetts Institute of Technology (MIT). She is presently a professor of Media Arts and Sciences at MIT.

Picard is the founder and Director of the Affective Computing Research Group at MIT and also the co-founder of *Affectiva*, which provides technology to help measure and communicate emotion. She is also the co-founder and Chief Scientist of *Empatica,* which works to improve lives with clinical-quality wearable sensors and analytics. She is the author of a well-read book *Affective Computing* which was published in 1997, and the author of more than two hundred and fifty peer-reviewed articles.[84]

Picard started her youths as an atheist but converted to Christianity. She firmly believes that there is always beyond what science and scientists can see. She feels that her faith plays a great role in her involvement with Affective Computing. She says as a faithful believer,

> When you first start understanding how the brain works, it's amazing. Even scientists who have no old-time religion will feel that sense of awe at how wonderfully we're made. Digging into the models of how the emotions work, I find I feel even greater awe and appreciation for the way we are made, and therefore for the Maker that has brought this about. My trying to understand all this is an act of worship, an act of homage, not an act of trying to usurp the Maker.[85]

---

82 *https://www.pbs.org/wgbh/questionofgod/voices/collins.html* (11.01.2021).

83 *Ibid.*

84 *https://aaac.cs.nott.ac.uk/members/138/rosalind-wright-picard* (12.01.2021).

85 *The Atlantic*, April 29, 1998 in *https://www.theatlantic.com/past/docs/unbound/digicult/dc980429.htm* (12.01.2021)

By way of concluding my discussion on these Christian scientists, I want to underline the fact that these Christian scientists and many more whom we cannot include now have one thing in common – they are renounced scientists who enrich science and scientific research, but at the same time, they are devout Christians in possess of unwavering faith in God. They all claim that their commitment to religion, belief in God and active participation in Church's ministry do not deter their scientific works but rather catalyse their scientific research. These celebrated scientists unanimously assert that science and religion are compatible and mutually enriching one another. What else can we say?

Concluding Remark

It may be too much to claim that Christianity gave birth to modern science, but no one could rule out the role of Christianity in the delivery and development of modern science either. Churches were opened for scientific discoveries and encouraged scientific research so that new things may be discovered. Not only Christianity but also the Bible itself encouraged people to dig deeper into the natural world to discover what God had put therein. So, we may say without any hesitation that Christianity is greatly responsible for the birth and growth of modern science. This elucidates the possibility of positive relations between science and religion, which is supported by the fact that many scientists, as discussed above, are deeply committed to God and religion. I want to underline that these Christian scientists and many more whom we cannot include now have one thing in common – they are renounced scientists who enrich science and scientific research. Still, at the same time, they are devout Christians in possession of unwavering faith in God. They all claim that their commitment to religion, belief in God and active participation in Church's ministry do not deter their scientific works but rather catalyse their scientific research. These celebrated scientists unanimously assert that science and religion are compatible and mutually enriching one another. What else can we say?

Chapter 3

Scientific Explanations of the Cosmos

Human beings down the ages have tried to understand the universe and their place in relation to the sun, moon and stars. The mystery and beauty of the universe arrested the minds of the people of various races and places, making them develop various explanations of the universe. We may say that both science and religion are equally fascinated by and interested in the cosmos. That is why we have a number of scientific and religious explanations of the origin, nature and function of the universe. We should know that both their explanations are limited. It is unwise to hold on to one and discard the other; we should take these explanations as complementary rather than contradictory and try to see their harmony, having an understanding that they are the explanations of the universe from particular contexts and perspectives and are not and cannot be an absolute statement on the universe.

The terms 'cosmos' and 'universe' are synonymous. In a broader sense, cosmology is the study of the universe as a whole, but in a narrower sense, it refers to the study of the formation and development of the universe. Another term, 'astronomy', is very similar to cosmology, in fact, they are rather inseparable. However, astronomy is a natural science that deals with the study of celestial objects, such as stars, planets, comets, nebulae, star clusters and galaxies, with an emphasis on the position, motion and composition of celestial bodies. In this sense, cosmology is more general, whereas astronomy is more specific.

This Chapter deals with the scientific explanations of the cosmos, starting with the Greek philosophers and moving on to the scientific revolution where the contributions of cosmologists like Copernicus, Galileo and Kepler will be discussed with special reference to the controversy with the Church. Our discussion will be closed with the significant contribution of Newton in the field of motion that had given rise to the concept of a mechanical universe or universe as a machine.

1. The Greeks' Geocentric Cosmology

The Greeks were the first to advance scientific explanations of the universe. Without telescopes or other instruments at their disposal, the Greek philosophers and scientists observed the universe – the earth, the sun, the planets and the stars and proposed their theories that lasted for nearly two thousand years.

1.1. Plato

Plato (427—347 BCE.) was one of the earliest philosophers who came out with a concrete theory on the universe. He was taught by Pythagoras, Heraclitus and Socrates, and it was from the inspirations of their insights that he drew his own magnificent vision of the world. We see Plato's conception of the cosmos in one of his *Dialogues – Timaeus*, where he explained how God, or rather a Craftsman called Demiurge, crafted out the orderly universe out of chaos. Describing the works of Demiurge, Plato narrated how "of the heavenly and divine, he created the greater part out of fire, that they might be the brightest of all things and fairest to behold, and he fashioned them after the likeness of the universe in the figure of a circle, and made them follow the intelligent motion of the supreme, distributing them over the whole circumference of heaven, which was to be a true cosmos or glorious world spangled with them all over."[1] According to Plato, there were God and chaos in the beginning; and God imposed order on preexistent chaos to generate the ordered universe called cosmos. Plato viewed that the earth was static and was at the center of the universe.[2] This geocentric view of the cosmos was shared by most of the Greek philosophers and scientists, and it was the prevailing idea throughout the Greek world and outside for many centuries.

1.2. Aristotle

Aristotle (384-322 B.C.E) was definitely the most influential thinker of the Greeks, especially in connection with cosmology, and his legacy was instrumental in shaping the picture of the universe that dominated Western thinking for nearly two thousand years. Aristotle was a student of Plato and he followed Plato's geocentric and geostatic notion of the cosmos where earth is put at the center of the universe unmoved and the sun, stars and planets are revolving around it in perfect concentric circles.[3] For Aristotle, the cosmos is a gigantic spherical plenum that is beginningless and also endless. Everything exists within it, and

1 Quoted from *Timaeus* in Hartley B. Alexander, "Plato's Conception of the Cosmos" in *The Monist*, (Vol. 28, No. 1, January, 1918), p. 6.

2 Nancy Morvillo, *Science and Religion: Understanding the Issues*, (Chichester, West Sussex: Willey-Blackwell, 2010), p. 52.

3 *Ibid.*

there is no possibility of existence outside of it, not even empty space.[4] Aristotle's cosmology is characterized by the division of the whole cosmos into two regions – the celestial region or the heavens and the terrestrial region or the earthly area. These two areas are fundamentally different; the former is constant and changeless devoid of decomposition, a sign of perfection, whereas the latter is characterized by change and decay, a sign of imperfection. These two regions are separated by a concave surface of the lunar sphere. The terrestrial region, which lies below the concave lunar surface, is an imperfect region with constant change, decay and transformation. It consists of four elements – earth, water, air and fire. All bodies in this region are compounded of combinations of two or more elements, and bodies are always coming into being as differing compounds of the four elements. Also, bodies are always passing away because their elements are dissociated to combine with other elements to form a new body. The upper atmosphere of the terrestrial region just below the conclave lunar surface is the home for comets, shooting stars and other similar objects and phenomena.[5] These are included in the earthly area or terrestrial region because of their impermanent nature.

The celestial region, according to Aristotle, is perfect and permanent within which lie planets and stars. This region is filled with the fifth element, i.e. ether, which is "an incorruptible, eternal substance that suffers no change, except change of place. It did not come into being and will never pass away."[6] Aristotle's division of the cosmos into two regions is the reflection of his concept of two types of motions – natural and unnatural motions. According to him, the direction of movement is determined by a kind of 'homing instinct' – everything going towards its proper place in the universe. For example, fire and smoke go up as their home is above, whereas a stone dropped goes vertically downwards because the earth is the home for stone. This is a natural movement. The unnatural movement, on the other hand, is a movement forced upon by some external agents. The trajectory of an arrow and pushing a physical object upwards away from the earth are examples of unnatural movement.[7] On the other hand, the motion of stars and planets are a totally different kind. According to Aristotle, as these things are made up of different elements, that is, ether, "things that are made up of the ether possess a perfectly circular, constant, continuous, and unforced motion."[8] This idea was the foundation of Aristotle's cosmology.

---

4 Edward Grant, *Science and Religion 400 BC- AD 1550: From Aristotle to Copernicus*, (Westport, Connecticut: Greenwood Press, 2004), p. 41.

5 *Ibid.*

6 *Ibid.*, p. 42.

7 Colin A. Russell, *Cross-Currents: Interactions between Science and Faiths*, (Grand Rapids: William B. Eerdmans Publishing Company, 1985), pp. 28-29.

8 Phil Dowe, *Galileo, Darwin and Hawking: The Interplay of Science, Reason, and Religion*, (Grand Rapids: William B. Eerdmans Publishing Company, 2005), p. 11.

1.3. Eudoxus

Before Aristotle, another Greek cosmologist, Eudoxus (408-353 BCE), a friend of Aristotle's teacher Plato, offered a schema for the movements of the heavenly bodies centred on the earth. According to his model, the universe is something like a beach ball with the fixed stars painted on the inside and the earth at the exact centre. Between the earth and the fixed stars move the sun, the moon and the planets, which were known during those times as the 'wandering stars.' According to Eudoxus, these moving heavenly bodies move in spheres where a series of concentric spheres are required to accommodate the total system.[9] The cosmological explanation advanced by Eudoxus encountered several problems. The biggest problem was that when the astronomers observed the movement of Mars, let's say, for six months, they noticed that it appeared to travel forward and came back and then went forward. Such phenomena need to be explained, and Aristotle introduced more spheres of movement to solve this problem. In fact, he posited the existence of fifty-five spheres of motion which is far more complicated than the original scheme proposed by Eudoxus.[10]

1.4. Ptolemy

Aristotle's model is not without a problem. According to this system, all the planets should appear to be the same brightness at all times because they are travelling in a perfect circle. But for the observer on the earth, planets appear with varying brightness at different times of the year, and Aristotle's system has no explanation for this anomaly. It was Ptolemy (100-170 CE) who modified Aristotle's model with a more sophisticated mathematical system so as to explain the looping motion and the variation in the brightness of the planets. Just like Aristotle, Ptolemy also assumed that planets travel in uniform motion along the circular path. But, the paths of the sun, moon and planets, which were considered as moving around the earth, were not circular when observed from the earth. He, therefore, introduced the idea that these heavenly bodies move around the earth in an eccentric way. He also brought out the idea of epicycle or smaller circular motion. According to this idea, the planets revolve uniformly along the small circular path or epicycle, and while revolving in an epicycle, they revolve around the earth along a larger circular path. So, the planet's motion is the sum of these two circles. With these devices, Ptolemy explained the motions of planets and the variations in their brightness by arranging various epicycles in the right way.[11]

1.5. Aristarchus

All the Greek philosophers and cosmologists were not in agreement concerning the position and movement of the earth. Though geocentric and geostatic

9 *Ibid.*

10 *Ibid.*

11 *Ibid.*, pp. 11-12.

cosmology was the prevailing idea, there were other opinions as well. The lesser-known Greek philosopher by the name Aristarchus of Samos (c. 310 – c. 230 BCE), way back in 270 BC, had advanced the idea that the earth and the other planets moved around the sun, but it was not much recognized. Copernicus also cited Aristarchus as an ancient authority in support of his new discovery in his unpublished work but later on deleted, and Aristarchus' name was not mentioned in his famous book, *On the Revolutions of the Celestial Spheres*. Most Pythagoreans held the view that the earth moved, where some of them believed that the sun and the earth move about a central 'fire.' Heraclides of Pontus (c. 388-c.310 B.C.E) also proposed that the earth rotates on its axis.[12] Though the heliocentric system of cosmology, propounded by Aristarchus was essentially correct, it did not gain widespread acceptance as Aristotle's influence was too strong and his followers too numerous. Thus, Aristotle's geocentric and geostatic cosmology improved and modified by Ptolemy became the unchallenged cosmological theory until the sixteenth century when it was challenged and finally dethroned by Copernicus and Galileo.

The geocentric and geostatic model of the universe went well with the Church for two reasons – *firstly*, it supports the superiority of the earth and of human beings by putting them at the center of the universe where all the celestial bodies are revolving around them. Again, as Morvillo puts it, with this model, "there is a location for heaven in the perfect celestial realm and a place for hell in the corruptible terrestrial realm."[13] *Secondly* and most importantly, this model apparently reflects some of the Biblical texts, such as sun and moon standing still until the people of Israel defeated their enemies (Josh. 10:12-13); the unmoved world in Psalm 93:1, and the sun coming forth from his chamber, rising from the end of the heavens (Ps. 19:4-6). Thus, the Church held this theory as 'eternal truth' for so many centuries, and any move against this would meet with serious opposition from the Church.

2. Scientific Revolution

The So-called 'Scientific truth' is not always a permanent truth or an absolute truth. That which was held for so many centuries as scientific truth could be proven wrong! Even what the Church had fervently and reverently embraced as truth can be falsified. This was exactly what happened in the scientific revolution.

What we called the *Scientific Revolution* technically started with the publication of Copernicus' work – *On the Revolutions of the Celestial Spheres* in 1543, where he challenged the geocentric conception of the universe and argued for the heliocentric cosmos, and ended with Newton, who proposed universal laws and a mechanical universe in the last part of the seventeenth century. During this period, the new development in natural philosophy (the term used for science

12 Nancy Morvillo, *Science and Religion*, p. 53.

13 *Ibid.*, p. 56.

till the late 18th century) is known as 'modern science.' We should remember that the word *science* replaced the term *natural philosophy* only in the late 18th century when the study of nature acquired a more technical, less humanly inclined ethos. Modern science began to take shape with the works of Kepler and Galileo around the year 1600, where mathematical calculation was emphasized in the study of physical nature.[14]

During this period, many scientific discoveries were made that changed the way we perceive the cosmos. Copernicus' sun-centered cosmology dethroned the age-old geocentric understanding of the universe. Kepler's law of planetary movement rectified the Greeks' postulation of the circular motion of the heavenly bodies by establishing that planets moved in ellipses, not in circles. Galileo observed more things in the heavens than had ever been dreamed of through his telescope: moons of Jupiter and myriads of stars invisible to the naked eye. Newton formulated his inverse-square law for gravity, which explained the planetary orbits. In the words of his contemporary, Edmond Halley, Newton had penetrated the secret mansions of the gods.[15] This indeed was a scientific revolution! The earlier systems of belief were categorically overthrown.

The basic features of modern science include – the mechanistic model of nature, the emphasis on unprejudiced observation or purely objective research, emphasis on experimentation to get the precise answer to research questions, and the use of Mathematics in describing natural phenomena and trying to formulate mathematical equations for it. The Scientific Revolution was, by and large, felt a necessity and Richard Westfall may not be wrong when he says that it is the most important event in Western history. He maintains,

> The Scientific Revolution was the most important 'event' in Western history… For good and ill, science stands at the center of every dimension of modern life. It has shaped most of the categories in terms of what we think, and in the process has frequently subverted humanistic concepts that furnished the sinews of our civilization. Through its influence on technology, it has helped to lift the burden of poverty from much of the Western world. But in doing so has accelerated our exploitation of the world's finite resources… Through its transformation of medicine, science has removed the constant presence of illness and pain, but it has also produced toxic materials that poison the environment and weapons that threaten us with extinction… I am convinced that the list describes a large part of the reality of the late twentieth century and that nothing on it is thinkable

---

14 Peter Barrett, *Science and Theology since Copernicus: The Search for Understanding*, (London: T&T Clark International, 2004), p. 15.

15 John Hedley Brooke, *Science and Religion: Some Historical Perspectives*, (Cambridge: Cambridge University Press, 2014, first published in 1991), p. 69.

> without the Scientific Revolution of the sixteenth and seventeenth centuries.[16]

I will discuss four important scientists who brought about the Scientific Revolution in the following pages.

2.1. Copernicus

Nicholaus Copernicus (1473–1543) was phenomenal in the way he could turn the whole understanding of the universe upside down. His heliocentric model of the universe was the beginning of the end of the Aristotle-Ptolemy model of a geocentric universe. The publication of his book - *De Revolutionibus Orbium Coelestium* (*On the Revolutions of the Celestial Spheres*) in 1543, just before his death, is considered as a major landmark in the history of natural philosophy, triggering what is known as the *Copernican Revolution* and making an indelible contribution in the Scientific Revolution. In other words, we may say that Scientific Revolution formally began with the publication of this book.

Copernicus was born in 1473 at Torun in Poland. When he reached the age of ten, his father died, and he was under the hands of his maternal uncle, Lucas Watzenrode, who became the bishop of the northernmost Roman Catholic diocese in Poland. Copernicus was thus brought up in a highly religious and ecclesiastical atmosphere. He had a good education at the University of Cracow, Poland, especially in mathematics and painting. Though he did not take astronomy classes at that time, he developed a growing interest in it and collected a number of books from which he was acquainted with the prevailing cosmological issues. Upon graduation, he was appointed as a Canon at Frombork Cathedral under the influence of his uncle. Though a Canon's position was typically available to the priest only, Copernicus was able to hold onto the job without ordination into priesthood mainly because of his uncle. He went to Italy to study medicine and canon law, where he earned a degree in canon law. After coming back to Poland, he continued to hold on to the position of Canon with an additional charge of a personal secretary to his uncle; he was also made the principal legal officer of the Cathedral Chapter. He held these positions till he died in 1543.

It is thus clear that though Copernicus was not an ordained priest, he was very much a churchman, closely attached to the Church, highly responsible for the welfare of the Church. However, in spite of his positions in the Church and his allegiance to Church doctrines, dogmas and administration, his scientific discovery had to go against the Church as the Church during that time held the idea that the earth is at the centre of the universe whereas the sun, the planets and the stars were going around it.

16 Quoted in Peter Barrett, *Science and Theology since Copernicus*, p. 16.

2.1.1. Heliocentric Cosmology

Copernicus never studied astronomy or cosmology at the university, but his main scientific contribution was in the field of astronomy. He already did his own studies on astronomy during his undergraduate studies at Cracow and continued to develop his knowledge on the subject while studying canon law in Bologna, Italy.[17] It was said that Copernicus' interest in cosmology arose within an ecclesiastical setting. A Church Council wanted to reform the Church calendar based on the predictions of the motions of the planets but the Church Council realized that this was impossible as not enough was known at this time about cosmology. As he was also part of the Church's administrative body, Copernicus felt that it was necessary to provide a cosmology adequate for the ecclesiastical reform of the calendar. He, thus, saw his work in astronomy as being part of his service to the Church.[18]

In 1514 he had written a booklet called *Commentariolus (Small Commentary), where he summarized his heliocentric cosmology. It has the following axioms:*[19]

- Planets do not revolve around one fixed point.
- The earth is at the center of the moon's orbit.
- The sun is at the center of the universe, and all celestial bodies rotate around it.
- The distance between the earth and sun is only a tiny fraction of the stars' distance from the earth and sun.
- Stars do not move, and if they appear to, it is only because the earth itself is moving.
- Earth moves in a sphere around the sun, causing the sun's perceived yearly movement.
- Earth's orbit around the sun causes the planets to orbit in the opposite direction.

These were highly provocative statements in those days because they challenged both the age-old 'scientific truth' as well as the Church's understanding of the position of the earth in the universe. Himself being a church official, Copernicus probably had no courage to publish such a book that was sure to hurt the feelings of the Church members and create theological controversy. Thus, *Commentariolus* was not printed until it was discovered in the 1880s, more than 340 years after the death of Copernicus. After he wrote *Commentariolus,* Copernicus worked more intensely on the issue, and after some 30 years, he came out with more detailed arguments for the heliocentric universe. But, it is said that

---

17 Owen Gingerich, "The Copernican Revolution," in *Science and Religion: A Historical Introduction*, (Baltimore: The Johna Hopkins University Press, 2002), p. 96.

18 Phil Dowe, *Galileo, Darwin and Hawking,* p.13.

19 *http://www.biography.com/people/nicolaus-copernicus-9256984* (accessed 14.05.2016).

because of his allegiance to the Church, the position he held, and his uncle being a Bishop, he felt that it would not be appropriate to publish a work against the Church's beliefs. Moreover, to say that the earth rotates is against the everyday experience of humans because one could imagine that if the earth rotates, clouds will float westwards, and a stone thrown up vertically in the air would not come back on the same spot. Again, given the fact that little was known about gravitational force, loose objects would fall away from the earth's surface. Copernicus was going against all common sense.

So, it is no wonder that he was very reluctant to publish his work. Owen Gingerich may be right when he says, "It is quite possible that Copernicus would never have published his hypotheses except for the persuasive intervention of a young Lutheran astronomer from Wittenberg, Georg Joachim Rehticus (1514-1574)."[20] Possibly due to the encouragement from friends like Rehticus, and more importantly, because of his own commitment that astronomical truth should not be kept away from the people, Copernicus, towards the end of his life, permitted the publication of his work. Thus, *De Revolutionibus* was published in 1543, the year Copernicus died, and he could hold the copy of his book on his death bed a few days before he died. The *Preface* – "To the Reader" was written by the anonymous person, but later on, it was found out that Lutheran clergyman Andreas Oslander (1498-1552) was the one who wrote it and he was also responsible for the printing of this book. He warned the readers in the following lines:

> For these hypotheses need not be true nor even probable… However, since different hypotheses are sometimes offered for one and the same motion (for example, eccentricity and an epicycle for the sun's motion), the astronomer will take as his first choice that hypothesis which is the easiest to grasp. The philosopher will perhaps rather seek the semblance of the truth. But, neither of them will understand or state anything certain, unless it has been divinely revealed to him… So far as hypotheses are concerned, let no one expect anything certain from astronomy.[21]

On the Revolutions of the Celestial Spheres has six books or sections. It begins with discussions on the philosophical foundation of the sun-centered universe and the moving earth. In Book 1, chapter 10, Copernicus brought out forcefully the heliocentric cosmology and stated: "And so the sun, as if resting on a kingly throne, governs the family of stars which wheel around…Therefore in this ordering, we find that the world has a wonderful commensurability and that there is a sure bond of harmony for the movement and magnitude of the orbital circles such cannot be found in any other way." He also discussed basic trigonometry,

---

20 Owen Gingerich, "The Copernican Revolution," p. 97.

21 See the *Preface* of Nicholaus Copernicus, *On the Revolutions of Heavenly Spheres*, (Amherst, New York: Prometheus, 1995).

a catalogue of fixed stars, the theory of the sun, the theory of the moon, and the movement of planets, etc.

2.1.2. Church Responses

Copernicus took great care not to hurt the feelings of the Church and adopted a number of measures to ensure that people receive his work positively - He dedicated the book to the Pope so that the Church may take it positively. He made his presentation in such a way that it looked more like a fictional hypothesis rather than the factual presentation of physical reality. Copernicus' work did not evoke much response in the beginning due to several reasons. *Firstly*, he died few days after the publication of his book and could not publicise it or defend it. *Secondly*, as there was no astronomical evidence produced in the Copernican hypothesis, the scientific community could not find much difference between Copernicus' hypothesis and that of Ptolemy's because both are mathematically equivalent with no conceivable observational test that could distinguish between them.[22] *Thirdly*, many people, both natural philosophers (scientists) and clergies did not pay much attention to it as they doubted the reality of the hypothesis. As many people did not believe in the probability of Copernicus' theory, it had fewer followers. *Fourthly*, as Owen Gingerich has said, the astronomers and theologians at the University of Wittenberg, where Copernicus' book received its first detailed study, were convinced that it was just a mathematical hypothesis and not to be taken as the presentation of a physical fact, because in those days astronomers used fictional circles in their modelling of the cosmos.[23] *Fifthly*, *De Revolutionibus* was written in Latin, only a few people could read it, and the influence could not be great. Possibly because of these, the full-scale Church's reaction to the hypothesis came only after 70 years.

A.D. White said that all branches of the Protestant Church – Lutheran, Calvinist, and Anglican denounced the Copernican hypothesis as contrary to the scripture. However, on a closer examination, this claim seems to be far too sweeping. Martin Luther and John Calvin never mentioned Copernicus' theory in their writings though Calvin did deny the moving earth in his sermon on the basis that it conflicts with common sense, not with the scripture.[24] Martin Luther was reported to have learnt about Copernicus' cosmology from his friends before the book *De Revolutionibus* was published. He said, "Whoever wants to be clever has to do his own thing. This is what that fool does who wants to turn astronomy upside down."[25] Gingerich comments: "His remark has gained publicity out of proportion to its significance."[26] The most noted opposition

22 Colin A. Russell, *Cross-Currents*, p. 38.

23 Owen Gingerich, "The Copernican Revolution," p. 98.

24 Colin A. Russell, *Cross-Currents*, p. 42.

25 Cited in Owen Gingerich, "The Copernican Revolution," p. 99.

26 *Ibid.*

from the Protestant side was represented by Philip Melanchthon, the right-hand man of Martin Luther, who took the support of Biblical verses like - the sun coming out like a bridegroom (Ps. 19:5), the earth being established and stood fast (Ps. 119:90). However, in spite of attempts here and there from the Protestant side, the opposition was muted and ineffective. Russell notes, "The atmosphere was, at worst, sultry rather than explosive, with occasional rumblings of distant thunder."[27] This may be due to the absence of substantial opposition of Copernicus' hypothesis from the Roman Catholic Church. Copernicus' idea of the heliocentric universe was strongly opposed by the Church only when it was supported by Galileo, more than 70 years after the publication of the *De Revolutionibus*. It was only in 1616 that *De Revolutionibus* was declared erroneous and heretical and placed it on the Index of Prohibited Books.

2.2. Kepler

Johannes Kepler (1571-1630) was a German astronomer who was the first great Protestant scientist. He was basically known for his three laws of planetary movement, which supplement a serious shortcoming in Copernicus' cosmology. Kepler came from a very humble and poor family in a small German town called Weil der Stadt. When he was just five years old, his family moved to Leonberg, where he did his education in German as well as in Latin. He was fortunate enough to get a scholarship that made possible his studies at the Lutheran Stift, or seminary, at the University of Tübingen, where he began his university studies in 1589. He continued his education at Maulbronn, and while he was still at Maulbronn, he had officially been registered as a student at Tübingen for almost a year. Thus, he completed his undergraduate studies at Maulbronn and passed by examination at Tübingen, earning a BA degree without having attended classes there. His dream was to proceed to the university to pursue an MA degree and then get advanced training in theology to enter service in the Church. It was expected that the boys who graduated from these schools would go on to become schoolteachers, ministers, or state functionaries. Kepler's teacher at Tübingen University in Mathematics and astronomy was Michael Maestlin, who was well versed in Copernicus' cosmology, and he believed that it was true.[28]

Kepler learnt both the classical cosmology and the new one proposed by Copernicus from his teacher and he readily accepted the latter. He finished his Master degree in 1591 and pursued theological studies. In early 1594, however, came a devastating change of plans. Within months of completing an additional three years of theological studies, Kepler was forced to cut them off as the Tübingen University selected him to work as a mathematics teacher at the Protestant seminary school in Graz, Styria in Austria. This post was vacant due

27 Colin A. Russell, *Cross-Currents*, p. 42.

28 See James R. Voelkel, *Johannes Kepler and the New Astronomy*, (Oxford: Oxford University Press, 1999), pp. 14-17.

to the demise of the former teacher. He was in great trouble and dilemma. His aspiration to become a Pastor was high, and to take up a job which was considered much lower, that also in a faraway foreign land, was not easy, but he understood that this was a call of duty. Finally, he decided to go to Austria with a commitment that he would someday return to Church's ministry.[29] This decision might have been the right decision for him because we could have a Kepler, an astronomer who had left an indelible mark in the history of cosmology.

Kepler did not stay long at Graz. Roman Catholic authorities did not receive his teaching well as he was inclined towards believing in the sun-centred cosmology expounded by Copernicus. So, he was forced to leave Graz in 1598. He went to Prague in 1600, where he worked as an assistant to Danish astronomer Tycho Brahe (1546-1601). Kepler inherited all the astronomical data of Tycho after his death, which proved to be very helpful for him in his studies of planetary movements.

2.2.1. Kepler's Laws

Kepler's main contribution lies in the area of planetary movement, and his laws of planetary movement changed the way human beings perceive the movements of the planets forever. From Aristotle down to Copernicus, it was considered that heavenly bodies move in perfect circular ways. As we have seen before, this circular motion could not explain phenomena like variation in the brightness of the planets at night, etc. To address this problem, they introduced epicycles. Even Copernicus, though he rectified a flaw in Aristotle-Ptolemy's cosmology by proposing a heliocentric universe, retained the prevailing idea that planets moved around the sun following a circular path. Kepler was unwilling to accept the centuries-old obsession with a circular motion and found out that the orbit of planets were ellipses. He himself acknowledged the importance of his discovery and thus says, "I was almost driven to madness in considering and calculating this matter… I have laid a monstrous egg."[30]

In the early 1600s, Kepler proposed three laws of planetary motion. They are as follows:

(a) Planets move around the sun in elliptical orbits with the sun at a focus of the ellipse.
(b) The imaginary line drawn between the sun and any planet marks out equal areas in equal times.
(c) The ratio of the squares of the periods of any two planets is equal to the ratio of the cubes of their average distances from the sun.

The first law of planetary motion was published in 1609 in one of Kepler's books, *Astronomia Nova* (*New Astronomy*). Another of Kepler's important works

29 *Ibid.*, pp. 22-23.

30 Quotes in Peter Barrett, *Science and Theology since Copernicus*, p. 29.

- *Epitome Astronomiae Copernicanae* (*Epitome of Copernicus Astronomy*), was published in volumes between 1618 and 1621. This book was a defence of the Copernicus system. He used many of his own ideas in this book, for example, an analogy between the arrangement of the universe and the Holy Trinity.[31] It may be mentioned here that though Kepler's efforts to explain the underlying reasons for planetary motions are no longer accepted, the actual laws themselves are still considered as an accurate description of the motion of any planet and any satellite.

2.2.2. Kepler and the Church

Kepler was a dedicated protestant Christian who aspired and was deemed to be a Pastor. Though he adopted Copernicus' heliocentric doctrine of the universe, his protestant churches did not give him much problem. He studied theology and was eager to enter full-time Church ministry. As noted before, he had to abandon his aim in life with much reluctance for a job as a mathematics teacher in a Lutheran school in Graz. So, there is no question of his loyalty to the Church and to the teachings of the Bible. However, he followed Copernicus' model of the universe that earned him expulsion from Graz by Roman Catholic authorities in 1598. His book *Epitome Astronomiae Copernicanae* (*Epitome of Copernicus Astronomy*), where he defended Copernicus' theory, was placed in the Roman Catholic Church's *Index of Forbidden Books*.

Kepler was highly responsible for changing our knowledge about the universe, especially how planets move around the sun. One of his important contributions is the use of mathematics in scientific research. His laws of planetary movement not only rectified the wrong knowledge of the movements of the heavenly bodies and cleared some of the profound astronomical problems but also became one of the bases of Newton's laws of motion. His perception of the works of God in and through sciences is enlightening, and he himself is a living example of the integral relationship between science and religion.

2.3. Galileo

It is frequently noted that Galileo Galilei (1564-1642) was born on the day of Michelangelo's death and that he died in the year of Newton's birth. These facts are significant as they placed Galileo's position between the Renaissance with its reverence for the opinions of the Greek philosophers and the age of exact science with its demand for experimental confirmation of its theories.[32] Some people called him the father of modern science, and with him dawned the age of science where experimental proof became the most important method in scientific research. It has been said of Galileo that "he belongs among that small group of men such as Petrarch, Erasmus, and Voltaire, whose lives stand for a transitional epoch in the history of men's minds, who at once bear the marks of the age they

31 Nancy Morvillo, *Science and Religion*, p. 68.

32 N.A., *The Mathematics Teacher*, (Vol. 24, No. 2, February, 1931), p. 118.

help to supplant, and in their thoughts create and anticipate the development of succeeding ages."[33]

2.3.1. His Life and Works

Galileo was born in Pisa, Italy, in 1564. His father, Vincenzio Galilei, was of noble birth and well educated, especially in Greek, Latin, Mathematics, and Music. Galileo was the eldest of six children, and the family was poor, which meant that Galileo would have to work for a living. His father decided that the boy should follow in his footsteps and go into the business of selling cloth but agreed to give him a good education first. At the age of thirteen, he was sent to a famous monastery near Florence. Here, he excelled in Greek and Latin language and literature, wrote essays and poems, played well on several musical instruments, and showed considerable skill as an artist.[34] Galileo's father seeing his son's talent and great ability, wanted him to study medicine; and he sent him to the University of Pisa so that he could become a professor of medicine, which was the highest-paid of all professors during that time. Galileo, however, became interested in Mathematics, and at the age of twenty-five, he accepted a poorly paid position as lecturer in Mathematics at Pisa.[35]

He then went to Padua to become a professor of Mathematics at the University of Padua. Here, he invented sector compasses and made the first thermometer. While at Padua he embraced Copernicus' heliocentric model of the universe. A Dutch spectacle-maker of Middleburg made a toy by glueing two lenses to a stick a few inches long. If you looked through the lenses at a weathercock, it appeared enlarged and upside down. Some Italian travellers saw the toy and mentioned it when they returned home. Galileo heard of it and immediately began to make his own telescope, improving the Dutch idea. The news of his invention spread like wildfire. His salary was immediately increased from $340 to $1000 a year. He made more than 200 telescopes and the largest one had a lens 2.25 inches in diameter and 5.5 feet focal length. He then turned one of his telescopes up to the heavens in 1609 to study planets, stars and their movements.[36] In the first month of 1610, he could announce that four satellites are revolving around planet Jupiter just as the moon revolves around the earth. This suggested that if Jupiter, which has satellites, is a planet, satellite-carrying earth could also be just a planet! It also revealed that all the heavenly bodies did not revolve around the earth directly. Galileo also noticed that the moon was not the perfect unblemished ball as Aristotle thought it to be, but having rough

33 Martha Ornstein, *The Role of Scientific Societies in the Seventeenth Century*, (Chicago, 1928), p. 23 cited in *Ibid.*

34 Frederick Slocum, "Galileo Galilei, A Pioneer in Scientific Research," *Publications of the Astronomical Society of the Pacific*, (Vol. XLV, No. 265, June, 1933), p. 103.

35 N.A., *The Mathematics Teacher*, p. 118.

36 Frederick Slocum, *Galileo Galilei*, pp. 109-110.

mountains and valleys. The new discovery was a death blow to Aristotelian-Ptolemaic geocentric cosmology.

For eighteen years, he lectured, taught private pupils, and carried on his researches at Padua. Among the works that he had wholly or partly finished were two books on the system and structure of the universe, an immense work full of philosophy, astronomy, and geometry; three books on natural and violent motions; three books on mechanics; one on sound and speech; one on light and colour; one on the tides; one on the composition of continuous quantity; one on the movements of animals; and several on military tactics. In addition to his writings, he had invented various things - There was what he called the military compass, a computing device somewhat on the principle of a slide rule. Several thousand of these were made and sold or given away. He also made magnets, magnetic compasses for ships, thermometers, microscopes, and, of course, telescopes in huge numbers.[37] Towards the end of his stay at Padua, his experience and new discoveries made him convinced that the Copernican heliocentric doctrine was right. Galileo was looking for proof and final vindication of the Copernican system. In August 1597, he wrote to Kepler, "I adopted the opinion of Copernicus many years ago."[38] Though he knew instinctively that Copernicus was right, he had yet to find the scientific observational proof that came only after discovering the telescope and pierced through the sky by it.

In spite of his successful carrier, he felt that in Padua he had less time for research and writing as much of his time was taken up by private tuition. At the invitation of Cosimo II, Grand Duke of Tuscany, who was his former student, he shifted to Florence. The University of Padua was very liberal and could accommodate radical teachings, whereas Florence was controlled by the Church and was next door to Rome. It was sure that in Florence, Galileo would not have the same academic freedom he enjoyed in Padua.

After he settled in Florence, he visited Rome at the invitation of the Pope. Frederick Slocum reports:

> He was right royally received. The church dignitaries vied with the nobles and learned laymen in doing him honor. Galileo showed cardinals and others his telescope, and to as many as would look through it, he showed Jupiter and its moons, and other 'celestial novelties.' He talked, he harangued, he held forth in the midst of a dozen or more disputants at once, and enjoyed himself immensely... He had a long audience with the Pope and the two parted good friends. Apparently all were greatly impressed by what they saw and heard.[39]

---

37 *Ibid.*, p. 116.

38 Quoted in I. Bernard Cohen, "The Progress of Science: The Heritage of Galileo," *The Scientific Monthly*, (Vol. 54, No. 3, March, 1942), pp. 283.

39 Frederick Slocum, *Galileo Galilei,* pp. 118-119.

2.3.2. The Controversial Book

In 1616, when Galileo was still in Rome, Pope Paul V commissioned several theologians to look into the matter of heliocentric doctrine. They reported back to the Pope, saying that placing the sun, not the earth, at the center of the universe was a deviation from biblical truth. Consequently, Copernicus' *De Revolutionibus* was declared heretical by the Roman Catholic Church and put in the *Index of Forbidden Books.* Moreover, Pope Paul V directed Cardinal Bellarmine to warn Galileo of the danger of heresy. Galileo was summoned on 25 February 1616 and was told: "to relinquish altogether the theory that the Sun is at the center of the world and at rest and that the Earth moves."[40] In stark contrast to the initial warm reception he received, Galileo left Rome dejected and returned to Florence. For some seven years, Galileo kept a low profile and decided not to do anything that would provoke the anger of Church authorities.

Pope Paul V died and was succeeded by Cardinal Barbarini as Pope Urban VIII in 1623. This man was not only one of Galileo's best friends but also quite liberal in his theological outlook and was a deeply learned person. Galileo was so delighted and hoped that the Church's decision on heliocentrism would be revoked. He quickly visited the new Pope to congratulate him on assuming the top position of the Church. He had several meetings with the new Pope and it seemed that the new Pope had a positive attitude towards what he had been doing and discovering. Encouraged by this, Galileo began at once what has proved to be his most popular work, *The Dialogues on the Two Principal Systems of the World.*

Although the work, carried on at intervals, was interrupted by Galileo's serious illness in 1628, it was finally completed in 1630. The greatest difficulty was experienced in obtaining a license to print from the ecclesiastical authorities, and it was granted only on the following conditions – (a) that the beginning and the end of the four days dialogues were dealt with more circumspectly; (b) that the Copernican doctrine regarding the motion of the earth was treated hypothetically, and (c) that however effective the arguments in favour of that doctrine might be, they must be subordinated to the evidence in the Holy Scriptures. However, the fact remains that Galileo's impulsive and scornful character led him to transgress all the limits laid down by the ecclesiastical authorities.[41] The book was published in 1632.[42] It was about a series of four conversations in four days between three

---

40 Eduardo Rodrigues da Cruz, "It Started with Galileo," *Zygon*, (Vol. 42, No. 3, September 2007), p. 591.

41 Giorgio Abetti, "Galileo Galilei as a Pioneer in the Physical Sciences," *Publications of the Astronomical Society of the Pacific*, Vol. 43, No. 252 (April, 1931), p. 134.

42 The actual tile of the book was - *Il Dialogo di Galileo Galilei, Linceo, matematico sopraordinario dello Studio di Pisa, e filosofo e matematico primario del Seremissimo Gran Duca di Toscana. Dove ne i congressi di quattro giornate si discorre sopra i due Massimi Sistemi del Mondo, Tolemaico e Copernicano, proponendo indeterminatamente le ragioni filosofiche e naturali tanto per l'una quanto per l'altra parte* (*The Dialogue of Galileo Galilei, Lyncean, mathematician extraordinary of*

characters: Salviati, a Copernican philosopher; Sagredo, a wit and scholar, keen and critical; and Simplicio, an Aristotelian philosopher who propounds the stock arguments in favour of the Ptolemaic theory. The conversations are conducted with good temper and fairness, and, discreetly enough, no definite conclusion is arrived at.[43] Though he made it clear in the title as well as in the *Preface* that he would deal with both doctrines impartially, one must admit that his convictions of the truth of his arguments gained the upper hand, so that the Copernican system triumphs all through the *Dialogues*. Frederick Slocum notes, "The arguments in favour of the Earth's motion around the Sun are so strong and so popularly stated that they did more in a few years to undermine the old system than all that had been written or spoken before."[44]

2.3.3. The Church's Reaction

Soon after the publication of *The Dialogues*, Pope Urban VIII appointed a special commission to look into the matter. The commission discovered the injunction given to Galileo by Cardinal Bellarmine, which was unknown to Pope Urban VIII. Immediately Galileo was summoned to Rome to appear before the Church's authorities. By this time, Galileo was already around seventy years old and in poor health. Still, he had no choice but to travel to Rome to appear before the Inquisition. There were two main legal questions at the trial – (a) whether Galileo had kept his promise to fulfill the conditions laid down by the Church's authority before the publication of the book; (b) more importantly, whether Galileo had violated the injunction supposedly served on him in 1616 by Cardinal Bellarmine. The historic trial took place in June 1633. The Holy Office brought out an Injunction that was supposedly served to Galileo in 1616. But, it is said that Galileo had never seen this injunction before. Galileo, on his part, produced before the court Bellarmine's letter of 1616, previously unknown to the prosecutors, which made no mention of any injunction but contained the weaker restriction on 'defending and holding' Copernicanism.[45] The court ruled in favour of the Holy Office. In both cases, Galileo Galilei was found guilty! At the age of 70, with poor health, Poor Galileo was not able to clear the accusations labelled against him.

He was sentenced, *first,* to abjuration or disowning; *second*, to formal imprisonment for life; *third*, to recite the seven penitential Psalms every week.

---

the University of Pisa, and philosopher and first mathematician of the Most Serene Grand Duke of Tuscany. Where in meetings of four days the two Principal Systems of the World, the Ptolemaic and the Copernican are discussed, and impartially pointing out the philosophical and natural augments as much for the one side and for the other). See *Ibid.*, pp. 134-135.

43 Frederick Slocum, *Galileo Galilei,* p. 120.

44 *Ibid.*

45 Richard J. Blackwell, "Galileo Galilei" in *Science and Religion: A Historical Introduction*, (Baltimore: The Johns Hopkins University Press, 2002), p. 114.

The last one was done for him by his daughter, Sister Marie Celeste. His book – *The Dialogue* was banned and put in the **Index of Prohibited Books**. His imprisonment consisted in being confined to the little town of Arcetri where he lived. When he wanted to go to Florence for medical treatment, he had to get permission from the Inquisitors. The abjuration was read out by him while kneeling, and the copies were sent to all the colleges and churches; professors read it before their classes; priests read it in the churches, and copies were sent to all of Galileo's friends and to the literati of all Europe.[46] A portion of abjuration reads:

> I, Galileo Galilei, son of the late Vincenzio Galilei, of Florence, aged seventy years, being brought personally to judgment, and kneeling before you Most Eminent and Most Reverend Lords, Cardinals, General Inquisitors of the universal Christian republic against heretical depravity, having before my eyes the Holy Gospels, which I touch with my own hands, swear that I have always believed, and now believe, and with the help of God will in the future believe, every article which the Holy Catholic and Apostolic Church of Rome holds, teaches, and preaches. But because I have been enjoined by this Holy Office altogether to abandon the false opinion which maintains that the sun is the centre and immovable, and forbidden to hold, defend, or teach the said false doctrine in any manner, and after it hath been signified to me that the said doctrine is repugnant with the Holy Scripture, I have written and printed a book, in which I treat of the same doctrine now condemned, and adduce reasons with great force in support of the same, without giving any solution, and therefore have been judged grievously suspected of heresy; that is to say, that I have held and believed that the sun is the centre of the universe and is immovable, and that the earth is not the centre and is movable; willing, therefore to remove from the minds of your Eminences, and of every Catholic Christian, this vehement suspicion rightfully entertained towards me, with a sincere heart and unfeigned faith, I abjure, curse, and detest the said errors and heresies, and generally every other error and sect contrary to Holy Church; and I swear that I will never more in future say or assert anything verbally or in writing, which may give rise to a similar suspicion of me…[47]

There was a rumour that after he read out the abjuration, as he was rising from his knees, Galileo was heard saying, "but it (the earth) does move." However, it is impossible to verify whether this was true or false; it was unlikely that Galileo could have enough courage to utter such words under such a situation in front of such audiences.

---

46 Frederick Slocum, *Galileo Galilei,* p. 122.

47 *Ibid.*, pp. 122-123.

The 1633 condemnation of Galileo had been reformed several times: in 1741–1744, with the Church's *imprimatur* (official permission) for the publication of the *Dialogue*; in 1757–1758, with the abolition of the general prohibition of Copernican books; in 1820–1822, with the explicit permission of books advocating the earth's motion as a thesis; and in 1835, with the removal from the Index of Copernicus's and Galileo's books.[48] Pope John Paul II finally admitted in 1979 that the Church was wrong in condemning Galileo.[49]

Galileo was a devout Catholic, deeply committed to the biblical truth. According to him, the author of the Bible and the universe is the same and only one God, and there can be no contradiction when understood both of these correctly. His intention was to help the Church to know the truth of God's creation. Unlike Copernicus, he wrote in Italian, not in Latin, so that his works could be read by a wider audience. He proved himself to be a pioneer in the history of both science and religion in the sense that from him, we learnt that science could err, so also the religious interpretation of truth. He not only became a pioneer in scientific experimentational research but also set the stage for future scientists like Newton to work on and unveil the mysteries of the universe. His experiments on the falling body became the foundation of Newton's law of motion. It is no wonder that Galileo is remembered as the father of modern science.

2.4. Newton

Isaac Newton (1642-1727) was one of the most important persons in science. He is generally recognized as one of the greatest creative men of genius who ever existed. His most important book – *Mathematical Principles of Natural Philosophy* or simply known as *the Principia*, published in 1687, was, according to Stephen Hawking, "probably the most important single work ever published in the physical sciences."[50]

2.4.1 His Life and Carrier

Newton was born prematurely on Christmas day 1642 in the manor house of Woolsthorpe, a tiny hamlet a few miles south of Grantham. He was so tiny that his mother often remarked that he was small enough to fit into a quart pot at birth. His father, an illiterate, had died three months before Newton was born. His mother looked after him with complete dedication till he was three years old, and then remarried. She abandoned him, leaving him at the hands of his maternal

48 Maurice A. Finochiaro, "The Church and Galileo," *The Catholic Historical Review*, Volume 94, Number 2, April 2008, p. 279.

49 *Ibid.*, p. 275. For a detailed discussion on Galileo and the Church see Ernan McMullin, *The Church and Galileo*, (Notre Dame: University of Notre Dame Press, 2005).

50 Stephen Hawking, *A Brief History of Time: From the Big Bang to Black Holes*, (London: Bantam Books, 1989), p. 5.

grandmother. When Newton was about eleven years old, his mother returned home due to the death of her husband.

In 1655 he was sent to the Grammar School at Grantham and boarded with a chemist in the town so that he might get his education free. Here he seemed to have come under an excellent master, one Henry Stokes. Newton was described as a sober, silent, thinking lad, respected but not popular. His skill in drawing and in constructing toys, clocks, kites, etc., amazed his friends in school. He already showed scientific aptitude rare in a boy of his age: for instance, in making his kites, he tried all kinds of shapes and investigated by experiment the best point to which to attach the string. These kites acquired local fame, for at night he flew them with lanterns attached, which frightened some of the country folk.[51] In June 1661, when he was 18, Newton was sent to Trinity College, Cambridge. In February 1664 he was elected scholar and took his BA in 1665. In 1667 he became a minor fellow; in 1668, an MA and major fellow. In 1669, at the age of 27, he became Professor of Mathematics at Cambridge.[52] In 1696 he left Cambridge, and the rest of his career covered some thirty years during which he lived in London, holding in succession the offices of Warden and Master of the Mint. Rouse Ball describes Newton's condition of life in London as follows:

> He was now comparatively wealthy, which gave him opportunities he much valued for generosity, enjoyed a well-appointed home, knew everyone whom he desired, and was universally honoured and esteemed, while, being past middle life, his fits of abstraction and his untidiness in dress and manners were looked on as mere eccentricities of genius. In such circumstances his character mellowed.[53]

He was widely regarded as the foremost Mathematician and physicist of Europe. He was elected as the President of Royal Society in 1703 and was knighted in 1705.[54]

2.4.2. His Scientific Contributions

It is characteristic of physicists and mathematicians to make their major contributions early in life. Newton's main discoveries were made in 1664-1666, between the ages of 21 and 23. During those two years, Newton formulated his basic laws of mechanics, his optical observations on the nature of light, the calculus, and the law of universal gravitation.[55] His most celebrated work – *Philosophiae Naturalis Principia Mathematica* (*Mathematical Principles of Natural Philosophy*)

---

51 W. W. Rouse Ball, "Newton," *The Mathematical Gazette*, (Vol. 7, No. 112, July, 1914), p. 349.

52 Anthony Storr, "Isaac Newton," *British Medical Journal (Clinical Research Edition),* (Vol. 291, No. 6511, Dec. 21-28, 1985), p. 1780.

53 W. W. Rouse Ball, "Newton," p. 352.

54 See Peter Barrett, *Science and Theology since Copernicus*, p. 50.

55 Anthony Storr, "Isaac Newton," p. 1783.

was published in 1687, where he underlined a number of his scientific discoveries. The *Principia,* as it is commonly known, marks the climax of the Scientific Revolution inaugurated by Copernicus' *De Revolutionibus*. The *Principia* covers various topics in three sections. The first section deals with the general principles governing the motion of bodies, the second section talks about the application of these principles to the motion of celestial bodies like planets and satellites under the force of gravity, and the third section is about fluid mechanics, the theory of waves and other aspects of general physics.[56]

Let us discuss in brief some of the important elements in Newtonian mechanics that changed the way humans perceive the universe:

(a) Newton's Laws of Motion

The three famous laws of motion are explained in brief as follows –

First Law - *A body remains at rest or in uniform motion unless acted upon by a force.* If we see a body at rest or in uniform motion, we know that the force acting on the body is zero. In other words, an object in motion will stay in motion in the same direction in a straight line unless there is a force acting upon it. A bullet fired from a gun will be in the same motion with the same velocity, in the same direction forever were it not for the simultaneous forces of gravity and the resistance of the atmospheric air. Likewise, an object which is at rest will be at rest forever until and unless some forces act upon it.

Second Law – If a force is applied to an object, it will move in the direction of the force, *the amount of force exerted is directly proportional to the mass of a body.* [$F = ma$, where F is a force, m - mass and a – acceleration]. Let's take examples to illustrate – A shopping cart, when empty, needs less force to make it move, whereas we need to apply more force to make it move if the cart is full. If the same force is applied to the moving carts, the empty cart will move faster than the full one. Again, if two distinct bodies are moving at a constant acceleration, the object with the larger mass will produce the greater force. For example, a car and a train that are travelling towards each other at an equal rate of speed collide, the force exerted on the car will be much greater due to the much greater mass of the train.

Third Law – *To every action (force), there is an equal and opposite reaction (force).* If two bodies exert forces on each other, these forces are equal in magnitude and opposite in direction. For instance, the force that a Cricket ball exerts on a bat is equal and opposite of the force that the bat exerts on the ball.

(b) Universal Law of Gravity

Newton synthesized the discoveries of Kepler, who had been able to describe the motions of the planets around the sun, and of Galileo, who had described the laws of motion of objects upon the earth to produce his famous universal law of gravity. Until Newton, no one could see the connection between planetary movements

56 Cf. Peter Barrett, *Science and Theology since Copernicus*, p. 49.

and falling bodies on the ground. Newton combined the discoveries of Kepler and Galileo in such a way that the motions of bodies in the heavens and bodies on earth are known to obey the same universal laws. Thus, he established that gravity was universal. Newton's law of gravitation, which states that "everybody in the universe attracts every other with a force directly proportional to the product of their masses and inversely proportional to the square of the distance between them," has been described as the greatest generalization achieved by the human mind. To prove his law, Newton had to show that the path of the moon around the earth could be accounted for by the interaction of the gravitational force on it, which he supposed the earth to be exerting, together with the centrifugal force of the moon, the formula for which had already been discovered by a Dutch Mathematician and Physicist, Huygens. He then computed the sun's attraction on the planets and showed that their orbits, which Kepler had described, but he could not account for, comply with the same laws. Newton left a diagram that anticipates the possibility of artificial satellites by showing that increasing the velocity of a projectile will eventually result in its circling the earth at the same velocity forever.[57]

The new discovery of Newton was the foundation of modern physics. For example, Newtonian physics help modern scientists to send a spacecraft on a planetary mission. In the words of Capra, "It was indeed a most formidable foundation supporting, like a mighty rock, all of science and providing a firm basis for natural philosophy for almost three centuries."[58]

(c) Absolute Universe and Absolute Time

The Newtonian universe was a three-dimensional space. It was an absolute space, always at rest and unchangeable. In the words of Newton, "Absolute space, in its own nature, without regard to anything external, remains always similar and immovable." All changes in the physical world were described in terms of a separate dimension, called time, which again was absolute, having no connection with the material world flowing smoothly from the past through the present to the future – "Absolute, true, and mathematical time, of itself and by its own nature, flows uniformly, without regard to anything external," says Newton.[59] So, for Newton, the universe is fixed, absolute and unchanged, time is also unchanged and absolute. However, the Newtonian *absolute universe* and *absolute time* were rejected by scientists like Albert Einstein, etc. as we shall see later.

(d) Universe as a Cosmic Machine

One of the main contributions of Newton was his idea of a mechanical universe that changed totally the way people perceive the universe. He explained the

57 Anthony Storr, "Isaac Newton," p. 1783.

58 Fritjof Capra, *The Tao of Physics: An Exploration of the Parallel between Modern Physics and Eastern Mysticism*, (London: HarperCollins Publishers, 1982, first published in 1975), p. 63.

59 *Ibid.*

universe on mechanical principles governed by the three laws of motion and the law of universal gravitation. In the words of Peter Barrett, this fulfils Descartes' vision of nature as a perfectly ordered machine governed by mathematical laws.[60] But the interesting point is Newton did not believe that natural cause could have helped planets and the moon to move in such a precise manner. There must be a controller which or who is very well skilled in mechanics and geometry. It is nothing but God, who is divine intelligence, skilled in mechanics and geometry, having gravitational force as 'puppet strings,' maintains and regulates the movements of heavenly bodies.

In spite of this, the Newtonian mechanistic worldview had led to the development of a new religious ideology. It is assumed that Newton's emphasis on the regularity of nature and mechanical movement of heavenly bodies encouraged the rise of 'Deism.' The term 'deism' (from the Latin *deus*, 'god') is often used in a general sense to refer to that view that God was the creator but deny a continuing divine involvement with, or special presence within, that creation. It is thus often contrasted with 'theism' (from the Greek *theos*, 'god'), which allows for continuing divine involvement within the world.[61]

Newton was not only a great scientist but also a devout Christian and a serious theologian, deeply committed to the word of God. His theological writings, though not as popular as his scientific writings, were far more numerous than his scientific writings. He was not popular as a theologian, most probably due to his theological belief in Unitarianism. Most of his theological writings were unknown during his lifetime as they were not published. When Newton died, he left a huge amount of writings - correspondences, notes, and manuscripts, making up some 10 million words which may be equivalent to about 150 normal books. Around half of these are theological writings. Newton's theological position was unorthodox; he rejected the doctrine of the trinity. It appeared that Newton's heir, John Conduitt feared that his heretical theological position may be discovered and that his fame would be turned into hatred; thus, he kept those controversial works unpublished. It was only after the 1960s that some of Newton's theological works were known to the world. Now, most of his works are available online.

From these works and the works published during his lifetime such as, *Principia* and *Opticks*, we come to know Newton's religious commitment. He never saw science and religion as opposing each other. He assumed that his scientific theories did not stand on their own but were dependent on God. In his *Opticks,* he wrote: "Does it not appear from phenomena that there is a Being incorporeal, living, intelligent, omnipresent, who in infinite space . . . sees the things themselves intimately and thoroughly perceives them and comprehends them wholly." In tune with this, he also has these lines in his *Principia*: "This

60 Peter Barrett, *Science and Theology Since Copernicus*, p. 51.

61 See Alister E. McGrath, *Science and Religion: An Introduction*, (Oxford: Blackwell Publishers, 1999), p. 18.

Being governs all things, not as the soul of the world, but as Lord over all… And from his true dominion, it follows that the true God is a Living, Intelligent, and Powerful Being; and from his other perfections, that he is Supreme or most Perfect." These indicate that Newton has a theocentric scientific approach. His scientific theories are meant not to challenge God's words revealed in the Bible or dispute with the Church, but for the people to know that God is behind all these scientific truths. In his letter to Richard Bentley, the Master of Trinity College, Cambridge, Newton said: "When I wrote my treatise about our system, I had an eye upon such principles as might work with considering men for the belief of a Deity; and nothing can rejoice me more than to find it useful for that purpose."

Concluding Remarks

Science understood as a systematically organized body of knowledge and religion understood as a human response to God or Ultimate reality are both limited and imperfect because they are by and large the product of imperfect and limited human beings. So, 'scientific truth' and 'religious truth' about the universe will also be imperfect and cannot be absolute truth. Though limited and imperfect, they are both important as they reveal some truth about the universe and the laws operating in it. They both express the truth in so far as they could perceive it within their limited methodological frameworks. Science (or rather physical science in our case here) and religion (represented by Christianity here) are both operated by limited human beings with limited cognitive faculties, and it is no wonder that sometimes they come in conflict with one another. This does not mean that science and religion are essentially opposing one another. As we see in this Chapter, the crux of the problem is the incomplete understanding of facts and realities produced by the limited cognizing faculties of humans that operate both in the arena of science and religion but not the reality of science and religion themselves.

We need to understand that both science and religion are meant for complementing one another as they are fellow travellers on the path of truth. They should not be considered conflicting because insofar as the history of the interaction between science and religion is concerned, the conflict happened because of spurious interpretation of truth but not at the level of the real scientific and religious truths. The real scientific truth is the highest religious conviction, and there is no way of conflicting. Galileo was right, though it was not recognized then, in stating that the author of the Bible and the universe is the same, and there can be no contradiction when understood both of these correctly. As both science and religion are dynamic, scientific theories and discoveries, as well as religious convictions, are subject to change and modification. Therefore, conflict is temporary, originated from a limited grasp of the unlimited divine truth revealed in and through the universe.

Chapter 4

Scientific Developments in the Nineteenth and Twentieth Centuries

The nineteenth and twentieth centuries witnessed a mushrooming of scientific theories and discoveries. Out of so many scientific developments during this period, we will discuss here three major groundbreaking works in the scientific world, such as the *Theory of Evolution* propounded by Charles Darwin and Church's reactions, *Theories of Relativity* by Albert Einstein, and the whole concept of *Quantum Mechanics*.

1. Charles Darwin and Evolution Theory

One of the greatest scientific theories, and that was in direct conflict with religious conviction concerning creation, was the theory of evolution propounded by an eminent English scientist and naturalist, Charles Darwin. Just as Newton and Einstein are monumental for their works in physics, Darwin's contribution in the field of natural science is significant. Bernard Davis maintains that Darwin's theory of evolution by natural selection is "a unique product of the scientific method," which was "based almost entirely on historical inferences rather than on hypotheses validated by experimental tests," and therefore, "is one of the greatest triumphs of that method" which "is clearly the most important generalization in biology." This theory "provides a realistic picture of man's origin that places him at a unique pinnacle in evolution, replacing earlier speculations that tried to account for his obviously unique qualities in other ways."[1]

1 Bernard D. Davis, "Evolution, Human Diversity, and Society," *Zygon*, (Vol. 11, No. 2, June 1976), pp. 81-82.

Darwin is one of the most controversial scientists during his time and after. There are as many admirers as enemies among the scientists then and now. His works not only came in direct conflict with the teachings of Christianity and other religions on the creation and the origin of life on the earth but also divided the scientific community into two halves. Writing on Darwin in the early part of the twentieth century, R.W. Wallace explained the division Darwin brought to the people:

> In Darwin's own day his theories divided the scientific household. Able nature students willingly grouped themselves on his side, while others just as able found themselves compelled to antagonize his hypothesis. Many scientific societies in Europe and America loaded him with honors, while in his homeland he was made a Fellow of the Royal Society. On the other hand, by a vote of 48 to 15, the French Academy declined to give him a place among the 'Immortals' on the ground that his works were 'not science, but a mass of assertions and absolutely gratuitous hypotheses, often evidently fallacious.'[2]

Whether we like the theory he put forward or not, the fact remains that Charles Darwin is one of the greatest scientists, and his works are still considered as the milestone in the studies of natural lives.

1.1. His Life

Charles Robert Darwin (1809-1882) was born in Shrewsbury to a wealthy family. His father Robert Waring Darwin, a physician and his mother, Susannah Wedgwood Darwin, both came from considerably well-to-do families. Charles Darwin inherited a scientific brain from his father and his grandfather, Erasmus Darwin, who was noted for his scientific research and theories and his book *Zoonomia* became quite famous. In this book, the idea of evolution was already born, which was fully developed by his grandson Charles Darwin. His mother died when he was eight, and Darwin was brought up by his elder sister Caroline.

He was sent to Shrewsbury Grammar school, where he was mainly taught Greek and Latin, and it was said that Darwin was not inspired by these subjects to work hard. Although he developed good habits of study, he attained only an average school record. He was regarded by his teachers, father, and probably also by his sisters 'as a very ordinary boy, rather below the common standard of intellect.'[3] Though he was not interested in Greek and Latin studies and could not score high marks, he showed remarkably distinctive powerful mental ability

2 R. W. Wallace, "Charles Darwin," *The Journal of Education*, (Vol. 69, No. 6, February 11, 1909), pp. 146-147.

3 Ralph Colp Jr., "Charles Darwin: Man and Scientist," *The Centennial Review*, (Vol. 27, No. 2 Spring 1983), p. 97. See also Nora Barlow, ed., *The Autobiography of Charles Darwin, 1809-1882*, (London: Collins, 1958), p. 28.

when it came to dealing with nature – plants and animals. In his *Autobiography*, he wrote: "My taste for natural history, and more especially for collecting, was well developed. I tried to make out the names of plants and collected all sorts of things, shells, seals, franks, coins and minerals."[4] He used to go to the countryside all by himself to study insects, animals and birds and he was enchanted by the beautiful and unusual scenery of the natural world. Such a deep interest in nature had already developed in him before he was ten years old.

In 1825 when Darwin was sixteen, his father sent him to Edinburgh University to study medicine. However, he was not interested in medicine and felt lectures on human anatomy disgusting and could not stand even watching a surgical operation. He left the university after spending two unsuccessful years as a student of medicine. But during his stay at Edinburgh University, he joined the *Plinian Society*, where a group of students held weekly meetings to discuss scientific subjects. He then became friends with Robert Grant, a zoologist and a physician, who was his senior by several years. It seemed that Grant used to discuss with him the evolutionary views of Chevalier de Lamarck, which reminded him of similar views of his paternal grandfather, Erasmus Darwin – of which he had heard about previously or might have read his book. He then probably read Lamarck's first published work on the idea that species change through time as a result of natural events but not through the intervention of God.[5] His interaction with his friends in *Plinian Society* seemed to have left an indelible mark on the life of Darwin.

In 1827 his father sent him to Christ College, Cambridge, to study theology in order to become a minister in the Church of England. He graduated in 1831. During his stay at Cambridge University, two of his teachers deeply influenced him: Adam Sedgwick, who taught geology, and John Stevens Henslow, who taught botany. It was Henslow who recommended Darwin for a position as naturalist on the H. M. S. Beagle, which was preparing for a South American voyage. At the age of twenty-two and half, after getting permission from his reluctant father, who feared that the Beagle expedition would injure his character, reputation, and clerical career,[6] he sailed with the Beagle, which became one of the most decisive events in his life. Wallace narrates how Darwin had spent his life during this voyage:

> During this voyage, which lasted six years, Darwin had the opportunity of studying at close range the luxuriant tropical life of Brazil, the stunted life of Patagonia and Terra del Fuego, and the novel life of Chile and Peru. Nothing escaped his eye; nothing was forgotten in his registration… Darwin became noted among his fellow voyagers as an observer and a commentator on natural history subjects. The monkeys

4 Nora Barlow, ed., *The Autobiography of Charles Darwin*, pp. 22-23.

5 Ralph Colp Jr., "Charles Darwin: Man and Scientist," p. 99.

6 *Ibid.*, p. 102.

> of the Amazon forests, the condors amid the peaks of the Andes, the colossal turtles of the Galapagos Islands, the degenerates of Fuego, and the myriad marvels of marine life came under his inspection and found a place in his painstaking register.[7]

This trip had, so to say, made Darwin to be a mature naturalist as Addison Gulick observes, "When he returned to England in 1836, at the age of 27, his characteristics as a scientific man were fully formed."[8] However, towards the end of Beagle voyage, his father's apprehension had become fulfilled - Darwin had given up his intention to be a clergyman! "He saw himself rather as a scientist who aspired to add 'a little to natural science' and 'to take a fair place among scientific men.'"[9] And for a reason unknown to us, his father also agreed with his intention to abandon the church's service and gave him full freedom to do whatever he wanted to do. Darwin then married his cousin, Emma Wedgwood, in 1839 and settled in Downe, Kent. A *Journal* published by the American Academy of Arts & Sciences that came out few months after his death contains details of how he spent his daily life in his little home:

> Mr. Darwin lived a very quiet and uneventful life... here, attended by every blessing except that of vigorous health, he lived the secluded but busy life which best suited his chosen pursuits and the simplicity of his character. He was seldom seen even at scientific meetings, and never in general society; but he could welcome his friends and fellow-workers to his own house, where he was the most charming of hosts. At his home, without distraction and as continuously as his bodily powers would permit, Mr. Darwin gave himself to his work.[10]

1.2. Darwin's Ideological Context

There were a number of new scientific ideas prevalent during Darwin's time that had probably influenced his thought and eventually shaped his Evolution theory. Nancy Morvillo summarizes scientific ideas prevalent during Darwin's time as follows:[11]

- Advancements in the fields of taxonomy, anatomy, palaeontology, and geology were changing ideas in both science and religion.

---

7 R. W. Wallace, "Charles Darwin," *The Journal of Education*, (Vol. 69, No. 6, February 11, 1909), pp. 146-147.

8 Addison Gulick, "Charles Darwin, the Man," *The Scientific Monthly*, (Vol. 15, No. 2 Aug., 1922), p. 135.

9 Ralph Colp Jr., "Charles Darwin: Man and Scientist," p. 103.

10 N.A., "Charles Darwin," *Proceedings of the American Academy of Arts and Sciences*, (Vol. 17, June, 1881- June, 1882), p. 450.

11 Nancy Morvillo, *Science and Religion: Understanding the Issues*, (Chichester, West Sussex: Willey-Blackwell, 2010), p. 148.

- Gradualism and the notion of Old Earth were discussed in the writings of Lyell.
- Concepts of evolution, as described by Lamarck and outlined in Erasmus Darwin's book *Zoonomia*, were widely known.
- Thomas Malthus described what would happen to human populations as a result of competition for limited food supplies.
- Natural theology, as described by Paley and others, was widely accepted by scientists of the day, including Darwin.

We will elaborate on some of these to locate Darwin's exact position in relation to the prevailing scientific ideas and to see how far these ideas influenced him. Darwin came in contact with several new publications where new scientific ideas and theories were elaborated. John Herschel's book, *A Preliminary Discourse on the Study of Natural Philosophy,*[12] challenged him to contribute something in the field of natural science. He said in his *Autobiography* that after reading this book, he developed "a burning zeal to add even the most humble contribution to the noble structure of Natural Science."[13] He was also convinced by the argument of Lyell in his book *Principles of Geology* which was revolutionizing geological thinking. Lyell propounded the theory of Uniformitarianism over against the theory of Catastrophism. Uniformitarianism held that the present state of the earth was not due to the action of extraordinary past catastrophes but instead was due to present-day forces which were either inaction or, temporarily, inactive.[14] He explained the origin of the earth's most dramatic topographical features like mountain ranges, etc., as the result of slow, gradual and completely naturalistic processes of change.

Again in 1838, Darwin read a book called *Essay on the Principle of Population* by a British economist, Thomas Malthus (1776-1834). Malthus stated that a human population growing unchecked would double every 25 years. Resources such as food, air and water cannot increase at the same rate, Malthus argued. Thus, human beings are involved in an intense 'struggle for existence,' competing for the limited resources. Darwin himself confessed that this book helped him to conceptualize his theory of Natural Selection.

It was way back in Edinburgh that Darwin learnt about Chevalier de Lamarck's (1744-1829) work on the possibility of evolution. Lamarck's main argument was that species of animal was not fixed but changed through time; they were not designed by God but "were formed according to blind, random forces… change took place as a result of natural events, not through the intervention of

12 See John Frederick William Herschel, *A Preliminary Discourse on the Study of Natural Philosophy*, (Cambridge: Cambridge University Press, first published in 1830, digitally printed version in 2009).

13 Nora Barlow, ed., *The Autobiography of Charles Darwin,* p. 68.

14 Ralph Colp Jr., "Charles Darwin: Man and Scientist," pp. 102-103.

God."[15] This idea was already there in Erasmus Darwin's *Zoonomia*. This possibly shaped Darwin's understanding of nature; he elaborated this idea with the help of other scientific theories and methodologies and eventually came out with his theory of evolution.

1.3. Darwin's Evolution Theory

Darwin's first systematic treatment of evolution came out in the form of a book in 1859 after incubating the theory for more than twenty years. He wrote two papers in 1842 and in 1844 where he explained his idea of evolution, but these two papers were not published. While working on his book, Darwin received a letter from another naturalist Alfred Russel Wallace (1823-1913). The letter contained Wallace's paper entitled – "On the Tendency of Varieties to Depart Infinitely from the Original Type" where he argued for the evolution of new species very similar to the way Darwin was putting this in his book. Both Darwin's 1844 paper and Wallace's paper, which was sent to Darwin, was read on 1st July, 1858, at a meeting of the Linnean Society, the world's oldest biological society. Society used to hold debates and discussions on natural history. These two papers were published in the third volume of the *Journal of the Linnean Society*.[16]

Darwin finished his book – *On the Origin of Species by Means of Natural Selection* and published it on 22 November 1859. The book became very popular, and it went through six editions in Darwin's lifetime.[17] In this book, Darwin did not include explicit discussion on the evolution of human beings though it was implicit. Only ten years later did he develop the courage, after witnessing the intense intellectual controversy that the book had created, to disclose his final conclusion concerning the evolution of human beings in another book - *The Descent of Man*.

The theory of evolution was built on a long time scale. Life on earth began as one-celled organisms about three billion years ago. Only about three million years ago, did the hominid line, leading to humans, branch off from the other apes.[18] Darwin's main argument in his book *On the Origin of Species* was not the evolution of life or the origin of life as such but the diversity of species as a result of modification by natural selection. Darwin's main intention was to demonstrate that the doctrine of fixity of species was not plausible scientifically and that transmutation and speciation had occurred and were occurring. It is maintained that all species had descended from a common ancestor; they had not

15 Nancy Morvillo, *Science and Religion*, p. 146.

16 See Charles Darwin, *On the Origin of Species by Means of Natural Selection*, (London: Elec Book, 1997; first published in 1859 by John Murray), p. 14.

17 *Ibid.*, p. 150.

18 Bernard D. Davis, "Evolution, Human Diversity, and Society," p. 82.

been created independently or together at the same time, transmutation occurred that resulted in the evolution of new species.[19]

Darwin's most famous theory was what he called 'Natural selection', and according to this theory, evolutionary change comes through the production of variation in each generation and differential survival of individuals with different combinations of these variable characters. Individuals with characteristics that help their survival probability will have more opportunities to reproduce, and their offspring will also benefit from the heritable, advantageous character. So over time these variants will spread through the population. Natural selection can ultimately lead to the formation of new species. Changes that allow an organism to better adapt to its environment will help it survive and have more offspring. Those species which can most adapt to the changing climate and environment will survive, acquiring new forms and changing themselves to suit the environment. In this way, the process of evolution continues.

The mechanism of Natural Selection has the following three essential elements:

(a) The existence of variation between the individuals of any species.
(b) That some of the differences that distinguish one organism from another are heritable, that is, they may be passed from parent to offspring.
(c) That individual of this heritable variation affects the individual's chances of survival (fitness) and hence is likely to produce its own offspring.

Thus, these three concepts – the variation, heritability and differential survival are the general requirements for the process of evolution by natural selection, according to Darwin.[20]

In the first two Chapters of *The Origin of the Species,* Darwin discusses the issue of variation among organisms - that within a species, organisms vary. This variation is basically produced in sexual reproduction, and therefore, it is inherited and is passed on to the next generation. The Third Chapter talks about the struggle for existence due to competition. As organisms increase in number in a given place with limited resources, there is natural fight and competition for food, air, light and space, etc. Chapter four can be considered as the main Chapter as he discussed in this Chapter his main thesis – that some species with more suitable variations and modifications survived the competitive atmosphere and lived on reproducing, and this process continued by natural selection. By means of Natural Selection, favourable variations are preserved, and detrimental variations are rejected. In other words, organisms with suitable variations will

19 Keith A. Francis, *Charles Darwin and the Origin of Species*, (London: Greenwood Press, 2007), pp. 56-57.

20 Christopher Southgate, *et.al, God, Humanity and the Cosmos: A Companion to the Science-Religion Debate*, (London: T&T Clark International, 2005), p. 162.

survive, whereas organisms without favourable variations will become extinct. Nature, not God alone, selects the best-adapted organisms, and they pass on their adaptive advantage to their offspring.

In simple words, the main features of Darwin's evolution theory may be summarized as follows:

(a) Organisms are descended from one or several common ancestors and have diversified from this original stock.
(b) Species come and go through time, while they exist, they change.
(c) The diversification of life involves individuals of one species diverging until they become two separate species; this has probably occurred billions of times on earth!
(d) Evolutionary change occurs through small incremental changes within populations; that means it take many years for new species to be born.
(e) Evolutionary change occurs through variation between individuals; some variants give the individual an extra survival probability. Nature selects the best-adapted species to survive and reproduce; thus, the process continues endlessly. As there is fierce competition for survival among the individuals in each generation, and since all individuals are not alike, those which have variation advantages will be more likely to survive, and those with unfavourable variations will be eliminated.

1.4. Christians' Response to Evolution Theory

There are three theological issues raised by Darwin's evolution theory:

Firstly, Darwin's theory refuted the notion that God had individually designed creatures and that the diversified organisms we have today were there from the beginning.

Secondly, the earth and the creatures in it were very old as against the time-line suggested by the chronology in the Bible, and that no literal reading of the Scripture could accord with the scientific account.

Thirdly, though Darwin did not explicitly mention in his *Origin of Species* how human beings evolved, which he did in his book *The Descent of Man*, published in 1871 twelve years after the publication of *The Origin*, it is implied that apes and humans share a common ancestor. This goes directly against the biblical account of humans, created distinctly by God in his image to have a unique position among all the creations.

These are some of the important issues that have emerged from Darwin's evolutionary theory, which needs a theological response, either to say that Darwin was utterly wrong in his presumption or we need to reinterpret the Bible in the light of evolutionary science. Then and now, Christians all over the world are not one in the way they respond to evolutionary theory. One group totally rejects the idea that there was a constant evolution of species, some species died, and new species were born, and people who adhere to this group find it all the more difficult to accept that human beings and apes have the same ancestor. Whereas some Christians felt the need to reinterpret the Bible, saying that literal interpretation is not doing justice to the text and that Darwin's evolution theory could not be rejected altogether, they could accept evolution, including that of the human body, but the human soul must be a divine creation, and divine intervention is necessary to explain the appearance of the human mind.

There is a wide range of reactions to Darwin's evolution theory among the Roman Catholic theologians. Cardinal Newman, one of the most influential Catholic theologians of the 19th century, remarked that he did not see Darwin's theory of evolution of organic beings as inconsistent with divine design.[21] In contrast to this charitable response to Darwin, Joseph Scheeben (1835-88), another very influential Catholic theologian, declared that any evolution theory, not only Darwinism, which includes human's evolution, is heretical.[22]

According to the E. C. Messenger of Louvain, a clergyman, writing in 1949 on the position of the Roman Catholic Church,

> Most theologians down to very recent times repudiated any form of evolutionary theory, even of plants and animals. Wiser counsels now seem to prevail, and a decided modification of the attitude of theologians is now being witnessed on the possibility of applying some restricted form of evolution to man. Theologians still seem to hold fast to the absolutely literal interpretation of the narrative of the formation of Eve. But the day may come when it will be more generally recognised that, in addition to the core of historical truth, the narrative contains figurative elements... A different attitude is surely desirable, and it would at least have the merit of a more wholehearted recognition that Science as well as Theology reveals to us truth concerning God and the world which He has made.[23]

The Roman Catholic Church began to adopt a different position, accepting that evolution might be an indirect mechanism of creation for the body but refusing to extend the argument to include the creation of the human soul. By the 1920s, a significant body of opinion began to build up among Roman Catholic scholars in favour of this position. They began to argue that there was nothing in the writings of the Church Fathers that prevented acceptance of evolution, provided the process was seen as a manifestation of divine creativity. This movement paved the way for the modern Roman Catholic view on

21 Charles Stephan Dessain and Thomas Gornall (ed.), *The Letters and Diaries of John Henry Newman*, Vol. 24 (Oxford: Claredon Press, 1973), p. 77.

22 Mariano Artigas, et al., *Negotiating Darwin: The Vatican Confronts Evolution 1877-1902,* (Baltimore: The Johns Hopkins University Press, 2006), p. 19.

23 John C. Greene, "Darwin and Religion," in Proceedings of the American Philosophical Society, (Vol. 103, No. 5, Oct. 15, 1959), p. 717.

evolution, in which natural processes which are assumed to be of divine origin have formed the human body, while the soul has been introduced by direct divine intervention.[24]

In 1950, Pope Pius XII addressed the question of human's origins more specifically in his letter to bishops titled 'Humani Generis,' which we may summarize as follows:

(a) The Church allows research and discussions with regard to the doctrine of evolution, in as far as it inquires into the origin of the human body as coming from pre-existent and living matter. (b) Catholics must believe, however, that the human soul was created immediately by God. Since the soul is a spiritual substance, it is not brought into being through the transformation of matter but directly by God, whence the special uniqueness of each person. (c) All humans have descended from an individual, Adam, who has transmitted original sin to all humankind. Catholics may not, therefore, believe in 'polygenism', the scientific hypothesis that humankind descended from a group of original humans.[25]

Almost half a century later, in a 1996 letter to bishops, Pope John Paul II came out more strongly for Darwin's theory, calling evolution "more than a hypothesis." On the subject of the soul, however, Pope John Paul II agreed with Pope Pius XII. The soul, John Paul agreed, could not emerge "from the forces of living matter, or as a mere epiphenomenon of this matter."[26] The Pope Francis of the Roman Catholic Church comes out with the idea that can be interpreted as supporting the Big Bang theory and some forms of evolution. Speaking at the Pontifical Academy of Sciences on 28th October 2014, Pope Francis says:

> When we read about creation in Genesis, we run the risk of imagining God was a magician, with a magic wand able to do everything. But, that is not so. He created humans and let them develop according to internal laws that he gave to each one so they would reach their fulfillment. The Big Bang, which today we hold to be the origin of the world, does not contradict the intervention of the divine creator but, rather, requires it. Evolution in nature is not inconsistent with the notion of creation, because evolution requires the creation of beings that evolve.[27]

---

24 Peter J. Bowler, "Evolution" in *The History of Science and Religion in the Western Tradition: An Encyclopedia*, edited by Gary B. Ferngren, (New York: Garland Publishing, Inc., 2000), pp. 529-530.

25 James B. Stenson, "Evolution: a Catholic Perspective," in *https://www.ewtn.com/library/HUMANITY/EVOLUTN.TXT* (accessed 26.11.2016)

26 Taylor Wofford, "Pope Francis's Remarks on Evolution are not that Controversial Among Roman Catholics", in *http://www.newsweek.com/pope-franciss-remarks-evolution-are-not-controversial-among-roman-catholics-281115* (accessed 25.11.2016).

27 *Ibid.*

The Church of England initially reacted strongly against Darwin's evolution theory. An overwhelming majority of the members and clergymen rejected Darwin's theory but liberal Anglicans strongly supported Darwin's natural selection saying that it is an instrument of God's design. The most famous confrontation took place at the Oxford in 1860 in a public debate during the meeting of the British Association for the Advancement of Science. The Bishop of Oxford Samuel Wilberforce argued against Darwin's theory, whereas Thomas Huxley, nick named 'Darwin's bulldog', was the chief spokesperson for Darwin's theory. The famous debate ended up in exchange for harsh words. After explaining his position at length, Bishop Wilberforce turned to Huxley and asked him whether he was descended from an ape through his grandfather's side or grandmother's side. Huxley replied with equal sarcasm that he would rather have an ape for his ancestor than a man who misused his position to attack a theory he did not understand.

In the USA, the first Christian organisation which vehemently opposed Darwin's Evolution theory was the World's Christian Fundamental Association (WCFA), formed in 1919. This organization was responsible for banning the teaching of Darwin's theory in public schools in several US states. The WCFA, along with several other fundamentalist groups, viewed evolution as a heretical challenge to the Biblical account of creation. They believed that evolution represented a sacrilegious movement of atheists and humanists whose views threatened the foundation of human existence. These fundamentalist groups were quite successful in removing Darwinian theory from the public schools during the early part of the 20th century. They introduced anti-evolution bills in over 20 state legislatures in the USA, and as a result of this, states like Tennessee, Mississippi and Arkansas passed laws during the 1920s, making the teaching of evolution a crime. The state legislatures of Texas and Florida passed non-binding resolutions that opposed the teaching of Darwinian theory in schools.[28]

The debate continues. Many non-scientists are strongly against evolution by natural selection because of moral and philosophical reasons; biologists are slowly and slowly on the road to believe that Darwinian theory may be the most promising theory in explaining the vast diversity of living beings. Some theological and scientific movements emerged in the USA in the middle of the twentieth century and the latter part of the century that opposed Darwin's evolution theory. One such movement is *creationism* which has two streams - scientific creationism and biblical creationism. While rejecting the theory of evolution, these creationists proposed that the whole universe was created as it is now, except for some minor changes at some point in time by a Creator. Another creation theory is *Intelligent design* which holds that the complex structures of life cannot be explained by natural selection and random mutation as suggested by Darwin but must be

28 Karen O'Connor and Gregg Ivers, "Creationism, Evolution and the Courts," *PS: Political Science and Politics,* (Vol. 21, No. 1, Winter, 1988), p. 11.

explained by some force of willful design. Till today most evangelical Christians in the USA and around the world do not subscribe to Darwin's theory of evolution.

Darwin brought revolutionary ideas into the public sphere about how life had started and developed. But the idea of evolution did not originate with Darwin himself. There were a number of biologists before him and during his time who proposed more or less the same idea. Darwin developed and systematized those scattered ideas on the evolution of life, and he, thus, became recognized as the originator of evolutionary science. The literal reading of the Bible, especially the creation story in the book of Genesis, comes in stark contrast to evolution theory. Till today, conservative Christians who take the Bible literally – God created the entire universe with all the living entities as they are now in just literally six days – and for whom the earth is only some six thousand years old, evolution theory is simply false. But not only from evolutionary science but also from the discovery of fossils, it is quite clear that the earth is not as young as 'the young earth biblical creationists' are projecting it to be. In fact, our day to day experience betrays the idea that God created everything as they are today in just 144 hours (six days). Considering a large number of organisms, insects, animals and different species of plant that were already extinct and numerous new species that are being formed due to mutation, it is almost impossible to say that evolution never happened. At the same time, the belief in God and the belief that human beings are endowed with a soul, which makes them unique among all creations could not allow holding human beings as evolved from animals. Thus, Darwin's evolution theory cannot be taken as correct and reliable in *toto* – after all, it is a theory.

The literal rendering of both Genesis creation story and Darwin's evolution theory seems to have missed the reality of the origin of species and its development thereafter. We may propose that evolution had indeed happened and is still happening, not of course exactly as propounded by Darwin, resulting in the extinction, formation and modification of some species. But, there is God who created things to evolve and guided the whole process of evolution. Thus, the belief that there is an intelligent all-knowing and all-powerful Creator and that a human being endowed with soul is a unique creature created by a Creator with a purpose should not be taken as inconsistent with the belief in evolution and the old earth.

1.5. Neo-Darwin Synthesis

Neo-Darwinism or sometimes referred to as 'modern synthesis' is the integration of Charles Darwin's theory of evolution by natural selection with modern genetics, especially Gregor Mendel's theory of genetics, resulting in a more comprehensive evolutionary theory. Julian Huxley, an English evolutionary biologist, coined the term 'Modern Synthesis' in his book *Evolution: The Modern Synthesis* published in 1942. Though the term 'neo-Darwinism' was used way back in 1896 by George John Romanes to designate the type of Darwinism advanced by August

Weismann, it has been the popular and scientific use of expression since the 1930s. A number of evolutionary biologists developed the synthesis in the 1930s and 1940s. Several names were given to the synthesis that includes – modern synthesis, evolutionary synthesis, neo-Darwin synthesis and neo-Darwinism.[29]

The neo-Darwin synthesis emphasizes the genetic basis of evolution and proposes a new definition of evolution as changes in *allele* frequencies within a population. *Allele*s are alternate forms of the same gene, characterized by differences in the DNA sequence that result in the construction of proteins that differ in amino acid composition. Four forces of evolution contribute to changes in *allele* frequencies – *random genetic drift*, *gene flow*, *mutation pressure* and *natural selection*. Out of these four, natural selection is the only evolutionary force that makes organisms better adapted to their environments. *Genetic drift* accounts for changes in allele frequencies in a population, whereas *Gene flow* describes allele frequencies due to immigration and emigration of individuals from a population. On the other hand, *mutation* is a weak but crucial evolutionary force because all genetic variation arises originally from mutation.[30]

There are differences between classical Darwinism and neo-Darwinism: *Firstly*, in neo-Darwinism, mechanisms of evolution other than natural selection are recognized as playing an important role. *Secondly*, neo-Darwinism or the Modern Synthesis succeeds in explaining the persistence of genetic variation, a problem that Charles Darwin could not explain satisfactorily. With the help of Mendel's theory of inheritance, in which the *alleles* of a gene remain separate instead of emerging, this problem was solved.[31]

A number of scientists and their works contributed to the modern synthesis or neo-Darwinism. The theory drew insight from the population genetics work of R. A. Fisher and Sewall Wright. Theodosius Dobzhansky's extensive studies on *Drosophila* (fruit fly) supported many aspects of the theory. The works of Ernst Mayr, George Gaylord Simpson, G. Ledyard Stebbins, etc., are making an immense contribution towards the emergence of neo-Darwinism synthesis.

2. Albert Einstein and Theory of Relativity

The mechanistic model of the universe propounded by Newton was the dominating theme in the physical sciences for nearly one hundred years. It was generally believed that the universe was a huge mechanical system running according to the Newtonian laws of motion. Developments in the understanding of the physical world through the nineteenth century slowly unearthed the

29 Cf. https://www.encyclopedia.com/earth-and-environment/ecology-and-environmentalism/environmental-studies/modern-synthesis (19.04.2021); https://www.newworldencyclopedia.org/entry/Neo-Darwinism (19.04.2021).

30 https://www.encyclopedia.com/earth-and-environment/ecology-and-environmentalism/environmental-studies/modern-synthesis (19.04.2021).

31 *Ibid.*

limitations of the Newtonian model, and finally, at the beginning of the twentieth century Albert Einstein, we may say, put the last nail in the coffin of the Newtonian model of the universe and physical movements therein. Fritjof Capra observes that in the first three decades of the twentieth century, two separate developments – that of relativity theory and of atomic physic (quantum mechanics) – shattered all the principal concepts of the Newtonian world view, such as the notion of absolute space and time, the elementary solid particles, the strictly casual nature of physical phenomena, and the ideal of an objective description of nature.[32] Two scientific papers published by Einstein in 1905 – the special theory of relativity and the theory concerning electromagnetic radiation, which become the basis for quantum mechanics – stood as the intellectual monuments, the milestones of modern civilization.

2.1. Albert Einstein

Albert Einstein was born on March 14, 1879, in Ulm, Württemberg, Germany, to Jewish parents. His father, Hermann Einstein, was a salesman and engineer and his mother, the former Pauline Koch, ran the family household. Einstein had one sister, Maja, born two years after him. Einstein attended elementary school at the Luitpold Gymnasium in Munich. However, he felt alienated there and struggled with the institution's rigid pedagogical style. But he developed a passion for classical music and playing the violin that would stay with him into his later years. Most significantly, Einstein's youth was marked by deep inquisitiveness and inquiry.[33]

His family migrated to Milan, Italy, in the mid-1890s leaving behind Albert at a relative's boarding house in Munich to complete his schooling at the Luitpold Gymnasium. He joined his family in Milan without finishing his school education. He secured admission into the Swiss Federal Polytechnic School in Zurich, specifically due to his superb mathematics and physics scores on the entrance exam. As he was still required to complete his pre-university education, he attended a high school in Aarau, Switzerland. Einstein later renounced his German citizenship and became a Swiss citizen at the dawn of the new century.[34]

After graduating from Polytechnic, Einstein faced major challenges in terms of finding academic positions. As he studied advanced subjects on his own, he often skipped classes; this earned him the ill-feeling of some professors, especially Heinrich Weber. Unfortunately, Einstein asked Weber for a letter of recommendation. Einstein was subsequently turned down for every academic position that he applied to. In 1901 he was writing to several universities to find an academic position; there is even a letter from his father to the famous chemist W. Ostwald saying, 'My son is profoundly unhappy with his current state of

32 Fritjof Capra, *The Tao of Physics,* (London: Flamingo, 1991), pp. 69, 70.

33 *http://www.biography.com/people/albert-einstein-9285408* (accessed 22.11.2016).

34 *Ibid.*

unemployment, and every day the idea becomes more firmly implanted in him that he is a failure in his career...' His father's pleas were unsuccessful.[35]

Einstein eventually found work in 1902 for a clerk position in a Swiss patent office in Bern. Soon after that, his father passed away, and he married Milena Maric the following year. The couple went on to have two sons, Hans and Eduard. The Marriage was not very successful and the two divorced in 1919. Einstein married his cousin Elsa Lowenthal the same year. Einstein lived and worked for nine intensely creative and productive years in a non-academic environment mostly as a patent examiner. It was during this period that Einstein conceived four important scientific papers that altered the course of modern physics.[36] In the year 1905, often called Einstein's "miracle year," he not only earned a Ph.D. degree from the University of Zurich but more importantly published four papers in the *Annalen der Physik*, one of the best-known physics journals of the era, each of which would alter the course of modern physics:[37]

(a) "On a Heuristic Viewpoint Concerning the Production and Transformation of Light," in which Einstein applied the quantum theory to light in order to explain the photoelectric effect. If light occurs in tiny packets (later called photons), then it should knock out electrons in a metal in a precise way.

(b) "On the Movement of Small Particles Suspended in Stationary Liquids Required by the Molecular-Kinetic Theory of Heat," in which Einstein offered the first experimental proof of the existence of atoms. By analyzing the motion of tiny particles suspended in still water, called Brownian motion, he could calculate the size of the jostling atoms and Avogadro's number (i.e. the number of atoms or molecules in one mole of a substance).

(c) "On the Electrodynamics of Moving Bodies," in which Einstein laid out the mathematical theory of special relativity.

(d) "Does the Inertia of a Body Depend Upon Its Energy Content?," submitted almost as an afterthought, which showed that relativity theory led to the equation $E = mc^2$. This provided the first mechanism to explain the energy source of the sun and other stars.

His success earned him important posts quickly. In 1909 he became Professor Extraordinary at Zurich, in 1911, Professor of Theoretical Physics at Prague, returning to Zurich in the following year to fill a similar post. In 1914, he was appointed Director of the Kaiser Wilhelm Physical Institute and Professor

35 John N. Murrell and Nicole Grobert, "The Centenary of Einstein's First Scientific Paper," *Notes and Records of the Royal Society of London*, (Vol. 56, No. 1, Jan., 2002), p. 89.

36 Paul Forman, "Einstein and Newton: Two Legacies," *The Wilson Quarterly*, (Vol. 3, No. 1, Winter, 1979), pp. 109-110.

37 *https://www.britannica.com/biography/Albert-Einstein* (accessed 23.11.2016).

in the University of Berlin. He remained in Berlin until 1933 and renounced his German citizenship for political reasons, and emigrated to America to take the position of Professor of Theoretical Physics at Princeton.[38]

In November 1915, Einstein completed the 'General Theory of Relativity,' which he considered the culmination of his life research. He was convinced of the merits of general relativity because it allowed for a more accurate prediction of planetary orbits around the sun, which fell short in Newtonian theory. Einstein's assertions were affirmed via observations and measurements by British astronomers Sir Frank Dyson and Sir Arthur Eddington during the 1919 solar eclipse, and that made Einstein a world-renowned physicist. In 1921, Einstein won the Nobel Prize for Physics. His theory of general relativity was still considered by many as questionable, so, Nobel Prize was given for his explanation of the photoelectric effect. Einstein still opted to speak about relativity during his acceptance speech.[39]

Einstein remained at Princeton for the rest of his life. He died in 1955 at the age of 76. During the autopsy, Thomas Stoltz Harvey removed Einstein's brain, reportedly without the permission of his family, for preservation and future study by doctors of neuroscience. Einstein's remains were cremated, and his ashes were scattered in an undisclosed location, following his wishes. After decades of study, Einstein's brain is now located at the Princeton University Medical Center.[40]

Albert Einstein is an icon of the twentieth century. Though he is most famous for his theory of relativity, he also made enormous contributions to quantum mechanics and cosmology. A self-pronounced pacifist, humanist, and late in his life, democratic socialist, Einstein was also deeply concerned with the social impact of his discoveries. He has a deep humanitarian concern and he was the one who warned US President Roosevelt about the danger of nuclear weapons. Einstein was offered the second Presidency of Israel but he turned it down. It is no wonder that the *Time Magazine* declared him as the person of the century. The Inventions of the atomic bomb, laser, telecommunication satellites, and cell phones are all based on Einstein's works.

2.2. What is Relativity?

In the 1920s, the theory of relativity was so famous that Einstein was practically like a Rock star, and every people wanted to know what theory of relativity really was. There was a competition organised in the USA to explain the theory of relativity to common people in about 3000 words. With his sense of humour, Einstein said that he would not enter the contest because he did not think he could do it!! The theory of relativity is full of mathematical calculations, very difficult to explain to the common people. For instance, in the theory of relativity,

38 *http://www.nobelprize.org/nobel_prizes/physics/laureates/1921/einstein-bio.html* (22.11.2016).

39 *http://www.biography.com/people/albert-einstein-9285408* (accessed 22.11.2016).

40 *Ibid.*

one finds the phrases like 'curved space', 'four dimensions' and 'finite universe.' Though these phrases are all familiar, people are struggling to understand just how can space be curved? How could there possibly be another dimension besides height, length and width? In what way could the universe be bounded? The terms are familiar, but the meaning is difficult to make out. Einstein himself conceded that his theory was difficult to explain to lay people. It was said that Einstein himself warned the publisher of his book, saying there were probably only twelve persons in the whole world who would be able to understand it. The Washington Post contained this statement when it reported the arrival of Einstein in USA:

> Less than two years ago Einstein published a little book made up principally of mathematical formulae. It wasn't a good bet for the publishers and Einstein himself admitted that there were probably only twelve living men in the world who would be able to understand it. But it seems those twelve men, who were the greatest scientists, immediately got it and read it. And when they had finished they set up a shout- it was almost an amazed and outraged yelp - that immediately echoed around the world (*Washington Post*, 3 April, 1921, p. 1).[41]

It is said that when Einstein was asked to explain his theory of relativity, he answered amusingly: "Put your hand over a hot stove for a minute that seems like an hour, sit beside a beautiful woman for an hour that would seem like a minute. That is relativity."

Einstein's special theory of relativity made both duration and length relative to motion, undercutting the assumption that the universe is framed by a stable or absolute container of time and space. Incorporating gravity into this theory in 1915 to produce his general theory of relativity, Einstein showed that space and matter act on one another so as to deform space itself: space tells matter how to move, and matter tells space how to curve. In Einstein's non-Euclidian world of diverging and intersecting parallel lines, the shortest path from one point to another in the presence of a gravitational field can become a curved line. Thus gravity is said to 'bend' light.[42]

Theory of relativity denies that there is such thing as a unique right frame of space because all frames of space are relative. Motion, distances, length, mass, and volumes are all relative. They can only be defined relatively to one specified observer. Likewise, magnetic fields are also relative, time can dilate, it is not absolute. Mass is energy, and energy has mass – the property which gives matter

41 Marshall Missner, "Why Einstein Became Famous in America," *Social Studies of Science*, (Vol. 15, No. 2, May, 1985), p. 276. For further investigation on the life of Einstein may I suggest two books - Walter Isaacson, *Einstein: His Life and Universe, (London: Pocket Books, 2008), and* Jürgen Neffe, *Einstein: A Biography, Trans. by Shelley Frisch, (New York: Farra, Straus and Giroux, 2007).*

42 Ted Peters, "Science and Religion," in ***http://www.academicroom.com/topics/science-and-religion*** (accessed 27.7.2015).

its characteristic solidity, that is, its mass is simply energy. Thus, energy becomes the ultimate material of the universe.[43] There is one constant, that is, the speed of light which is the same for all observers; and that no object which has mass could travel at the speed of light. As the speed increases, the mass also increases. As an object approaches the speed of light, its mass rises ever more quickly, so it takes more and more energy to speed it up further. It can never reach the speed of light because by then, its mass would become infinite.[44]

The general theory of relativity shows us that space is not three dimensional and time is not a separate entity either. Time and space are connected to form the fourth dimension: space-time.[45] Before 1915 people thought that space and time were a fixed arena in which events took place, and these events did not affect them. But according to Einstein's general relativity theory, space and time are dynamic quantities, and because of the force of gravity, space-time is curved. When a body moves or a force acts, it affects the curvature of space and time, and in turn, the structure of space-time affects the way in which bodies move and forces act. So, with the theory of relativity absolute space and time, the unchanging and infinite universe lost their meaning, and they are replaced by dynamic space and time and finite universe. Thus, Stephen Hawking and Roger Penrose concluded that Einstein's general theory of relativity implied that the universe must have a beginning and possibly an end.[46]

3. Quantum Mechanics

Quantum mechanics is considered one of the century's most innovative and fruitful scientific insights into the workings of nature. Some people even considered it as the greatest intellectual achievement of the human mind,[47] which of course, is debatable considering the works of Galileo, Newton, Darwin and Einstein, among others. Quantum mechanics deals with the behaviour of matter and light on the atomic and subatomic scale. It attempts to describe and account for the properties of molecules and atoms and their constituents - electrons, protons, neutrons and other more esoteric particles such as quarks and gluons. These properties include the interactions of the particles with one another and with electromagnetic radiation, such as, light, X-rays, and gamma rays.[48]

---

43 Arthur F. Smethurst, *Modern Science and Christian Beliefs*, (New York: Abingdon Press, 1955), p. 77.

44 Stephen Hawking, *A Brief History of Time: From the Big Bang to Black Holes*, (London: Bantam Press, 1989), p. 21.

45 Fritjof Capra, *The Tao of Physics*, p. 71.

46 Stephen Hawking, *A Brief History of Time*, p. 36.

47 Victor F. Weisskopf, "What Is Quantum Mechanics?" in *Bulletin of the American Academy of Arts and Sciences*, (Vol. 33, No. 7, Apr., 1980), p. 27.

48 *https://www.britannica.com/science/quantum-mechanics-physics* (accessed 29.11.2016).

Some one hundred years ago, the causes of a number of quite obvious phenomena were completely unknown. For example, why a piece of coal, when heated, first becomes red, then yellow and then white? Why do materials have specific properties? Why is copper brown? Why does it conduct electricity so well? Why does oxygen mix with hydrogen forms water? Why does sodium gas emit yellow light when heated? These and many more were not known before. But the reasons for all these are known to us now, thanks to the emergence of quantum mechanics.

The scientific development that led to the formation of Quantum mechanics started with Max Planck in 1900 when he discovered that light, X-ray and other waves could not be emitted at an arbitrary rate, but only in certain 'energy packets' that he called '*quanta.*' Planck postulated that light and all other electromagnetic radiation could appear not only as electromagnetic waves but also in the form of these quanta. Light quanta, which gave the quantum theory its name, have been accepted as *bona fide* particles and are now known as photons.[49] It was Einstein who concluded that the energy of light beam could not be indefinitely subdivided. Light occurs in finite pieces of energy – the light quanta or photons.[50]

Quantum Mechanics was formulated by a group of scientists that included Werner Heisenberg from Germany, Erwin Schrodinger from Austria, Paul Dirac from England, etc., in the 1920s. The theory was based on the famous uncertainty principle articulated by Heisenberg which says that there is fuzziness in nature - the position and the velocity of an object cannot both be measured exactly, at the same time. The very concepts of exact position and exact velocity together, in fact, have no meaning in nature. So, particles no longer had separate, well-defined positions and velocities. Instead, they had a quantum state, which was the combination of position and velocity. Stephen Hawking notes, "Quantum mechanics, therefore, introduces unavoidable element of unpredictability or randomness into science."[51] This is because movement at the subatomic level or movement of electrons and protons within the atom does not follow Newtonian mechanical law where everything follows clear-cut laws on how to move, and prediction is easy if you know the starting conditions. The discovery that nature's smallest particles, such as electrons, do not behave mechanistically, rather, their behaviour seems unpredictable and indeterminate shocked the community of scientists.

One of the most striking features of the atom which quantum theory reveals, is that the small particles within the atom have dual aspects, that is, the subatomic units of matter are both *particle* and *wave*! Depending on how we look at them, they sometimes appear as particles, but sometimes as waves. The same thing is

49 Fritjof Capra, *The Tao of Physics,* p. 77.

50 Victor F. Weisskopf, "What Is Quantum Mechanics?" p. 29.

51 Stephen Hawking, *A Brief History of Time*, p. 60.

true of light which can take the form of electromagnetic waves or particles.[52] Thus, it is not possible to predict the atomic event with certainty; we can only say how likely it will happen. Capra, thus, notes, "Quantum theory thus demolished the classical concept of solid objects and of strictly deterministic laws of nature. At the subatomic level, the solid material objects of classical physics dissolve into wave-like patterns of probabilities."[53]

Quantum mechanics has far-reaching consequences on the way we see the material world. *Firstly*, science's ability to predict and determine has a limit, indicating that science is not always reliable to determine the universal laws. There are things, movements, properties that science could not explain. So, the role of God cannot be ruled out. *Secondly*, quantum mechanics reveals that scientific knowledge is not always objective knowledge, but a fair amount of subjectivity is involved, thereby making scientific knowledge more like theological knowledge. According to Ted Peters, "the act of observing subatomic behaviour influences such behaviour, thereby compromising the Newtonian sense of objectivity or nonparticipatory observation in scientific method. Subjectivity seems constitutive of the reality being observed."[54] *Thirdly*, according to Capra, the subatomic particles have no meaning as isolated entities but can only be understood as interconnections between the preparation of an experiment and the subsequent measurement. Quantum theory thus reveals a basic oneness of the universe. We cannot separate things in the universe. As we penetrate deep into the matter, we do not see isolated basic building blocks but a complicated web of relations between the various parts of the whole where the observer is part of the web. Capra concludes,

> These relations always include the observer in an essential way. The human observer constitutes the final link in the chain of observational processes, and the properties of any atomic object can only be understood in terms of the object's interaction with the observer. This means that classical idea of objective description of nature is no longer valid.[55]

Concluding Remarks

The three scientific developments we have discussed, such as theory of evolution, theory of relativity and quantum mechanics changed the way we look at the world and the whole universe, including our own existence in relation to the whole creation. Though Darwin's evolution theory is 'still a theory' without sufficient

52 Fritjof Capra, *The Tao of Physics,* pp. 76-77.

53 *Ibid.*, p. 78.

54 Ted Peters, "Science and Religion", in *http://www.academicroom.com/topics/science-and-religion* (accessed 27.7.2015).

55 Fritjof Capra, *The Tao of Physics,* p. 78.

scientific proof, more and more scientists and lay people adhere to it. The Christian community around the globe is divided in the way they treat evolutionary science. Conservative and evangelical Christians reject the idea almost totally, whereas others are inclined to believe in the possibility of evolution but snub the idea that humans and apes share the same ancestor; furthermore, they question the possibility of the human soul being evolved from anything other than God.

Einstein's theory of relativity dethroned Newtonian mechanics by projecting some of the strangest ideas like 'dilation of time,' 'curved space, four-dimensional and finite universes' and the 'relativeness of motion, distances, length, mass, and volumes.' These things look ridiculous, but they are proved to be true, and they changed drastically the way we look at the whole universe and our place in it. People start questioning even in the religious sphere to speak of absolute truth in the world of relativity. This can affect the way we perceive sin and morality, good and bad – because what is good or sinful is to a great extent determined by the context – in relation to the contextual realities.

Quantum Mechanics, the science of small things, reveals the weakness of science in determining the reality of things. As the movement of electrons in an atom is indeterminate, which follows no fixed law, it is clear that matters are not controlled by scientific laws. Furthermore, the dualistic nature of the subatomic particles – existing as a particle as well as a wave at the same time demolished the concept of absolute at least at the atomic level. Again, the fact that movements of subatomic particles are affected by the observer, so the role of the observer is paramount in determining the reality of subatomic particles. This, in turn, questions the validity of scientific objectivity but opens the role of subjectivity in scientific research.

Chapter 5

Theories of the Origin of the Universe

Our knowledge of the universe has increased tremendously during the past five centuries. Until the first half of the seventeenth century, the earth was considered the centre of the universe, and all the planets, sun, and stars were revolving around it. Thanks to the incredible works of Copernicus and Galileo, which shifted our whole idea of the universe from a geocentric universe to a heliocentric one; we have come to know our real position in the universe. And with more scientific discoveries in the past one hundred years, more and more unbelievable and fascinating facts concerning the universe have been revealed. In the 1920s, Edwin Hubble discovered that there are a number of galaxies in the universe. He spotted several galaxies and could measure the distance between such nine different galaxies. With modern telescopes, we have come to know that there are some hundred thousand million galaxies in the universe, each containing some hundred thousand million stars!! Our sun is just an ordinary average-sized yellow star among such hundred thousand million stars.[1] Our galaxy, known as Milky Way, contains about 100,000 million stars like the sun. It is bun shaped with a diameter of nearly 100,000 light-years. It is estimated that there are nearly 3000 million other galaxies in the observable universe. A typical galaxy has a diameter of 30 million parasecs (1parasec is equal to slightly more than three light-years). The distance between neighbouring galaxies could be of the order of 3 to 4 million parsecs.[2] Such incredible facts have come down to us!

---

1 See Stephen Hawking, *A Brief History of Time: From the Big Bang to Black Holes*, (London: Bantam Press, 1989), pp. 38-39.

2 K. K. Theckedath, "Dialectics and Cosmology: The Big Bang and the Steady State Theories", *Social Scientist*, (Vol. 31, No. 1/2, Jan. - Feb., 2003), p. 63.

The question is, how did this universe start? Scientists, philosophers, theologians, various religions, etc., have proposed several theories as to how such a huge universe with unbelievable numbers of stars came into existence. We will now discuss various theories of the origin of the universe, taking into consideration both religious and scientific views.

1. Creationism

The term Creationism or Creation Science, as creationists would love to call it, broadly refers to a belief in the creation of the universe by a Creator. Though they differ greatly in their opinion, Creationists reject the theory of evolution and hold that the whole universe was created as it is now, except for some minor changes at some point in time by a Creator. They hold the idea that not only the Creator or God created the universe but also that God constantly involves himself in creation, giving sustenance and causing destruction as the need arises. Henry M. Morris (1918 – 2006) and Duane Gish (1921 – 2013), both of the Institute for Creation Research, San Diego, USA, are well-known proponents of this theory. Creationism emerged basically as a challenge to Darwin's evolution theory, so its main target is to dismantle the growing popularity of evolutionary science and finally defeat it.

According to Henry M. Morris, the Founder and President Emeritus of the Institute for Creation Research, Creationism can be studied and taught in any of three basic forms, as follows:[3]

(1) Scientific creationism (no reliance on Biblical revelation, utilizing only scientific data to support and expound the creation model).

(2) Biblical creationism (no reliance on scientific data, using only the Bible to expound and defend the creation model).

(3) Scientific Biblical creationism (full reliance on Biblical revelation but also using scientific data to support and develop the creation model).

He maintains that these three forms of creationism are not contradictory to one another but rather complimentary.

1.1. Scientific Creationism

According to Henry Morris, the tenets of scientific creationism are as follows:[4]

(a) The physical universe of space, time, matter and energy has not always existed but was supernaturally created by a transcendent personal Creator who alone has existed from eternity.

---

3 Henry M. Morris, "The Tenets of Creationism" in ***https://www.icr.org/article/168/*** - An Official Website of Institute for Creation Research (accessed 19.12.2016).

4 *Ibid.*

(b) The phenomenon of biological life did not develop by natural processes from inanimate systems but was specially and supernaturally created by the Creator.

(c) Each of the major kinds of plants and animals was created functionally complete from the beginning and did not evolve from some other kind of organism. Since their first creation, changes in basic kinds are limited to 'horizontal' changes (variations) within the kinds, or 'downward' changes (e.g., harmful mutations, extinctions).

(d) The first human beings did not evolve from an animal ancestry but were specially created in fully human form from the start. Furthermore, the 'spiritual' nature of humans (self-image, moral consciousness, abstract reasoning, language, will, religious nature, etc.) is a supernaturally created entity distinct from mere biological life.

(e) As preserved especially in the crustal rocks and fossil deposits, Earth pre-history is primarily a record of catastrophic intensities of natural processes, operating largely within uniform natural laws, rather than one of the uniformitarian process rates. Therefore, there is no a priori reason for not considering the many scientific evidence for a relatively recent creation of the earth and the universe, in addition to the scientific evidence that most of the earth's fossiliferous sediments were formed in an even more recent global hydraulic cataclysm.

(f) Processes today operate primarily within fixed natural laws and relatively uniform process rates. Since these were themselves originally created and are daily maintained by their Creator, there is always the possibility of miraculous intervention in these laws or processes by their Creator. However, evidence for such intervention must be scrutinized critically because there must be a clear and adequate reason for any such action on the part of the Creator.

(g) The universe and life have somehow been impaired since the completion of creation, so imperfections in structure, disease, aging, extinctions, and other such phenomena result from 'negative' changes in properties and processes occurring in an originally perfect created order.

(h) Since the universe and its primary components were created perfect for their purposes in the beginning by a competent and volitional Creator, and since the Creator does remain active in this now-decaying creation, ultimate purpose and meaning exist in the universe. Teleological considerations, therefore, are appropriate in scientific studies whenever they are consistent with the actual data of observation, and it is reasonable to assume that the creation presently awaits the consummation of the Creator's purpose.

(i) Although people are finite and scientific data concerning origins are always circumstantial and incomplete, the human mind can explore the manifestation of that Creator rationally and scientifically and reach an intelligent decision regarding one's place in the Creator's plan.

1.2. Biblical Creationism

Henry Morris again puts forward the following points as the basic tenets of Biblical Creationism:[5]

(a) The Creator of the universe is a triune God - Father, Son and Holy Spirit.

(b) The Bible is the divinely inspired revelation of the Creator to humans. Its unique, plenary, verbal inspiration guarantees that these writings, as originally and miraculously given, are infallible and completely authoritative on all matters with which they deal, free from error of any sort, scientific and historical as well as moral and theological.

(c) All things in the universe were created and made by God in the six literal days of the creation week described in Genesis 1:1-2:3, and confirmed in Exodus 20:8-11. The creation record is factual, historical and perspicuous. All things which now exist are sustained and ordered by God's providential care.

(d) The first human beings, Adam and Eve, were specially created by God, and all other men and women are their descendants.

(e) The Biblical record of primaeval earth history in Genesis 1-11 is fully historical and perspicuous, including the creation and fall of humans, the curse on the creation and its subjection to the bondage of decay, the promised Redeemer, the worldwide cataclysmic deluge in the days of Noah, the post-diluvial renewal of human's commission to subdue the earth and the origin of nations and languages at the tower of Babel.

(f) The final restoration of creation's perfection is in the future, but individuals can immediately be restored to fellowship with their Creator, on the basis of His redemptive work on their behalf, receiving forgiveness and eternal life solely through personal trust in the Lord Jesus Christ, accepting Him not only as estranged Creator but also as reconciling Redeemer and coming King.

(g) The eventual accomplishment of God's eternal purposes in creation, with the removal of His curse and the restoration of all things to divine perfection, will take place at the personal bodily return to the earth of Jesus Christ to judge and purge sin and to establish His eternal kingdom.

---

5 *Ibid.*

1.3. Scientific Biblical Creationism

The third form of creationism, would be the blend of the above two - Scientific and Biblical Creationism, where relying fully on Biblical revelation, it uses scientific data to support its position. There are again three prominent groups that can be put within Scientific Biblical creationism:

1.3.1. Young Earth Creationism

As the name indicates, people who hold this position believe that the earth is not as old as many people projected it to be. Taking the Genesis account of creation literally, they hold on to the idea that the Bible is a simple historical record that has to be accepted at face value. Each day of the Genesis creation account is a natural solar day and is to be taken as such. As a result of this belief, the earth is considered quite young, around 4000 - 10,000 years old only. Thus, Literalists are commonly known as 'Young earth Creationists.'[6]

1.3.2. Old Earth Creationism

In contrast to the young earth creationists, the old earth creationists are diverse in their beliefs but share in common the view that the earth is much older than what the literalists contend. One camp holds the view, which is often referred to as the 'gap theory', that life created became extinct and there was a re-creation of life, and the process continues till human beings were created in the last. This allows room for accepting old age and fossils as well as the recent creation of Adam and Eve.[7] The old earth creationist, Allen Higley, who was the founding president of the Science and Religion Association in the 1930s, attributed much of the fossil record to Satanic activities before the creation of Eden. He said that Lucifer was the first being created on this world and that he was here several million years ago and that his fall was the cause of several million years of chaos in which the earth was without form and void. That was the time when the stratification of rock took place.[8]

Another group within this believes that each day of creation listed in Genesis should be interpreted to be indeterminately long periods of time, possibly millions or billions of years, equating somewhat to the ages of geology. Living forms were introduced via supernatural creation throughout these various long days. There was no macroevolution. Still, another group within the old earth creationism believes in the possibility of limited evolution within God's creations. People who hold this creationism are called Progressive Creationists and they believe that over millions of years of evolution, occasional interventions occurred in which

6 Brian J. Alters, "What Is Creationism?" in *The American Biology Teacher*, (Vol. 61, No. 2, Feb., 1999), pp. 104.

7 *Ibid.*

8 Ronald L. Numbers, "Clarifying Creationism: Five Common Myths," *History and Philosophy of the Life Sciences*, (Vol. 33, No. 1, 2011), p. 132.

new kinds of organisms were specially created, such as horses or humans, thus providing a theological explanation for gaps in the fossil record-a supernaturally punctuated evolution.[9]

1.3.3. Theistic Evolutionary Creationism

There is still another group of creationism that we may call "theistic evolutionary creationism" because it holds both the role of God as well as evolution in the process of creation. This group is characterized by those who believe that evolution did occur to create new organisms, including humans with supernatural intervention along the way. There are two main groups within this creationism. The first group holds that the randomness involved in evolution is minimal. They are commonly referred to as *theistic evolutionists* because they basically accept evolutionary theory with the condition that a supreme being was responsible for the human outcome by directly guiding the process. The second group holds that the process of evolution does involve an authentic random element but that a supreme being employed that randomness to produce the desired end-human.[10]

2. Intelligent Design

This is another theory of the origin of the universe that negates the validity of Darwin's evolution theory. Intelligent design is a belief or theory that the complex structures of life cannot be explained by natural selection and random mutation as suggested by Darwin but must be explained by some force of willful design. According to intelligent design proponents, the inner workings of the cell and the complexity of the eye, etc., are so intricate that they require a creative intelligent force to have set them in motion.[11] This theory holds that living things show signs of having been designed, and that living creatures and their biological systems are too complex to be accounted for by the Darwinian theory of evolution, and that a designer or a higher intelligence may be responsible for their complexity.

2.1. The Emergence of Intelligent Design

Intelligent design theory was based on William Paley's work – *Natural Theology* published in 1802, with which Darwin was very familiar. Paley argued that the intricate and delicate structures and workings of the watch show that a creative and intelligent watchmaker has designed it; since the universe resembles a watch in its organization there must be a cosmic designer. In other words, just as we infer a watchmaker from the complex workings of a pocket watch, we must infer a creator of the universe from the complex systems of the natural order.

9 Brian J. Alters, "What Is Creationism?" p. 104.

10 *Ibid.*, p. 105.

11 Amy Binder, "Gathering Intelligence on Intelligent Design: Where Did It Come From, Where Is It Going, and How Should Progressives Manage It?" *American Journal of Education*, (Vol. 113, No. 4, August 2007), pp. 549-550.

The concept of intelligent design was quite old. Aristotle's inclusion of the final Cause in his analysis of the physical and biological worlds and the Stoics' inference of the existence of God from biological complexity point to the early existence of arguments regarding purpose and design.[12] However, the present intelligent design theory was developed by a group of American creationists who protested the court ruling which barred the teaching of 'creation science' in public schools as breaching the separation of church and state. The intelligent design only goes back to 1988, when it was first used by Charles Thaxton in a speech and later in the textbook he edited, *Of Pandas and People: The Central Question of Biological Origins.* Many consider Phillip Johnson, the real founder of the modern intelligent design movement.[13] From the mid-1990s, intelligent design proponents were supported by the Discovery Institute, which, together with its Center for Science and Culture, planned and funded the 'intelligent design movement.' They advocated the inclusion of intelligent design in public school curricula.[14]

2.2. Arguments for Intelligent Design

William Dembski, one of the most illustrious proponents of Intelligent design, in his book, *Intelligent Design: The Bridge between Science and Theology*, observes, "Intelligent design is three things: a scientific research program that investigates the effects of intelligent causes; an intellectual movement that challenges Darwinism and its naturalistic legacy; and a way of understanding divine action."[15] Supporters of intelligent design argue that many features of the natural world, particularly biological structures, are too complex to be explained by naturalistic causes and, thus, can only be explained as products of an intelligent designer. Stephen C. Meyer, Vice President of the Seattle-based Discovery Institute and program director for its Center for Science and Culture, the main center for the propagation of intelligent design, claims that DNA is like a software program or an advanced form of nanotechnology and that such a complex program must have been written by a programmer. Given that DNA holds such detailed, complex information, Meyer argues, something with intelligence must have had a role in the origin of DNA - since it could not evolve by merely natural causes. Meyer

12 Gregory R. Peterson, "The Intelligent-design Movement: Science or Ideology?" *Zygon*, (Vol. 37, No. 1, (March 2002), p. 8.

13 Allene Phy-Olsen, *Evolution, Creationism, and Intelligent Design*, (Santa Barbara, California: Greenwood, 2010), p. 62.

14 Verla Poole, *A Comprehensive Introduction to Intelligent Design: Concepts and Theory*, (Delhi: White Word Publications, 2012), p. 1.

15 W. A. Dembski, *Intelligent Design: The Bridge between Science and Theology*, (Downers Grove, Illinois: Inter Varsity Press, 1999), p. 12.

concludes that living organisms look designed because they really were designed and therefore had a designer.[16]

It is a form of creationism and a contemporary adaptation of the traditional teleological argument for the existence of God, but one that deliberately avoids specifying the nature or identity of the designer. Its leading proponents - all of whom are associated with the Discovery Institute, believe the designer to be the God of Christians.[17] Intelligent design, however, does not try to identify this designer with the God of a particular religion, though individuals within the movement are free to form their own theological views. The intelligent design further recognizes that religion has been the germinating force for the development of the sciences. Almost all the great scientists of the past built their theories on the acknowledgement of a Designer.[18]

Michael Behe, a well known American biochemist and proponent of Intelligent Design, introduced the term 'irreducible complexity' in his celebrated book *Darwin's Black Box: The Biochemical Challenge to Evolution,* published in 1996. According to him, 'irreducible complexity' is a single system composed of several well-matched interacting parts that contribute to the basic function, wherein the removal of any one of the parts causes the system to cease functioning effectively. Intelligent design advocates assert that natural selection could not create irreducibly complex systems because the selectable function is present only when all parts are assembled. Behe argued that irreducibly complex biological mechanisms include the bacterial flagellum of *Escherichia coli*, the blood-clotting cascade, cilia, and the adaptive immune system, etc.[19]

2.3. Intelligent Design Movement – A Scientific Movement

The proponents of the intelligent design maintain that their theory is scientific theory and not a religious doctrine. Like those scientists from an earlier era, the modern intelligent design movement seeks to explain biological and other forms of physical complexity in terms of the actions of a divine intelligent agent. They claim that such an explanation is scientific in character and, therefore, should be taught in the same manner as other scientific theories in schools and universities. Dembski, one of the most important proponents of this theory, suggests that intelligent design is a theory of biological origins and development. Its fundamental claim is that intelligent causes are necessary to explain the complex, information-rich structures of biology and that these causes are empirically detectable.[20]

16 Brett Clark, John Bellamy Foster and Richard York, "The Critique of Intelligent Design: Epicurus, Marx, Darwin, and Freud and the Materialist Defense of Science", *Theory and Society,* (Vol. 36, No. 6, Dec., 2007), p. 516.

17 Verla Poole, *A Comprehensive Introduction to Intelligent Design*, p. 1.

18 Allene Phy-Olsen, *Evolution, Creationism, and Intelligent Design*, p. 64.

19 *Ibid.*, pp. 9-10.

20 Gregory R. Peterson, "The Intelligent-design Movement: Science or Ideology?", p. 10.

However, this is not accepted by a number of authors. Gregory R. Peterson plainly states that science appears to play only a secondary role in the intelligent design theory literature, where the primary concerns are theology and philosophy. It is "an ideological agenda masquerading as science," concludes Peterson.[21] In the same vein, Niall Shanks and Keith Green also argue that intelligent design is more theological than scientific. Quoting Dembski who says, "Indeed, intelligent design is just the Logos theology of John's Gospel restated in the idiom of information theory,"[22] they conclude, "Intelligent design creationism, then, is deeply rooted in theological speculation."[23]

3. Big Bang

One of the most popular theories of the origin of the universe, which is accepted by most scientists and even many Christians, is the hot Big Bang theory. According to this theory, the universe was created from an explosion of indefinitely dense, small and extremely hot particle – the primaeval atom - that occurred some 10 – 20 billion years ago. It is claimed that the radiation from that super hot event can still be seen around in the universe coming from all directions. This radiation, which is in the form of microwave background radiation, has been observed, and this provides natural proof for the Big Bang theory.[24] The term 'Big Bang' was actually coined by physicist Fred Hoyle during a radio broadcast in 1949. He favoured the alternative 'steady-state theory' for the origin of the universe, and he used the term 'Big Bang' as a derisive nickname for the emerging theory of the origin of the universe.

3.1. Expanding Universe

Before we come to the discussion of this theory, it is important to discuss the concept of *expanding universe* because we can say that the Big Bang theory is the outcome of the scientific discovery that the universe is not static or fixed but it is expanding and keeps on expanding! Though the expansion of the universe was implicit in Einstein's general theory of relativity, Einstein himself believed in a fixed and static universe. It was a Russian physicist, Alexander Friedmann, at the beginning of the 1920s, who proposed, basing on Einstein's general theory of relativity, that the universe is not static. But Edwin Hubble was the first scientist

---

21 *Ibid.*, p. 22.

22 W. A. Dembski, "Signs of intelligence: A Primer on the Discernment of Intelligent Design," in W. A. Dembski & J. M. Kusiner (Eds.), *Signs of Intelligence: Understanding Intelligent Design*, (Grand Rapids, Michigan: Brazos Press, 2001), p. 192.

23 Niall Shanks and Keith Green, "Intelligent Design in Theological Perspective", *Synthese*, (Vol. 178, No. 2, January 2011), p. 309.

24 K. K. Theckedath, "Dialectics and Cosmology: The Big Bang and the Steady State Theories", *Social Scientist*, (Vol. 31, No. 1/2, Jan. - Feb., 2003), p. 61.

who established what has been accepted now as a scientific fact that the universe is not static but expanding.

Around 1928, Hubble undertook to determine whether the universe really was expanding. Before he began his work, the picture of an expanding Universe did not have a firm foundation; astronomers did not believe in it because the theory of expanding universe proposed by scientists was too theoretical and incomplete to be convincing. Hubble's first step was to find out what the mysterious spiral 'nebulas' were. Photographing these objects with the 100-inch telescope, then the world's largest, he found that they contained vast numbers of individual stars. Hubble's photographs convinced astronomers that spiral nebulas were true galaxies or island universes. Hubble's next step was to find out how far away the galaxies were. He proceeded to measure their distances, using, as a yardstick, a certain kind of star called a Cepheid, whose true brightness was known from studies of similar stars in our own galaxy. From the degree of faintness of Cepheid stars in other galaxies, he could estimate the distances between these galaxies.[25] He came to this conclusion after observing the different colour of lights coming from distant galaxies. He found out that other galaxies are moving away from us, and the velocity of their movement is proportional to the distance between us. The farther the galaxy is from us, the faster it moves away from us; at the double the distance, the recession velocity will also double! Though there were scientists like Friedmann and Lemaitre before him who proposed the theory of the expansion of the universe, Edwin Hubble was considered as the one who established this fact. That the universe is expanding is, indeed, one of the fascinating scientific discoveries. Stephen Hawking, one of the greatest scientists of our time, notes: "The discovery that the universe is expanding was one of the great intellectual revolutions of the twentieth century."[26]

The universe is just like a balloon with a large number of dots on its surface. When the balloon is blown up, the distances between the dots increase. As we keep on blowing the balloon, all the distances between the dots keep on increasing uniformly. If we are in any of these dots, we will see other dots moving away from us. The universe is expanding in the same fashion. The logical consequence of an expanding universe is that the universe should be smaller before, and many hundred million years ago, it should be very small. It follows thus – in the beginning (when time is zero, t = 0) the universe would have been infinitely small and dense, but with great power. Such an idea led to the emergence of Big Bang cosmology.

25 Robert Jastrow, *God and the Astronomers,* (New York: W. W. Norton & Company, 1978), p. 51.

26 Stephen Hawking, *A Brief History of Time,* p. 42.

3.2. Big Bang Cosmology

By using Hubble's law, that is, the relation between the distance of a galaxy and its recession velocity – *the farther away a galaxy is, the faster it moves*, one can calculate the age of the universe, that is, the starting point of the expansion. Assuming that there has been no change in the rate of expansion, one arrives approximately at the age of some 10 to 20 billion years. Today, most cosmologists believe that the universe came into being with the explosion of an infinitely dense and infinitely small particle some 10 to 20 billion years ago.[27] This explosion is popularly known as Big Bang. At that time, all the matter in the universe was packed into a dense mass, at temperatures of many trillions of degrees. The dazzling brilliance of the radiation in this dense, hot universe must have been beyond description. The picture suggests the explosion of a cosmic hydrogen bomb. The instant in which the cosmic bomb exploded marked the birth of the universe.[28]

Georges Lemaitre (1894–1966), a Belgian priest, astronomer and professor of physics at the Catholic University of Leuven, was the one who proposed the now famous Big Bang theory. According to him, the expansion of the universe could be traced back to a very dense state in the distant past, in which the particles of the whole universe existed as a single particle, the "primaeval atom" as he called it, which disintegrated in an explosion, giving rise to space and time and the expansion of the universe that continues to this day. His original publication appeared in an unpopular Belgian Journal, but Arthur Eddington, on seeing the prospect of the theory, republished it in the *Monthly Notices of the Royal Astronomical Society* and also in his own Book - *The Expanding Universe* (1933).[29]

Not only religious people but a number of scientists are unhappy with the idea that the world began in this way. Until recently, many scientists preferred the *Steady State theory* for the origin of the universe, which holds that the universe had no beginning and is eternal. But the latest evidence makes it almost certain that the Big Bang really did occur many billions of years ago: In 1965, two American physicists, Arno Penzias and Robert Wilson of the Bell Telephone Laboratories, discovered that the earth is bathed in a faint glow of radiation coming from every direction in the heavens. The measurements showed that the earth itself could not be the origin of this radiation, nor could the radiation coming from the direction of the moon, the sun, or any other particular object in the sky. The entire universe seemed to be the source. The two physicists were puzzled by their discovery. They did not realize that they had stumbled upon the answer to one of the cosmic mysteries. Scientists believed that this radiation came from the Big Bang explosion. The theory of the Big Bang had long asserted that the universe

---

27 Fritjo Capra, *The Tao of Physics*, (London: Flamingo, 1991), pp. 218-219.

28 Robert Jastrow, *God and the Astronomers*, p. 13.

29 Craig Sean McConnell, "Twentieth-Century Cosmologies" in Cary B. Ferngren (ed), *Science and Religion: A Historical Introduction*, (Baltimore: The Johns Hopkins University Press, 2002), p. 316-317.

must have resembled a white-hot fireball in the very first moments after the Big Bang occurred. Gradually, the fireball would have become less brilliant as the universe expanded and cooled, but its radiation would have never disappeared entirely. It was the diffuse glow of this ancient radiation, dating back to the birth of the universe, that Penzias and Wilson apparently discovered.[30] It is no wonder that Arno Penzias and Robert Wilson were awarded the Nobel Prize in 1978.

3.3. Big Crunch

There can be two assumptions as to the future of the universe as the logical consequence of the Big Bang. The first assumption is that the gravitational attraction between the different galaxies causes the expansion to slow down and eventually stop. The galaxies then start to move towards each other, and the universe contracts and finally comes back to its original infinite density – thus the Big Crunch! The second assumption is that the universe expands with such a strong force that the gravitational pull could never stop it. This means it will expand forever. Whether the universe will stop expanding and start contracting or it will expand forever can be known if we know the present rate of expansion and its present average density. It is impossible to calculate the present expansion rate accurately though only a rough calculation is possible. More difficult is to know the density of the universe accurately because we have to add up the masses of all the stars in our galaxy and other galaxies. After adding up the masses of all the stars and working out their density, even adding up the 'dark matters' that might be there in the galaxies which we cannot see, we get only one-tenth of the amount of density required to halt the expansion.[31] Taking into consideration these facts, Stephen Hawking concludes, "The present evidence, therefore, suggests that the universe will probably expand forever."[32] So, Big Crunch could never happen! Even if the universe is going to re-collapse, it will take at least 10 to 20 billion years, which is the amount of time it took to expand so far.

4. Black Holes

The term 'black hole' was coined by the American scientist, John Wheeler in 1969. But the idea of the existence of a black hole was some one hundred years old. With his general theory of relativity published in 1915, Einstein predicted the possibility of the existence of a black hole. Black holes are regions of space in which the gravitational field is so strong that nothing can escape, not even light. So much mass is compressed into such a small volume that gravity overwhelms all other forces, and nothing even light can escape. Instead of a normal surface, a black hole has an event horizon, a virtual surface that separates the outside

---

30 Robert Jastrow, *God and the Astronomers*, pp. 14-15.

31 Stephen Hawking, *A Brief History of Time*, p. 49.

32 *Ibid.*

world from the region of the black hole.[33] Mitchell Begelman remarks: "Within a finite region surrounding the center of a black hole, all light rays and physically realizable trajectories of particles are directed inward. Space and time are so distorted that there is literally no way out."[34] Stephen Hawking, who has done tremendous works on the black hole, explains the great phenomenon in space called black holes as follows:

> The light cones... are bent slightly inward near the surface of the star... As the star contracts, the gravitational field at its surface gets stronger and the light cones get bent inward more. This makes it more difficult for the light from the star to escape, and the light appears dimmer and redder to an observer at a distance. Eventually when the star has shrunk to a certain critical radius, the gravitational field at the surface becomes so strong that the light cones are bent inward so much that the light can no longer escape. According to the theory of relativity, nothing can travel faster than light. Thus if light cannot escape, neither can anything else; everything is dragged back by the gravitational field. So one has a set of events, a region of space-time, from which it is not possible to escape to reach a distant observer. This region is what we now call a black hole.[35]

Black holes are a striking example of a prediction of Einstein's theory of general relativity. Although, it took many decades before the black hole was fully understood and widely accepted; recent years have seen rapid advancement on both the observational and theoretical sides. Black holes have now become accepted as an astrophysical reality.[36] Supermassive black holes have been observed at the centers of many galaxies. Such supermassive black holes at the central region of large galaxies, like our Milky Way Galaxy, have millions, or even billions, of solar masses.[37] Black holes are of various sizes - some are as small as an atom but some black holes could be as big as one million suns. A black hole may be as small as the size of an atom, yet its matter would be so densely compacted that it would weigh something like 100 trillion tons! An even tinier black hole, say the size of an atom's nucleus, would still tip the scales at about a billion tons.[38]

---

33 Ramesh Narayan and Eliot Quataert, "Black Hole Accretion", *Science, New Series,* (Vol. 307, No. 5706, Jan. 7, 2005), p. 77.

34 Mitchell C. Begelman, "Evidence for Black Holes", *Science, New Series,* (Vol. 300, No. 5627, Jun. 20, 2003), p. 1898.

35 Stephen Hawking, *A Brief History of Time*, p. 90.

36 B. Brügmann, A. M. Ghez and J. Greiner, "Black Holes", *Proceedings of the National Academy of Sciences of the United States of America*, (Vol. 98, No. 19, Sep. 11, 2001), p. 10525.

37 Alexei V. Filippenko, "Black Holes in the Milky Way Galaxy", *Proceedings of the National Academy of Sciences of the United States of America,* (Vol. 96, No. 18, Aug. 31, 1999), p. 9993.

38 Don Nardo, *Black Holes*, New York: Lucent Books/Thomson Gale, 2004, p. 26.

Two populations of black holes have been established observationally. *Firstly*, the Stellar-mass black holes are presumably the collapsed remnants of massive stars. *Secondly*, Supermassive black holes are found, as pointed out above, at the centers of galaxies. They were first proposed to explain the prodigious energy outputs of quasars and are now understood to be the primary source of energy in all types of active galactic nuclei.[39]

4.1. How to Locate Black Holes?

As light and matter are trapped inside, a black hole cannot be directly detected; however, the presence of Black Holes can be located from the activities of stars around them. Scientists measure their gravitational influence on surrounding material and locate the black hole and calculate its size and power. The main celestial laboratories for such studies are binary star systems and galactic nuclei. If, for example, a visible star rapidly orbits a dark object, the process of elimination suggests that the latter is a black hole. Similarly, if the motion of stars and gas near the nucleus of a galaxy indicates that an enormous mass is confined to a very small volume, a black hole is probably present.[40] Black holes have been discovered primarily by measuring their gravitational effects on distant bodies. By applying the Newtonian laws of gravity, astronomers have established that dark masses exist at the centers of galaxies.[41]

4.2. How They Form?

It is known that stars have their own life span. When stars burned all their nuclear fuel, they collapsed and formed black holes. When massive stars end their lives, they explode violently as supernovae. If this is the case, "the number of black holes may be greater even than the number of visible stars, which totals about a hundred thousand million in our galaxy alone."[42] However, direct evidence linking supernovae and their black-hole remnants has been missing until now. Scientists think supermassive black holes, especially those at the center of the galaxy, were made simultaneously as the galaxy they are in. Super-dense mini black holes, which are as small as an atom, were probably formed during the Big Bang.

4.3. Supernovae

At average intervals of several centuries in the life history of any stellar system, a star suddenly blazes out to a maximum luminosity, perhaps 100 million suns and then slowly fades away until vanishes. These stellar explosions are called

39 See for a detailed explanation, Mitchell C. Begelman, "Evidence for Black Holes", pp. 1898-1899.

40 Alexei V. Filippenko, "Black Holes in the Milky Way Galaxy", p. 9993.

41 Mitchell C. Begelman, "Evidence for Black Holes", p. 1898.

42 Stephen Hawking, *A Brief History of Time*, p. 100.

supernovae. They are the rarest and most spectacular phenomena observed in the universe.[43]

Ordinary novae are those objects that suddenly emerge from the obscurity of apparently commonplace stars, and within a day or two, become about 20,000 times more luminous than our sun. Supernovae appear with similar abruptness, but they surpass ordinary novae in intrinsic brilliance by a factor between one and ten thousand. The Swedish astronomer Lundmark was apparently the first to use the term Supernovae. He used the term in a paper on pre-Tychonic novae in 1932 though Baade and Zwicky were also regarded as the first persons who introduced the term 'supernovae' in 1934 when they separated supernovae from the common novae. The relative frequency of normal novae to supernovae has been roughly estimated at 15,000 to one-normal novae occurring at the rate of twenty to thirty per year both in the local galaxy and in the Andromeda Nebula, whereas supernovae, according to a recent estimate by Zwicky, occur one per galaxy every six hundred years.[44]

Novae frequently occur in our galaxy, but supernovae are far more luminous and rare, only occurring once or twice a century in our own galaxy. The last supernovae observed in our galaxy were the Tycho and Kepler supernovae in 1572 and 1604, respectively. Supernovae can be so luminous that they outshine all the other stars in a galaxy. After a sharp rise to maximum light over a few days, their luminosity decays and slowly fades over weeks and months. Some have a light-curve plateau and remain at a constant brightness for up to four months before fading. The energy required to power a typical supernova display is similar to the amount of energy our sun will output over its 10 billion year lifetime. To produce that amount of energy over a few days, the progenitor star must be significantly altered in a supernova.[45]

4.4. Quasars

A 'Quasi-stellar-object' or a *Quasar* is a massive and extremely remote celestial object emitting exceptionally large amounts of energy, which typically has a star-like image in a telescope. It has been suggested that quasars contain massive black holes and may represent a stage in the evolution of some galaxies. Before Hubble, quasars were considered to be isolated star-like objects of a mysterious nature. Hubble has observed several quasars and found that they all reside at galactic centres. Today most scientists believe that supermassive black holes at the galactic

43 Edwin Hubble, "Supernovae", *Publications of the Astronomical Society of the Pacific,* (Vol. 53, No. 313, June, 1941), p. 141.

44 DorritHoffleit, "Observations of Supernovae", *Proceedings of the American Philosophical Society*, (Vol. 81, No. 2, Jun. 30, 1939), p. 265.

45 John J. Eldridge, "Massive Stars in Their Death Throes", *Philosophical Transactions: Mathematical, Physical and Engineering Sciences,* (Vol. 366, No. 1884, Astronomy, Dec. 13, 2008), p. 4441.

centres are the 'engines' that power the quasars.[46] But according to Roberto Terlevich of the Royal Greenwich Observatory and Brian Boyle of Cambridge University, the power source of quasars is most probably the synchronized bursts of star birth and death in the cores of young galaxies. Shining like beacons from the very edges of the universe, quasars emit such an astounding amount of energy the equal, in some cases, of the combined brilliance of 100,000 ordinary galaxies that scientists have turned to even more enigmatic constructs to explain them.[47]

The term 'quasar' was derived from how these objects were originally discovered in the earliest radio surveys of the sky in the 1950s. Away from the plane of the Milky Way Galaxy, most radio sources were identified with otherwise normal-looking galaxies. Some radio sources, however, coincided with objects that appeared to be unusually blue stars, although photographs of some of these objects showed them to be embedded in faint, fuzzy halos. Because of their almost star-like appearance, they were dubbed "quasi-stellar radio sources," or "quasi-stellar object" which by 1964 had been shortened to "quasar."[48]

Quasars rank among the brightest objects in the universe. Two independent surveys reveal that of 35 observed galaxies that host quasars, about half appear to have been ripped apart, to have suffered recent collisions, or to be about to merge with a nearby galaxy. These violent scenes suggest that many quasars light up when a collision or merger creates a fresh supply of gas and dust, reviving a dormant black hole at the center of a galaxy. The black hole embarks on a feeding frenzy, sucking in the new material. As the gas and dust spiral in, they radiate away much of their energy, generating the quasar's fierce emissions.[49]

The presence of black holes in our universe is now almost an established fact, and most scientists believe in it. However, it is not absolutely clear as to how they are exactly formed? Is there a connection between supernovae and black holes? It was opined that supernovae resulted in black holes, but there is no observational proof. How many black holes will be there? It is said that black holes occurred when a particular star contracted beyond a critical point that produced a great gravitational force, but scientists could not explain why stars should contract. There are many unanswered questions around black holes, and even some scientists are reluctant to believe in the presence of a black hole itself.

5. Steady-State Theory

The Steady-State Theory, as the name indicates, holds that the universe existed in the same state in contrast to the claim of the Big Bang model. Three scientists are

46 *http://www.spacetelescope.org/science/black_holes/* (03.01.2017).

47 Ray Jayawardhana, "Could Quasars Get Their Shine From Stars?" *Science, New Series*, (Vol. 259, No. 5102, Mar. 19, 1993), p. 1692.

48 *https://www.britannica.com/topic/quasar* (03.01.2017).

49 R. Cowen, "New View of Quasars Sheds Light on Origin", *Science News*, (Vol. 150, No. 21, Nov. 23, 1996), p. 326.

associated with the emergence of this theory – Hermann Bondi, Thomas Gold and Fred Hoyle who proposed this theory in 1948; Bondi and Gold together proposed this theory, and Hoyle proposed independently but in the same year 1948. The Steady-State theory was presented as an alternative to the Big Bang theory. In opposition to the Big Bang theory, which proposes the emergence of the whole universe at t = 0, the steady-state theory holds that the expanding universe might not result from the Big Bang and a singularity. This theory endorses the constancy of all parameters and Hubble's constant in the universe at all times. In order to explain the permanent identity of the expanding universe, the theory claims that new matter comes into existence in the interstices of space, which are created by moving away galaxies from each other.[50]

Criticizing the Bid Bang theory, Gold and Bondi argued that while using Doppler Effect in arguments, it was assumed that the atoms of the distant galaxies which emitted their light thousands of millions of years ago and are being observed today, obeyed the same laws of physics as the atoms today in our laboratories. How could the laws be obeyed in the past and today in a universe which was changing? Hence, it was assumed that the universe was unchanging in its characteristics over millions of years and should have the same features in all epochs.[51] Bondi and Gold have three assumptions upon which they built their theory: (1) The universe is homogeneous on a large scale; (2) The universe is isotropic, that is, it is the same in all directions; (3) The perfect cosmological principle holds, namely, the universe in its laws have the same features at all epochs.[52]

The assumptions of Bondi and Gold implied that the density of the universe should be the same at all epochs. However, according to Hubble's law which is universally accepted, the galaxies are moving away from each other. If the density could remain constant new galaxies should be formed while old galaxies move away. Only then the density of the universe remained constant in all epochs. This is the basic idea of creation in the Steady-State cosmology.[53] Fred Hoyle calculated the amount of matter required to be created second per cubic centimeter to maintain a steady density while the universe was expanding. Having found this rate of creation, he then modified Einstein's equations of gravitation in order to ensure that the law of conservation of matter and motion was disturbed. He posited a new field called the C-field, which explain the creation of matter. Hoyle's C-field was a reservoir in which matter could be created.[54] Hoyle says,

---

50 Mirsaeid Mousam Karimi, "Adolf Grünbaum on the Steady-State Theory and Creatio Continua of Matter Out of Nothing", *Zygon*, (Vol. 46, No. 4, December 2011), pp. 858-859.

51 K. K. Theckedath,"Dialectics and Cosmology: The Big Bang and the Steady State Theories" *Social Scientist*, (Vol. 31, No. ½, Jan. - Feb., 2003), p. 76.

52 *Ibid.*

53 *Ibid.*, p. 77.

54 *Ibid.*

"The theory of a steady-state universe leads to many startling conclusions: that the universe had no beginning and will have no end, that space as well as time is infinite, that matter is continually being created throughout space-to mention a few."[55] He further explains the Steady-State theory as follows:

> The steady-state theory holds that the large-scale features of the universe do not change with time. Only the galaxies and clusters of galaxies change; if we "smear out" their material uniformly through space and consider the general properties of the cosmos, it is unchanging. The expansion of the universe is a basic feature of the theory. The question arises: If the galaxies are moving apart from each other, why does space not become more and more empty? The answer of the theory is that new galaxies and clusters of galaxies are constantly being formed, their rate of formation just compensating for the separating effect of the expansion. So a stable situation is preserved.[56]

There are not many scientists who adhere to this theory. Stanley L. Jaki may be right when he said that this theory never secured a single piece of experimental verification. According to Mirsaeid Mousam Karimi, problems with the Steady State theory began to emerge in the mid-1960s, when observations showed that quasars and radio galaxies were found only at large distances, whereas the this theory predicted that such objects would be found everywhere, including close to our own galaxy. Moreover, the galactic red-shift plus the cosmogonic nucleosynthesis of the light elements were strong evidence against the theory.[57]

6. Anthropic Cosmological Principle

The Anthropic Principle was proposed by Brandon Carter in Poland in 1973, during a two-week Symposium commemorating Copernicus' 500th birthday. Brandon Carter had the idea that humanity did hold a special place in the universe, an assertion that is the exact opposite of Copernicus' now universally accepted theory. He devised the '*anthropic principle*,' a multifaceted argument for a contrived universe, a universe which had as its goal from the very beginning the creation of biological life or, in the stronger version, the creation of human life. The anthropic argument is based on the fact that there are an inconceivable number of apparent coincidences which together are necessary for significant life to have evolved. In a closer examination, such coincidences, however, should not be seen as coincidences at all, since they are better explained as the result of contrivance by 'an intelligent coordinator,' not as the product of mere chance.

55 Fred Hoyle, "The Steady-state Universe," *Scientific American*, (Vol. 195, No. 3, September 1956), p. 157.

56 *Ibid.*

57 Mirsaeid Mousam Karimi, "Adolf Grünbaum on the Steady-State Theory and Creatio Continua of Matter Out of Nothing", p. 859.

Among an infinite field of potentiality, the occurrence even of one of these apparent anthropic coincidences would have been almost infinitely unlikely. Yet when the intricate degree of cooperation displayed by all of the apparent coincidences is taken into account, as well as the intolerance to change of any of them by the smallest of variables, the conclusion that the universe is contrived seems unavoidable. This contrived creation, apparently, was coercively imposed on the chaos by a unilateral divine act that determined the entire process toward the evolution of significant biological and anthropic life.[58]

6.1. Models of Apparent Coincidences

John Jefferson Davies listed some of the so-called 'coincidences' in the universe or what may be called 'the cosmic fine tuning' that allowed life to exist:[59]

- If gravity were stronger by one part in 10 to the power 40, there would long ago have been a catastrophic collapse of the universe (the 'Big Crunch') instead of its present expansion.
- If matter in the universe were not spread out at an incredibly low density, the universe would long ago have collapsed in upon itself.
- If the initial explosion of the 'Big Bang' had differed in strength by one part in 10 to the power 60, the universe as we now know would not have existed.
- If the combined masses of the proton and electron were to become a little more rather than a little less than the mass of the neutron, the hydrogen atom would become unstable, and the sun would fade and collapse.
- If the strength of the electromagnetic and strong nuclear forces were only moderately different, the process of carbon formation in the cores of stars would not occur, and there could be no carbon-based life as we know it.
- If the mass of neutrinos were 5 x 10 to the power -34 kg instead of 5 x10 to the power -35 kg, because of their great abundance in the universe, the additional gravitational mass would result in a contracting rather than expanding universe.
- If the strong nuclear force were about 5% weaker, the deuteron could not exist; without deuterium, the main nuclear chain reaction used by the sun could not proceed. Stable, long-lived stars such as the sun would not exist, and there would be no life on earth.

58 Barry Whitney, "Divine Persuasion and the Anthropic Argument," *The Personalist Forum*, (Vol. 14, No. 2, The Hartshorne Centennial Conference, Fall 1998), pp. 143-144.

59 John Jefferson Davis, "The Design Argument, Cosmic 'Fine Tuning,' and the Anthropic Principle", *International Journal for Philosophy of Religion*, (Vol. 22, No. 3, 1987), pp. 140-141.

Barry White also listed several apparent coincidences which are numerous and impressive -The fact that there is a life-permitting and inexplicable asymmetry between matter and antimatter. Another is that the overall amount of matter in the universe is precisely what is necessary for life: had there been any more or any less matter, anthropic life would not have been possible. Further, given the infinite range of possible velocities, the Big Bang exploded at precisely the right velocity to permit the evolution of significant life. The universe, furthermore, is precisely as big and as old for intelligent life to have evolved as it has: the universe could not be less sparse, nor could life have evolved more quickly than it has. To cite another apparent coincidence, the temperature of nuclear stability insures the evolution of life, as does the development of deuterium, neutrinos, the ratio of protons to electrons and their respective electrical charges, and so on.[60]

Thus, Paul Davies concludes that physicists and astronomers who study the overall structure and evolution of the universe encounter cosmic cooperation of such a wildly improbable nature that "it becomes hard to resist the impression that some basic principle is at work."[61] Patrick A. Wilson also states - "in light of these and countless other 'cosmic coincidences,' the universe seems remarkably finely tuned for mankind. This extremely fine edge on which our presence in the universe balances cries out for an explanation."[62] The explanation is that this cosmic principle known as 'Anthropic Principle' (from Greek *anthropos* – human, meaning 'human centered') works in the universe so that there is the possibility of life in general and human life in particular.

6.2. Different Types of Anthropic Principles

Brandon Carter initially came up with what is now known as 'the Weak Anthropic Principle' and later on proposed the 'Strong Anthropic Principle.' The Weak Anthropic Principle states that as there are observers in our universe, the universe must possess properties that permit the existence of these observers. In other words, the universe must be consistent with the fact that it contains observers (whose position will necessarily be privileged). The Strong Anthropic Principle, on the other hand, states that the structure of the universe and the particulars of its construction are essentially fixed by the condition that at some point, it inevitably produces an observer.[63]

---

60 Barry Whitney, "Divine Persuasion and the Anthropic Argument," p. 145.

61 P. C. W. Davies, *The Accidental Universe* (Cambridge: Cambridge University Press, 1982), p. 77.

62 Patrick A. Wilson, "What Is the Explanandum of the Anthropic Principle?" *American Philosophical Quarterly*, (Vol. 28, No. 2, Apr., 1991), p. 167.

63 Reinhard Breuer, *The Anthropic Principle: Man as the Focal Point of Nature*, translated by Harry Newman and Mark Lowery, (New York: Springer Science+Business Medis, 1991), p. 8.

John Barrow and Frank Tipler, in their celebrated book - *The Anthropic Cosmological Principle* mention three different types of Anthropic Principles which they describe as follows:[64]

6.2.1. Weak Anthropic Principle: The observed values of all physical and cosmological quantities are not equally probable, but they take on values restricted by the requirement that there exist sites where carbon-based life can evolve and by the requirement that the universe be old enough for it to have already done so.

6.2.2. Strong Anthropic Principle: The Universe must have those properties which allow life to develop within it at some stage in its history. An implication of the Strong Anthropic Principle is that the constants and laws of nature must be such that life can exist. This speculative statement leads to a number of interpretations: (a) There exists one possible universe designed with the goal of generating and sustaining observers, (b) observers are necessary to bring the universe into being, and (c) an ensemble of other different universes is necessary for the existence of our universe

6.2.3. Final Anthropic Principle: Intelligent information-processing must come into existence in the universe, and, once it comes into existence, it will never die out.

> The Anthropic Principle itself does not talk about the role of God in the whole process of the fine-tuning of the universe for life to happen. However, it cannot be difficult to infer that if there are such contrivances in the universe for the possibility of life by an intelligent coordinator and not as the product of mere chance or coincidences, there must be God or Intelligent Ultimate Reality or whatever name we may give it, who acts behind all these contrivances so as to make the universe suitable for life in general and human life in particular.

7. Many Worlds Theory

The Many-Worlds Interpretation is an approach to quantum mechanics according to which, in addition to the world we are aware of directly, many other similar worlds exist in parallel at the same space and time. The existence of the other worlds makes it possible to remove randomness and action at a distance from quantum theory and thus from all physics. The theory is also referred to as the relative state formulation, the Everett interpretation, the theory of the universal wave function, many-universes interpretation, or just many-worlds. This theory originated in the Ph.D. thesis of Hugh Everett III (1930 -1982) – "The Theory of the Universal Wave function" submitted to Princeton University and published in 1957. But it was Bryce Seligman DeWitt (1923 - 2004), an American theoretical physicist, who coined the term 'many-worlds' and popularized Everett's theory.

64 John D. Barrow and Frank J. Tipler, *The Anthropic Cosmological Principle*, (Oxford: Oxford University Press, 1996, first published in 1986), pp. 16-22.

Everett speaks of 'the universal wave-function,' which is a quantum state of the totality of existence, regarded as the 'basic physical entity' or the fundamental entity, obeying at all times a deterministic wave equation. It is often taken to be a distinctive feature of his interpretation that the entire universe can intelligibly be said to have a wave-function. This contrasts with a version of the Copenhagen interpretation, which accepts as meaningful the attribution of a wave-function only to a system that may be subjected to a measurement performed on it by some object which is not part of the system. But on the other hand, according to the usual understanding of Everett's view, when a measurement-type interaction occurs, the entire universe splits into multiple 'copies,' each with its own individual wave-function.[65] According to Everett, whenever a quantum system is in a superposition of, let's say, 'N' quantum states, after the measure, the whole universe will split into 'N' copies, each containing a version of the measured reality, including the observers. In the simplest case that 'N' equals two, for example, the passing or not of a photon through a polarizer rotated forty-five degrees with respect to the initial polarization plan of the photon, the universe will split into two almost equal copies, in one of which we shall have a photon trapped by the polarizer and in the other one a photon having passed through it, and two identical observers, one in each universe, each of them thinking to be the only one and observing only one of the two versions of the quantum phenomenon.[66]

Everett's Many-Worlds theory is as difficult to explain as to believe. Let us try to explain in a simple way as follows: Hugh Everett agreed with much of what the highly respected physicist Niels Bohr had suggested about the quantum world. He agreed with the idea of 'superposition', as well as with the notion of 'wave functions.' But Everett disagreed with Bohr in one vital respect, and proposed a radical supposition that differed from the popular models of quantum mechanics. Everett did not believe that observation causes quantum matter to stop behaving in multiple forms. Instead, he argued that a measurement taken of a quantum object causes an actual split in the universe. The universe is literally duplicated, splitting into one universe for each possible outcome from the measurement.[67] Each of these universes offers a unique and independent reality that coexists with other parallel universes. If Everett's Many-Worlds Theory is true, it holds many ramifications that completely transform our perceptions on life. Any action that

65 Richard A. Healey, "How Many Worlds?" *Noûs,* (Vol. 18, No. 4, Special Issue on the Foundations of Quantum Mechanics, Nov.,1984), p. 591.

66 Luis Girela, "Many Simple Universes or Only a Very Complex One?" *Theoria: An International Journal for Theory, History and Foundations of Science,* (Vol. 14, No. 2(35), Mayo 1999), p. 331.

67 Josh Clark, "Do parallel universes really exist?" in *http://science.howstuffworks.com/science-vs-myth/everyday-myths/parallel-universe2.htm* (07.01.2017).

has more than one possible result produces a split in the universe. Thus, there are an infinite number of parallel universes and infinite copies of each person.[68]

While some hail this interpretation as the only serious contender for an interpretation of the quantum theory, capable of incorporating quantum mechanical considerations into cosmology, few working physicists take it seriously, and even one of its most influential erstwhile supporters has withdrawn his support. Part of the explanation for this lack of consensus is no doubt a failure to agree on precisely what the many-worlds interpretation is that the interpretation itself needs interpreting.[69]

8. Kalām Cosmology

Now, let me turn to discussing Islamic Cosmology known as *Kalām Cosmology*. The eighth to eleventh centuries A.D. can be regarded as the golden age of Islamic theology and philosophy. Islamic dialectical theology was technically known as *kalām*, literally meaning 'speech', but it connotes 'natural theology'[70] or 'philosophical theism.'[71] *Kalām*, when taken literally, means 'speech', came to denote "the statement of points of theological doctrine, and was later used to mean the statement of an intellectual position or the argument upholding such a statement. Ultimately, *kalām* became the name of the whole movement within Arabic thought that might best be called Arabic scholasticism."[72] The *kalām* argument is simply the old first cause cosmological argument based on the impossibility of an infinite temporal regress of events. It is as follows:[73]

(a) Whatever begins to exist has a cause of its existence.
(b) The universe began to exist.
(c) Therefore, the universe has a cause for its existence.

One of the most important Islamic theologians Al-Ghazali defended point no. (b) as follows:

An argument based on the impossibility of an actual infinite:

- An actual infinite cannot exist; an infinite temporal regress of events is an actual infinite; therefore, an infinite temporal regress of events cannot exist.

---

68 Jason Chu, "Parallel Universes and the Many-Worlds Theory", in *http://www.universetoday.com/113900/parallel-universes-and-the-many-worlds-theory/* (07.01.2017).

69 Richard A. Healey, "How Many Worlds?" p. 591.

70 Phil Dowe, *Galileo, Darwin, and Hawking: The Interplay of Science, Reason, and Religion* (Grand Rapids: William B. Eerdmans Publishing Company, 2005), p. 143.

71 Willian Lane Craig, *The Kalām Cosmological Argument* (Eugene, Oregon: Wipf and Stock Publishers, 1979), p. 4.

72 *Ibid.*

73 William Lane Craig, "Professor Mackie and the Kalām Cosmological Argument", *Religious Studies*, Vol. 20, No. 3 (Sept., 1984), p. 367.

An argument based on the impossibility of the formation of an actual infinite by successive addition: - A collection formed by successive addition cannot be actually infinite; the temporal series of past events is a collection formed by successive addition; therefore, the temporal series of past events cannot be actually infinite.

In the *kalām* argument for the beginning of the universe, there is no iota of doubt that the Cause of the existence of the universe is God. There are a number of Quranic verses that speak about the creation where God created the universe out of nothing. However, just like the Christian concept of the creation of human from dust, Quran testifies that the first human being, Adam was created from dust (30:20).

9. Creation Stories in Hinduism

As Hinduism is complex and diverse, it is not possible to discuss all the creation stories found in the many different religious literature and philosophies here. I will look at the Vedas, the Primary Scripture of Hinduism which is known as *Sruti* and discuss some of the important creation stories found therein. In the early Vedic hymns, we see descriptions of *Aditi* as the universal mother or mother goddess who gave birth to all the gods who in turn shaped or carved the world. We also have in the Rig Veda concept of the creation of the worlds emerging from *Hiranyagarbha*, the primaeval egg.

Two of the Rig Vedic Hymns – '*Purusa*' and 'Hymn of Creation' deal with the origin of creation. According to *Purusa-sukta* (Hymn of human: Rig Veda 10:90) gods are the agents of creation, while the material out of which the universe was made is the body of a primaeval giant called *Purusa*. The act of creation is treated as a sacrifice in which Purusa is the victim; the parts cut off becoming portions of the universe. According to *Purusa-sukta* everything and every being – mortal and immortal is contained in *Purusa*. A fourth of him is all beings, three-fourth of him are what are immortals in heaven; summer, autumn, animals of all kinds, human beings of all castes, Vedas, etc. are all made out of *Purusa*. His head was a Brahmin, his two arms were made the Kshatriya, his two thighs the Vaisya, and from his feet, the Sudra was born. Sun, moon, gods are all born of Purusa, so also air, earth, and so on.

Another Hymn of the Rig Veda – *Nasadiya Sukta* (Rig Veda 10:129) called 'Hymn of Creation' explains the origin of the world as the evolution of the existence (*sat*) from the non-existence (*asat*). Before creation, there was nothing but darkness. Water came into being first, from it was evolved intelligence by heat, and desire follows, and so on.

One of the most important scriptures of the Hindu religious tradition is the Upanishad, and so far as philosophical Hinduism is concerned, the Upanishad is by far the most important scripture. Upanishads are part of the Vedas, the primary scripture, and there are several Upanishads. The Upanishads, though looked upon as part of the Vedic literature, are a protest against the Vedic cult. In contrast to

Vedic polytheism, the chief topic of the Upanishads is the unity of the godhead. The one God, called Brahman or Atman, was recognised as behind all these gods and goddesses.[74]

Brahman is the ultimate reality, the source of everything. Brahman alone is real, and was understood in the Upanishads as the indwelling Spirit. It was Brahman which alone existed at the beginning (Brihadaranyaka Upanishad I.iv.1). Brihadaranyaka Upanishad explains the creations as follows: "As the spider comes out with its thread, or as a small sparks come forth from the fire, thus do all senses, all worlds, all *devas*, all beings, come forth from that Self" (II.i.20). A similar expression is found in Mundaka Upanishad as well. Apart from using the simile of spider and fire, Mundaka Upanishad uses another simile – "… as plants grow on the earth, as hair come out from a living person, so in this world does everything come out of the undecaying One" (I.i.7; see also II.i.1). There are several verses in Mundaka Upanishad that talk about the creation of the universe from the Ultimate Reality. We also see the same simile in Swetaswatara Upanishad (4:10). Another interesting creation story is recorded in Taittiriya Upanishad. Here, the Creator is named as Brahma, and he meditated and created the universe. "He wished – let me become many, let me be born. He meditated and created all this whatever is" (II.6). All these explanations of creation, according to Shakuntala Rao Shastri, "prove that creation is only the coming out of what already existed potentially in Brahman."[75]

As we observed above, the concept of *creatio ex nihilo* (creation out of nothing), which is the prevalent idea in Muslim and Christian creation theology, is generally not applied to Hindu creation stories especially seen in the Vedas. Either it is *Purusa*, *Hiranyagarbha* or Brahman, creation happened from the already existent eternal source. However, the 'Hymn of Creation' in Rig Veda is elusive as to what this myth tries to convey. By and large, Hindu creation stories in the Vedas give us a clear picture of the creation of the universe from the already eternally existent material, be it God or otherwise.

10. Biblical Doctrine of Creation and Creation *Ex Nihilo*

There is an unending debate about whether God created the entire creation out of nothing or from the preexistent matter. Those who follow the doctrine of creation out of nothing (*creatio ex nihilo*) based their argument on various Biblical verses from the Old Testament and New Testament. On the other hand, those who subscribe to the idea that God created heaven and earth and everything in them from the preexistent unorganized chaotic matter. In this sense, God can be looked upon as the one who organized and gave forms and systems to the preexistent chaotic matter. This group makes detailed exegesis on Gen. 1:1-2 to support their

74 Shakuntala Rao Shastri, *Aspirations From a Fresh World*, (Bombay: Bharatiya Vidya Bhavan, 1954), p. 97.

75 *Ibid.*, p. 147.

claim and also take the help of 2 Peter 3:5, where it is mentioned that the earth was formed out of water. For them, the doctrine of *creatio ex nihilo* (creation out of nothing) is a post-biblical doctrine developed from the second century to fight against heretical teaching, especially that of Gnosticism.

10.1. Creation Story in the Bible

The first two verses of the Bible read: "*In the beginning when God created the heavens and the earth, the earth was a formless void and darkness covered the face of the deep, while a wind from God swept over the face of the waters*" (Gen. 1:1-2). Here we see *tohû wabohu-* "without form and void" and "*tehôm*" – deep and "the face of water." Keith Norman argues, "This hardly signifies absolute nonexistence; rather, it speaks of the formless, primaeval chaotic matter, the Urstoff out of which the Creator fashioned the world."[76] In the same vein, C. H. Dodd, one of the well known New Testament scholars, concludes that "the Mosaic account of creation postulates two preexistent factors - the eternal God, and Chaos."[77] Blake T. Ostler also argues that God created heaven and earth by organizing preexistent chaos. "The waters represented the primordial chaos already present when God created the earth in Genesis 1:2 (and there is no indication in the text that the waters are ever created)."[78]

Thus, the argument is clear, that is, insofar as the creation story of Genesis is concerned, it is *not* out of nothing that God created heavens and earth, but from the pre-existing chaotic matter.

In the New Testament, the doctrine of creation from pre-existing matter found support from the Epistle of Peter. The 2 Peter 3:5 reads - "*They deliberately ignore this fact, that by the word of God heavens existed long ago and an earth was formed out of water and by means of water*." For several scholars, this verse is a clear indicator of creation from a preexistent matter. According to Blake T. Ostler, this verse supports the view that everything was organized from pre-existing chaos. Heaven and earth are said to be formed *ex hydatos kai di hydatos* - both "out of water" and also "through water." The heaven and earth are formed from water, which is recognized in the very next verse as the principle of chaos causing the flood or the deep in Genesis 1:2. The earth was created from water and destroyed by water through the flood because water represents the unformed and chaotic - the deep that is never said to be created in the Genesis account of creation. It is presented as already present at the time God undertakes to create heaven and

76 Keith Norman, "Ex Nihilo: The Development of the Doctrines of God and Creation in Early Christianity," *Brigham Young University Studies*, Vol. 17, No. 3 (Spring 1977), p. 296.

77 C. H. Dodd, *The Bible and the Greeks* (London: Hodder &. Stoughton, 1935), p. 105 quoted in *Ibid.*

78 Blake T. Ostler, "Out of Nothing: A History of Creation *ex Nihilo* in Early Christian Thought," *Review of Books on the Book of Mormon 1989–2011*: Vol. 17, No. 2, (2005, Article 9), pp. 256-257

earth. Lastly, the verb used in 2 Peter 3:5 is a form of the verb *synistēmi,* meaning to organize by combining together and not by creating out of nothing.[79]

Thus, scholars of this camp maintain that the creation story in Genesis supported by Peter's letter gives us a clear picture of God creating the heavens and earth from a pre-existing chaotic matter. The theologians in the second and third centuries changed the whole scenario. Therefore in the words of E. O. James:

> By the end of the second century, largely as a result of the conflict with Gnosticism, the view of the cosmos being fashioned from preexistent matter was abandoned in favor of the doctrine of creation ex nihilo. God alone, it was affirmed, was without beginning or end as the Ultimate Principle, existing in his own right as Creator. Therefore, the cosmos was created by him 'out of nothing.'[80]

10.2. Doctrine of Creatio *Ex Nihilo*

The doctrine of creation *ex nihilo* states that God alone is uncreated and eternal, while all else – human beings, angels, other living things, and matter itself - was created by God *out of nothing, ex nihilo,* and are thus of an entirely different order of being from the Creator. Most of the early Christian theologians and Church fathers adhered to this doctrine, and it may be safe to say that most contemporary Christians also cling to this doctrine.

Towards the end of the second century, Irenaeus, the Bishop of Lyon, strongly came out with the doctrine of creation out of nothing. This was done basically to fight against Gnostic dualism, which attempted to isolate the supreme God from the visible universe. Irenaeus countered by asserting the creation of the world out of nothing, i.e., God's will alone. He wrote in his *Against Heresies,* "While men, indeed, cannot make anything out of nothing, but only out of matter already existing, yet God is in this point pre-eminently superior to men, that He Himself called into being the substance of His creation, when it previously had no existence."[81] Another famous Church Father, Tertullian, is reported to have said that God did not create out of himself, nor out of eternal coexisting matter. So if it was neither out of God's self nor out of something, it must have been out of nothing.[82]

The first reference to creation out of nothing, it is often claimed, is found in 2 Maccabees 7.28 where it is written: "I implore you, my child, to look at the heavens and the earth; consider all that is in them, and realise that God did not

79 *Ibid.*, pp. 257-258.

80 E. O. James, *Creation and Cosmology*, p. 92, quoted in Keith Norman, "Ex Nihilo: The Development of the Doctrines of God and Creation in Early Christianity," *Brigham Young University Studies* , Vol. 17, No. 3 (Spring 1977), pp. 303-304.

81 *Ibid.*, p. 303.

82 Frances Young, 'Creatio ex nihilo': A Context for the Emergence of the Christian Doctrine of Creation," *Scottish Journal of Theology*, Vol. 44, (1991), p. 142.

create them from what already existed *(ouk ex ontori*), and that a human being comes into existence in the same way."[83] In the New Testament, there are two verses that are often quoted in support of this doctrine – "*In the presence of God, the God who makes the dead live and calls into being things that are not, Abraham had faith.*" (Rom. 4:17), and "*By faith, we understand that the universe was formed by God's command so that the visible came forth from the invisible.*" (Heb. 11:3). One of the noted New Testament scholars, James Dunn, in his commentary on Romans 4:17, notes: "As Creator he creates without any precondition: he makes alive where there was only death, and he calls into existence where there was nothing at all. Consequently, that which has been created, made alive in this way, must be totally dependent on the Creator, the life-giver, for its very existence and life."[84]

Another verse used to support creation *ex nihilo* is John 1:3 which reads, "All things were made by him; and without him was not anything made that was made." Paul Copan and William Lane Craig, commenting on this verse, assert: "The implication is that all things (which would include preexistent matter, if that were applicable to the creative process) exist through God's agent, who is the originator of everything."[85]

We know that Genesis creation story cannot be interpreted literally. Looking at the nature of God portrayed in the whole Bible, it is impossible to sustain that God is dependent on something for the creation or to claim that there is eternally existing chaotic material beside God with which God created the heavens and the earth. What Gary Anderson has said holds some waters, "Though Genesis 1 does not teach *creatio ex nihilo* in the way early Christian theologians might have thought, it does not rule it out as decisively as many modern readers have assumed."[86] As God is the source of all things, the material which he used, if at all he used, should also be his own creation. Therefore, it would be incorrect to maintain that *creatio ex nihilo* is a post-biblical doctrine developed by the early Christian theologians to fight against heretical teachings. I will conclude the discussion with the words of John Webster: "Creation out of nothing served to spell out the ontological entailments of the distinction between the eternal creator and the temporal, contingent creatures who are the objects of his saving regard, resisting ideas of the creator as one who merely gave form to coeval matter, and so accentuating the limitless capacity and freedom of God."[87] To have an idea

83 *Ibid.*, p. 143.

84 James D. G. Dunn, *Romans 1–8* (Dallas: Word, 1988), p. 237.

85 Paul Copan and William Lane Craig. "Craftsman or Creator? An Examination of the Mormon Doctrine of Creation and a Defense of *Creatio ex nihilo*" in *The New Mormon Challenge: Responding to the Latest Defenses of a Fast-Growing Movement,* ed. Francis J. Beckwith, Carl Mosser, and Paul Owen, (Grand Rapids, MI: Zondervan, 2002), pp. 117-118.

86 Gary A. Anderson, "*Creatio ex nihilo* and the Bible," p. 22.

87 Quoted in *Ibid.*, p. 26.

that God depended on the uncreated preexistent matter for creating the whole creation betrays the God of the Bible and Christian beliefs.

Concluding Remarks

There is vital cohesion in the creation stories of Christians, Hindus and Muslims – projecting God as the Creator. The universe did not eternally exist; there was a time when it was not. Then the Creator created everything in the universe. So, the role of God or the Ultimate Reality is paramount for the creation and sustenance of the universe and everything therein. Biblical creationism represents the typical traditional Christian understanding of the origin of creation, but this type of literal reading of the scripture is no longer popular among Christians. The creation story in Genesis cannot be interpreted literally to mean that God finished the creation of the whole universe and everything in it, as more or less as we have today, just in144 hours (six days). Taking into consideration the various theories, such as Intelligent design, Anthropic principle, Big Bang, Creationism and creation stories we see in various religions, and even evolution science, we may conclude by locating their point of meeting and the locus of harmony that there is this Ultimate Cause and Maintainer, whom we may call God, who is behind the fine-tuning and contrivance of the universe so that carbon-based life is possible in the universe, who is the Intelligent Coordinator and Omniscient Designer of the universe and everything in it, the Source and Power of the 'primaeval atom' which exploded in the big bang, who controls the expansion of the universe as well as the evolution process of living things, who makes the movement of proton and electron unpredictable and matter at the subatomic level to behave as particle and wave at the same time, to show that there is always something beyond. Human knowledge is limited. Scientific knowledge is limited. We have to accept with all humility that there will always be an unfathomable mystery.

Chapter 6

Philosophy and Sociology of Science

It has very often been considered that science and scientific discoveries are outside of the sphere of human influence and that science speaks in terms of facts; scientific laws, and discoveries are to be considered as true because scientific research is done rationally and objectively. In the past fifty years, many people questioned the validity of his claim. It is now argued by philosophers and sociologists of science that science is a social phenomenon because what is said and done in science is said and done by human beings. Thus, science is subject to our social norms, institutions, beliefs and practices. Now we know that scientific research is not altogether objective. In fact, human beings, who are influenced by their socio-cultural, political and religious context, could not achieve absolute objectivity in any research, including scientific research. The philosophers and sociologists of science stand firmly by their assumption that a fair amount of subjectivity is always involved in scientific research.

In this Chapter, I will explain the meanings and features of both philosophy and sociology of science; having a brief survey of the historical development of both disciplines, I will pick some of the prominent philosophers and sociologists of science to discuss their contributions and in the end close the Chapter with the argument that science is a social construct.

1. What is a Philosophy of Science?

The philosophy of science is the branch of philosophy that critically examines the foundations, methods, products, and implications of scientific activity. According to William Bechtel, a professor of philosophy at the University of California, philosophy of science is a field devoted to analyzing the character of scientific investigations. It attempts to answer such questions as: What is a scientific explanation? To what extent can scientific claims ever be justified or shown to be false? How do scientific theories change over time? What relations hold between old and new theories? What relations hold, or should hold, between theoretical claims developed in different fields of scientific investigation?[1] Merrilee H. Salmon explains the philosophy of science as the branch of philosophy that reflects and critically analyzes science. "As a discipline, it tries to understand the aim and methods of science, along with its principles, practices, and achievements."[2] Salmon underlines the following questions which the philosophy of science tries to address:[3]

- What are the aims of science?
- What is the role of observations and experiments in obtaining scientific knowledge?
- How do scientists justify their claims?
- What is scientific proof?
- How does scientific knowledge advance and grow?
- How do the historical and cultural settings in which scientific work occurs affect the content and quality of such work?, etc.

John Losee, in his book - *A Historical Introduction to the Philosophy of Science*, brings out four viewpoints on the philosophy of science.[4] The *first* view is that the philosophy of science is the formulation of worldviews that are consistent with, and in some sense based on, important scientific theories. The task of the philosopher of science is to elaborate on the broader implications of science. A *second* view is that the philosophy of science is an exposition of the presuppositions and predispositions of scientists. The philosopher of science may point out that scientists presuppose that nature is not liable to sudden, unpredictable change and that there exist in nature regularities of sufficiently low complexity to be accessible to the investigator. This view tends to assimilate the philosophy of science to sociology. A *third* view is that the philosophy of science is a discipline in which the concepts and theories of the sciences are analysed and clarified.

A *fourth* view is that the philosophy of science is a second-order criteriology. The philosopher of science seeks to answer questions like:

(a) What characteristics distinguish scientific inquiry from other types of investigation?

---

1 William Bechtel, *Philosophy of Science: An Overview for Cognitive Science*, (Hillsdale: Lawrence Erlbaum Associates, 1988), p. 1.

2 Merrilee H. Salmon, *et al., Introduction to the Philosophy of Science*, (Englewood Cliffs: Prentice Hall, 1992), p. 1.

3 *Ibid.*, p. 2.

4 See John Losee, *A Historical Introduction to the Philosophy of Science*, (Oxford: Oxford University Press, 2001, first published in 1972), pp.1-2.

(b What procedures should scientists follow in investigating nature?
(c) What conditions must be satisfied for a scientific explanation to be correct?
(d) What is the cognitive status of scientific laws and principles?

The principal task of the philosophy of science is to analyse the methods of enquiry used in the various sciences. The job of a philosopher of science is to question assumptions that scientists take for granted. But it would be wrong to imply that scientists never discuss philosophical issues themselves. We know from the history of science that many scientists have played an important role in the development of the philosophy of science; Aristotle, Galileo, Newton, Einstein, etc., are prominent examples. Each was deeply interested in philosophical questions about how science should proceed, what methods of enquiry it should use, how much confidence we should place in those methods, whether there are limits to scientific knowledge, and so on. All these questions still lie at the heart of the contemporary philosophy of science. So the issues that interest philosophers of science are not 'merely philosophical'; on the contrary, they have engaged the attention of some of the greatest scientists of all.[5]

2. A Brief Historical Survey of the Developments in Philosophy of Science

The words 'science' and 'scientist' came rather late, and it was only towards the end of the 18th century that 'science' was used in place of 'natural philosophy', and there was no real distinction between scientist and philosopher, and many of the great scientist-philosophers of ancient times were also theologians. Science gave philosophy a way of empirically testing theories and concepts, whilst philosophy has helped to develop the scientific method used today. Philosophy also dictates what areas science can and cannot test, delineating the boundary between physical and metaphysical questions. These boundaries and the rules governing research have developed over the centuries, and philosophy and science are intertwined.

To trace the history of the philosophy of science, especially in the Western world, we have to begin with the philosophers of Ancient Greece. Whilst many other philosophers contributed to the very beginning of the scientific process, we may say the genesis of science began with Aristotle, who is considered the Father of Science. With him born the idea of *deductive reasoning,* which has remained a cornerstone of the scientific method. This idea remained a common theme throughout the history of the philosophy of science. So, Aristotle was credited as the initiator of the scientific method.[6]

5 Samir Okasha, *Philosophy of Science: A Very Short Introduction*, (Oxford: Oxford University, 2002), p. 12.

6 Martyn Shuttleworth, "Philosophy of Science History" *in https://explorable.com/history-of-the-philosophy-of-science* (18.09.2014).

After the Greek world, we have the Roman world, and the Romans were the next to take the burgeoning science, developing the scientific method of the Greeks. The Romans were far more interested in the empirical, applied side of science, using mathematics and practical knowledge to create some great technological advances. They did not contribute much insofar the development of philosophical thinking about science is concerned. They simply relied on the methods used by Aristotle and Ptolemy. However, their contribution to practical science was immense, but they had a minimal effect on the history of the philosophy of science, leaving the field largely devoid of momentum for hundreds of years.[7]

The Islamic world preserved the philosophical knowledge of the Ancient Greek philosophers and greatly contributed to the development of the philosophy of science. Shortly after the inauguration of 'Abbāsid Caliphate (750-1258 A.D.), translations into Arabic began to be made of Greek scientific and philosophical works, and also of others like Sanskrit, Syriac, etc. Included in these translation projects were the works of Aristotle and Ptolemy. This translation works reached its climax during the time of Caliph al-Ma'mūn al-Rashid (reigned 813-833). Under him, an institution was set up called *bayt al-hikma* or "House of Wisdom," where books were translated and copied and where a library was kept for reference. For two centuries, this translation works was going on.[8] 'House of Wisdom' was the only institution of learning and knowledge of its time, and it was a place that treasures of knowledge from Greece, Persia and India were stored.[9] It is beyond doubt that Greek philosophy had exerted great influence upon the theological and philosophical thought of the Arabs.

The great philosopher, Ibn-Sina (980 - 1037), also known as Avicenna, built upon the scientific processes postulated by Aristotle but was one of the first philosophers to bring the metaphysical issue of God into the picture. He believed that general and universal questions were the first stage, and experiments uncovered the truth. Ibn al-Haytham is commonly regarded as the first scholar to define the modern scientific method, laying down the steps of the scientific process and attempting to unite the induction of predictions and generalizations with the deduction of experiments. He also pointed out that scientists should not regard themselves as infallible and that they should be open to criticism. Al-Biruni, another great Islamic philosopher, was the first philosopher to understand the importance of errors within scientific experimentation. He understood that

7 *Ibid.*

8 W. Mongtgomery Watt, *Islamic Surveys I: Islamic Philosophy and Theology,* (Edinburgh: Edinburgh University Press, 1962), pp. 41-42.

9 Asghar Ali Enginer, *Rational Approach to Islam*, (New Delhi: Gyn Publishing House, 2001), p. 76.

any experiment would contain small and random fluctuations and that repeated experimentation was the only way to neutralize these inaccuracies.[10]

During the Renaissance (roughly 14th to 17th century), there was a significant advancement in the philosophy of science. The history of the philosophy of science began to take shape with the meticulous and innovative work of Francis Bacon (1561-1626), who made a great contribution in determining the course of modern science by making a significant leap in the process of scientific reasoning and method. He developed the *inductive* method of reasoning over against *deductive* method developed by Aristotle. He redesigned the scientific method to utilize a largely induction based philosophy, where a series of observations could be applied to the universe as a whole. Galileo (1564-1642) was another important scientist-philosopher, and he took the Baconian views of science to another level by emphasizing the need for both empiricism and rationalist thinking. He was a great proponent of carefully designed experiments, but he also believed that it is essential to idealize concepts, especially in mathematics and geometry.[11] Galileo firmly believed that science and religion could peacefully go together because they originated from the same God. Rene Descartes (1596-1650), another important philosopher of science, was in agreement with Bacon that the highest achievement of science is a pyramid of propositions, with the most general principles at the apex. But in contrast to Bacon, who sought to discover general laws by progressive inductive ascent from less general relations, Descartes sought to begin at the apex and work as far downwards as possible by a deductive method.[12]

In the eighteenth century, the philosophy of science began to see another development where attempts were made to separate science from non-sciences. Christian Huygens (1629-1695), a prominent Dutch mathematician and scientist and a leading European natural philosopher argued that science and mathematics were actually different fields and could not be treated the same way. He stated that mathematics and geometry could prove something beyond doubt, whereas science can never prove something emphatically; instead, it merely gives a probability that a certain finding is true. Huygens was the first proponent of the *hypothetico-deductive* method, where a scientist proposes a hypothesis and then tries to deduce the probability that it is correct through observational and empirical observation. This built upon Bacon's work and developed the idea that scientists could approach the truth by constantly refining experiments and increasing the probability of their hypothesis being correct.[13]

This period saw the first divergence of the history of the philosophy of science from metaphysical philosophy. At this time, a great scientist and philosopher-theologian, Isaac Newton (1642-1727), also entered the fray. He did

10 Martyn Shuttleworth, "Philosophy of Science History."

11 *Ibid.*

12 John Losee, *A Historical Introduction to the Philosophy of Science*, p. 64.

13 Martyn Shuttleworth, "Philosophy of Science History."

not advocate hypotheses, believing that any research using a hypothesis could not be scientific. Newton argued that any scientific undertaking should begin with analysis, where a scholar performed observations and experiments and then made conclusions depending upon the results. Newton was also an example of a scientist/philosopher who believed that the almighty was behind every process in the universe because it was too complex to be explained by physics alone. Having firmly believed in God, he saw his works as uncovering the laws of the universe behind creation. Huygens and Newton agreed that science could not give definite answers, only a probability that something was correct because humanity could not possibly understand or comprehend the complexities behind the universe. The other main contributor of this period to the history of the philosophy of science was David Hume (1711-1776), who first highlighted the problem of induction, in that any inductively derived 'proof' could be undone by a single contrary observation.[14]

During the nineteenth century, the history of the philosophy of science took on a form recognizable to modern science, and the debate took a new turn. The discussion now addressed the link between science and theology, with the growing schism started during the Galileo debate beginning to widen. The Catholic Church felt that science was undermining the teachings of religious scripture, and philosophers began to address this issue. John Herschel (1792-1871) published a groundbreaking book, *A Preliminary Discourse on the Study of Natural Philosophy*, in 1830, which addressed this very issue, and attempted to breach the growing divide, possibly realizing the damage that this widening rift could cause. Herschel argued that science was not questioning religious beliefs, such as the existence of God or the immortality of the soul. He stated that rather than attempting to doubt the existence of God, science should be used as a tool to undermine the growing trend of atheism.[15]

In the twentieth century, the philosophy of science became almost completely separated from theology. The great scientist, philosopher and mathematician, Poincare (1854-1912), began the twentieth-century history of the philosophy of science. He questioned the very nature of scientific hypotheses, arguing that there were many different types. Poincare also brought the idea of 'convention' to the history of the philosophy of science, believing that scientists often used the most convenient methods to describe the universe. Poincare also argued that there were many types of hypotheses, some fulfilling the scientific ideal of empiricism, testing and generalization, whereas others were incorporated into the building blocks of scientific theory.[16] We will discuss some of the prominent philosophers of science in the twentieth century.

14 *Ibid.*

15 *Ibid.*

16 *Ibid.*

3. Some Prominent Philosophers of Science in the Twentieth Century

Five persons deserve our attention when discussing the development of a philosophy of science in the twentieth century. They are: Michael Polanyi, Karl Popper, Imre Lakatos, Thomas Kuhn, and Paul Feyerabend.

3.1. Michael Polanyi

Michael Polanyi (1891-1976) was born in Budapest, Hungary, into a Jewish family. He migrated to Germany and became a Chemistry professor at the Kaiser Wilhelm Institute in Berlin in 1926, and then, due to anti-Semitism, he moved to England in 1933. Here he continued his job as a professor of Chemistry, but later on, he became a social sciences professor at the University of Manchester. His main contribution in the field of philosophy of science lies in his idea that personal judgments and human values are the essential components of scientific research. In his famous book *Personal Knowledge: Towards a Post-Critical Philosophy*, Polanyi argued against *objectivism* as a final tool in scientific research and maintained that knowledge, including scientific knowledge, is personal, gained with experiences and personal involvement in the whole process of knowing.

Polanyi was highly critical of what he called 'the restrictions of the scientific outlook' or *objectivism*, which is one of the main themes of his book. His main intention was "to break out of this highly stabilized framework and to enter avenues of legitimate access to reality from which objectivism debars us."[17] He says, "Objectivism has totally falsified our conception of truth, by exalting what we can know and prove while covering up with ambiguous utterances all that we know and cannot prove, even though the latter knowledge underlies, and must ultimately set its seal to, all that we can prove."[18]

According to Polanyi, the act of knowing, as the act of perception, is essentially an acquired skill. Knowledge is possible only because of a knower's talent in integrating a variety of elements into a perspective around that particular point which is the focus of his or her attention. Thus, the understanding that results from this activity is essentially a specific reading or interpretation from within a general horizon, which is constituted by the knower's active arrangement of particulars so that they form a coherent whole. The participation of the knower in the whole system of knowing is important for gaining authentic knowledge. The knower-participant is actively and bodily present in the formation of knowledge. This presence, termed by Polanyi as 'indwelling,' establishes the organization of subsidiary factors according to the knower's intuitive imagining as to the feasibility of any particular focal explanation. Seen in such a manner, knowledge is the result of a successful application of creative and interpretive skills, and its preservation

17 Michael Polanyi, *Personal Knowledge: Towards a Post-Critical Philosophy*, (London: Routledge & Kegan Paul Ltd., first published in 1958), p. 308.

18 *Ibid.*, p. 302.

depends upon the continuation of such abilities. Thus, meaning is never secured once and for all; rather, its very appearance depends upon the maintenance of that particular subsidiary-focal perspective within which it first developed. In effect, all truth is traditional.[19]

James Wiser notes that knowledge is not explicit in Polanyi's scheme of thought; thus, access to it is possible only by participating in the community, which is structured according to the traditions that contain the prerequisite subsidiary-focal patterns. Traditions, therefore, and the communities which are formed in their service are the necessary means by which knowledge is preserved through the transmission of a particular heritage. To come to know is to participate in a subsidiary-focal structure that is sustained by the authority of its traditions because of its tacit dimension. The effect of Polanyi's argument on behalf of traditional knowledge is to suggest that belonging to a community, believing in its traditions, and thereby understanding the experience which engendered them are all aspects of a single process, i.e., the acquisition of knowledge.[20]

Polanyi is against the notion that science is purely based on objective research. He maintains that objectivity is a false idea because this posits a kind of knowing in which the knowing object is eliminated or ignored. Polanyi's unifying theme is the personal participation of the knower in all forms of knowledge. He maintains that belief is the source of all knowledge. "All truth is but the external pole of belief, and to destroy all belief would be to deny all truth." This reflects what St. Augustine had said: "Unless you believe, you will not understand." Polanyi suggests that scientist's work involves a long tradition of scientific research, the learning of skill and the personal gift of intuition, imagination, judgment, courage and patience and all these involve a certain amount of commitment and dedication. Thus for Polanyi, faith informs and shapes science, and the person is not divorced from science.[21]

3.2. Karl Popper

Karl Popper (1902 - 1994) is one of the biggest names in the history of the philosophy of science. He was an Austrian-British philosopher and is generally regarded as one of the greatest philosophers of science of the 20th century. He taught at Canterbury University College in Christchurch, New Zealand, and also at the London School of Economics and the University of London. Among his students were great philosophers like Lakatos, Feyerabend, etc. Popper tried to delineate the boundary between science and non-science, arguing that metaphysics was non-observational, and therefore, could not be science. He championed the

19 James L. Wiser, "Michael Polanyi: Personal Knowledge and the Promise of Autonomy", *Political Theory*, (Vol. 2, No. 1, Feb., 1974), pp. 81-82.

20 *Ibid.*, pp. 82-83.

21 Sarojini Henry. *The Encounter of Faith and Science in Inter-Religious Dialogue*, (Pune/Delhi; Indian Institute of Science and Religion/ISPCK, 2005), p. 50.

idea of *falsification*, where a hypothesis must be potentially disprovable for it to be regarded as scientific. Popper's idea of falsification may be summarized as follows – Our best theories are not those that have endless cases of confirming predictions, but rather, our best theories are those that have survived specific cases where they could have been shown to be wrong. It is primarily this characteristic, that is, being at risk in the sense of being shown to be incorrect, which distinguishes genuinely scientific theories.[22] According to him, theological, epistemological and metaphysical questions were not falsifiable, and therefore not scientific. Popper believed that how the hypothesis was derived was an unimportant part of the scientific method, but the only important issue was that the hypothesis was testable and falsifiable. He felt that instead of attempting to prove theories, scientists should try to falsify them, a belief still held by many scientists. Popper's idea of falsifiability earned him a place among the great philosophers of science.[23]

3.3. Imre Lakatos

Imre Lakatos (1922-1974), born Imre Lipsitz into a Jewish family in Debrecen, Eastern Hungary, received a profound education in the town's Jewish Real Gymnasium. He continued his studies at the University of Debrecen in 1940, where he studied Mathematics, Physics and Philosophy.[24] In 1947 he became a high-ranking official in the Hungarian Ministry of Education, but, being a man who found it difficult to bow to authority, his nature soon got him into trouble. In 1950 he was arrested and spent over three years in a Stalinist jail. After the Hungarian uprising in 1956, he fled to Vienna. From there, he went eventually to Cambridge, where his academic career began. He taught at the London School of Economics from 1960 until his untimely death in 1974.[25]

The outline of Lakatos' major contribution to the philosophy of science already appeared in his 1968 paper, with its emphasis on scientific growth rather than on falsification and its use of the notions of progressive and degenerating problem-shifts. But his 'methodology of scientific research programmes' is developed in detail only in his 1970 paper on "Falsification and the Methodology of Scientific Research Programmes."[26]

In this paper, Lakatos relates his ideas to the ideas of his teacher, Karl Popper. He accepts the general fallibilistic framework of Popper's philosophy.

---

22 Richard DeWitt, "Philosophy of Science", *Philosophies of Science: A Guide*, edited by Fritz Allhoff, (Chichester: Wiley-Blackwell, 2007), p. 17.

23 Martyn Shuttleworth, "Philosophy of Science History."

24 Gábor Kutrovátz, "Lakatos' Philosophical Work in Hungary", *Studies in East European Thought*, (Vol. 60, No. 1/2, *The Sociological Tradition of Hungarian Philosophy*, Jun., 2008), pp. 114.

25 John Worrall, "Nachruf auf Imre Lakatos: Imre Lakatos (1922-1974): Philosopher of Mathematics and Philosopher of Science", *Zeitschrift für allgemeine Wissenschaftstheorie/Journal for General Philosophy of Science*, (Vol. 5, No. 2, 1974), p. 211.

26 *Ibid.*, pp. 214-215.

The changes he introduces are: (a) standards are separated from rules of acceptance and rules of rejection; (b) they are not applied to individual theories, but to sequences of theories which are connected by certain techniques of modification, so-called research programmes; (c) the elements constituting a research programme need not be rewritten, or 'reconstructed' in accordance with the rules of a particular logical system, they can be used in the form in which they occur in science, leaving unchanged all the logical and empirical faults they possess; in this way both theories and the forms of life of which they are part can be examined; (d) the standards judge the evolution of a research programme over a period of time, not its shape at a particular time; and they judge this evolution in comparison with the evolution of rivals, not by itself; it is therefore possible for a research programme to remain within science even if all the theories it produces are self inconsistent and beset by oceans of anomalies; (e) the standards judge research programmes, they do not tell the scientist what to do; (f) the standards can be evaluated in a way that is very similar to the evaluation of empirical research programmes.[27]

The 'methodology of research programmes' is the result of Lakatos's creative development of two discoveries. *First*, the discovery that falsificationism could be developed so as to deal with these apparently anomalous aspects of scientific development; and *secondly*, the discovery of the critical role played in science by the heuristic principles whose importance for mathematics Lakatos had already stressed. According to this methodology, the basic unit of scientific discovery is not an isolated theory but rather a research programme. Such a programme, developing under the guidance of its heuristic, issues in a series of theories.[28] According to Lakatos, scientists work with a research programme at the heart of which is a 'hard core' theory that determines the shape and identity of the programme. The 'hard core' is not exposed to falsification so that its positive potentialities can be systematically developed and explored. A commitment to its central core maintains the continuity of a research programme. A protective belt of more tentative 'auxiliary hypotheses surrounded the hardcore or the core theory. Any revising of the hardcore would lead to abandoning the research programme. While the surrounding 'auxiliary hypotheses' serve to define and support the hardcore, they are themselves explained with reference to the core theory.[29] The research programme suggested by Lakatos is considered quite useful in several scientific research and theological formulation.

27 Paul Feyerabend, "Imre Lakatos", *The British Journal for the Philosophy of Science*, (Vol. 26, No. 1, Mar., 1975), pp. 11-12.

28 John Worrall, "Nachruf auf Imre Lakatos: Imre Lakatos" (1922-1974), p. 215.

29 Sarojini Henry. *The Encounter of Faith and Science in Inter-Religious Dialogue*, p. 52.

3.4. Thomas Kuhn

Thomas Samuel Kuhn (1922-1996) was a renowned American physicist and one of the most influential philosophers of science in the twentieth century. He earned a doctoral degree in physics from Harvard University and became a professor at the University of California. He left and went to Princeton, where he taught for many years. Kuhn's main contribution in the field of philosophy of science is his concept of *paradigm* and *paradigm shift* in the development of science. The publication of his groundbreaking work in 1962 – *The Structure of Scientific Revolutions* almost totally changed the way we look at science and scientific research. His work can be seen as negating the absolute validity, rationality and pure objectivity of scientific research.

Paradigm, according to Thomas Kuhn, is a "universally recognized scientific achievements that for a time provide model problems and solutions to a community of practitioners," and by choosing the name, paradigm, he means "to suggest that some accepted examples of actual scientific practise - examples which include law, theory, application, and instrumentation together - provide models from which spring particular coherent traditions of scientific research. These are the traditions that the historian describes as 'Ptolemaic astronomy' (or 'Copernican'), 'Aristotelian dynamics' (or 'Newtonian'), 'corpuscular optics' (or 'wave optics'), and so on."[30] Thus, a scientific paradigm is a standard of scientific achievement in terms of which scientific work is conducted and evaluated. According to Kuhn, the history of science is the history of the careers of various paradigms, some involving several disciplines, some involving only small groups of specialists. Science has to be defined in terms of paradigms, and that in the absence of a paradigm, there was no such thing as science.[31]

He explains 'paradigm' and 'paradigm shift' in terms of Normal science and Revolutionary science. According to Kuhn, 'normal science' means research firmly based upon one or more past scientific achievements; achievements that some particular scientific community acknowledges for a time as supplying the foundation for its further practice. These past 'scientific achievements' are put into science textbooks for schools and universities, and from them, students learn about science. Researchers in science worked within this paradigm. Those whose research is based on shared paradigms are committed to the same rules and standards for scientific practice. That commitment and the apparent consensus it produces are prerequisites for normal science, i.e., for the genesis and continuation of a particular research tradition.[32]

30 Thomas S. Kuhn, *The Structure of Scientific Revolutions*, (Chicago: The University of Chicago Press, 1996, first published in 1962.), pp. x, 10.

31 Del Ratzsch, *Philosophy of Science: The Natural Sciences in Christian Perspective*, (Downers Grove: Intervarsity Press, 1986), pp. 44-45.

32 Thomas S. Kuhn, *The Structure of Scientific Revolutions*, pp. 10-12.

A paradigm dictates such things as - what is studied and researched; the type of questions that are asked; the exact structure and nature of the questions and how the results of any research are interpreted. Meera Nanda remarks:

> Kuhn argued that scientific practice always takes place under a paradigm. The ruling paradigm decides what kind of problems scientists study, what criteria they use to evaluate a solution, and what experimental procedures they find acceptable. All aspects of what scientists do are so filtered through the paradigm they are in that no paradigm-neutral, objective evaluation of scientific 'facts' in two different paradigms is possible. Scientific theories in different paradigms are simply incommensurable, and there is no way to judge a more accurate representation of reality. Indeed, there is no 'reality' which is not relative to a paradigm.[33]

Paradigm continues as long as there is no alternative competing paradigm. "The presence of an anomaly or two is not sufficient to cause abandonment of a paradigm."[34] A paradigm can absorb some errors, but if anomalies eventually become insurmountable, like Ptolemy's epicycles, a paradigm shift needs to happen. Kuhn maintains that the logic of falsification is not applicable to the case of paradigm rejection. Science entered a revolutionary stage when a viable competing paradigm emerged. "A paradigm-rejection is three-term relation which involves an established paradigm, a rival paradigm, and the observational evidences."[35] A shift from Ptolemaic geocentric cosmology to the Copernican heliocentric cosmology and from Newtonian mechanics to Einstein's relativity are good examples of a paradigm shift in the history of science.

3.5. Paul Feyerabend

Paul Feyerabend (1924-1994) was an Austrian-born philosopher of science. He lived in various countries and finally landed in the USA, where he worked as a professor of philosophy at the University of California, Berkeley, for three decades from 1958–1989. He was one of the twentieth century's most famous philosophers of science. He was known for his critique of Karl Popper's "critical rationalism." An imaginative nonconformist, he became a critic of philosophy of science itself, particularly of "rationalist" attempts to lay down or discover rules of the scientific method. He was known for his attack on science which gave him the reputation for being an "anti-science philosopher," "the worst enemy of science,"[36] and he believed that the scientific method was an artificial construct and restricted the

33 Meera Nanda, *Prophets Facing Backward: Postmodernism, Science, and Hindu Nationalism*, (Delhi: Permanent Black, 2006), p. 22.

34 John Losee, *A Historical Introduction to the Philosophy of Science*, p. 119.

35 *Ibid.*

36 *https://plato.stanford.edu/entries/feyerabend/* (08.01.2017).

free thought of ideas. He suggested that very few scientists actually followed any such method, and took a very open view of science, implying that there can never be a strict definition of what constitutes science. His landmark book, *Against method,* published in 1978, coined the phrase *epistemological anarchy,* which holds that there are no useful and exception-free methodological rules governing the progress of science or the growth of knowledge. It holds that the idea that science can or should operate according to universal and fixed rules is unrealistic, destructive, and detrimental to science itself.[37]

4. Major Schools in the Philosophy of Science

The following are the major schools in the philosophy of science:[38]

4.1. Deductive Method – started by the Greeks, especially Aristotle. It is a series of deductions made from *a priori* truths.

4.2. Inductive Method - Modern science as we know it was born with the advent of the inductive approach. The power of inductive reasoning lies in its stress on observation as well as in its acceptance of the methodological rule that scientists must generalize from empirical observations to overarching natural laws. Many scientists still maintain that the defining mark of scientific practice is careful observation, followed by inductive inferences to general laws that describe the phenomena observed.

4.3. Falsification - The agenda for the last sixty-five years in the philosophy of science was set by Karl Popper's famous move from induction to falsification as the defining mark of scientific practice. According to Popper, what demarcates science from non-science is the practice of formulating risky hypotheses and then trying to falsify them. Each scientific hypothesis must make some testable prediction about what will be found in the world; if this prediction is later falsified by experimentation, the hypothesis should be rejected.

4.4. The Received View - The Received View holds that scientific theories and scientific rationality could be clearly delineated from all other human rational endeavours. It assumes a sharp distinction between theoretical and observation sentences: some sentences correctly express our immediate experience of the world, and they are the ones we use for testing theoretical proposals made by scientists. This model, which still is widely accepted, clearly presents a steep and presumably unattainable set of standards for religious accounts of divine action.

4.5. Subjective Research – From the 1950s onwards, more and more people realized that science is not 'theory-free', but 'theory-laden' and that scientific research is not altogether objective but also or rather mostly subjective. It is now held that scientists are engaged not merely in 'seeing' the world but in 'seeing

37 Martyn Shuttleworth, "Philosophy of Science History."

38 See Philip Clayton, "Philosophy of Science: What one Needs to Know", *Zygon,* (Vol. 32, No. 1, March 1997), pp. 96-98.

it as' something in particular, with the whole range of interpretive issues and presuppositions. It is generally perceived that scientific research is not presenting bare uninterpreted data, but expectations and conceptual commitments of the researchers influence the overall scientific research and interpretation of data.

5. What is the Sociology of Science?

Sociology of science deals with the social conditions and effects of science on society and *vice versa*, and it also deals with the social structures and processes of scientific activity. Science is a cultural tradition, preserved and transmitted from generation to generation partly because it is valued in its own right and partly because of its wide technological applications. Its most distinguishing characteristic is that the primary purpose of its cultivators, the scientists, is to change the tradition through discoveries. The sociology of science seeks to establish the social conditions under which science makes maximal progress as specifically and precisely as possible.[39]

That science is a social activity, and therefore as much subject to social scientific investigation as any other human activity is almost accepted truth now. Sociologists of science have concentrated on this characteristic of science as a tradition and as an institution. The questions they deal with are: How did this unique tradition of modern science emerge and become institutionalized? How is it maintained and controlled? How is research organized? What determine changes in scientific organization, and how are these changes related to research?[40] The Sociology of science also seeks answers to such questions: What property rights should an individual scientist have in his/her ideas? What are the advantages and disadvantages of different types of the political system for science? Do all political systems have a mixture of advantages and disadvantages? What religious and secular ideologies are most compatible with the development of science? What are the sources of economic support for science? What are the proper proportions of fundamental and applied scientific research? How can the different sciences best stimulate one another to progress? What are the responsibilities of science to predict and control its discoveries, meaning by 'responsibilities' those moral and rational considerations that affect the relations between scientists and other social groups in society? How are scientific facts made and verified? How do our social commitments on issues like gender or race affect our scientific vision? Where does science policy come from, and how does it involve different kinds of expertise?

According to Pierre Bourdieu, a French sociologist and philosopher, the sociology of science rests on the postulate that the objective truth of the product - even in the case of that very particular product, scientific truth - lies in a particular

39 Joseph Ben-David and Teresa A. Sullivan, "Sociology of Science", *Annual Review of Sociology*, (Vol. 1, 1975), p. 203.

40 *Ibid.*

type of social conditions of production, or more precisely, in a determinate state of the structure and functioning of the scientific field. The 'pure' universe of even the 'purest' science is a social field like any other, with its distribution of power and its monopolies, its struggles and strategies, interests and profits, but it is a field in which all these invariants take on specific forms.[41]

6. Development of Sociology of Science

The sociology of science has undergone considerable growth and diversification in recent years. Early sociology of science was developed within philosophical debates regarding the nature of science and the social bases of knowledge in general. Karl Mannheim and Max Scheler in the 1920s gave these discussions a specifically sociological bent. In the 1930s, the theme was made into explicit sociology of science both by Marxists and by the functionalist Robert Merton, and both approaches were followed up during the next 30 years. Sociology of science became a flourishing research area in the early 1960s, with the publication of works by several scholars, such as Derek Price, Thomas Kuhn, Joseph Ben-David and Warren Hagstrom. In the 1970s, sociology of science burgeoned into a variety of approaches: citation and network studies, conflict theory, social constructivism, ethnomethologically-influence studies of laboratory life, and others. The idealized functionalist image of science has largely given way to more critical, relativist, and highly empirical approaches to science.[42] Today, the sociology of science is becoming one of the blooming disciplines in sociology. Its contribution in estimating the influence of science on social conditions and vice versa is commendable.

7. Social Construction of Science

By 'social construction of science', we mean the social influences on science and scientific theories, research and discoveries and on the content of scientific knowledge. The predominant conception of science has been one of the accumulations of impartial, objective knowledge of nature by disinterested scientists. This conception is associated with an image of science as conflict-free and a reflection of natural reality. In reaction to this conception, contemporary studies in the sociology of science have drawn attention to the way scientific knowledge is socially constructed and to the relative rather than the absolute character of that knowledge.[43] Many sociologists of science now challenge the

---

41 Pierre Bourdieu, "The Specificity of the Scientific Field and the Social Conditions of the Progress of Reason", in *http://www.soc.ucsb.edu/ct/pages/JWM/Syllabi/Bourdieu/SpecificitySField.pdf* (06.01.2017).

42 Randall Collins and Sal Restivo, "Development, Diversity, and Conflict in the Sociology of Science", *The Sociological Quarterly*, (Vol. 24, No. 2, Spring, 1983), p. 185.

43 Raymond Murphy, "The Sociological Construction of Science without Nature", *Sociology*, (Vol. 28, No. 4, November 1994), p. 957.

age-old view that science is objective, rational, and the only reliable path to knowledge. However, the use of the term 'social construction' in science studies started to become common in the mid-1970s.

The social constructivist study of science is a variant of the constitutive position in that it assumes that social circumstances, not nature, constitute science. The social constructivist investigation of science presumes that scientific knowledge originates in the social world rather than the natural world. It presupposes that the natural world has more or less no role in the construction of scientific knowledge. The influence of nature is conspicuous by its absence in the descriptions by constructivists of the development of scientific knowledge.[44]

In the true mediative position, social circumstances intervene by mediating between nature and accounts of nature but do not eliminate the effect of nature. Sociological descriptions and explanations of the production of scientific knowledge from the true mediative position would incorporate both the effect of social circumstances and of nature. They would bring out how nature, as well as social circumstances, influences the accounts of scientists. It could plausibly be argued that the influence of nature on accounts has increased as science and its applications have developed because the specificity of science consists of its attentiveness to nature.[45]

Sociologists insist that our knowledge is socially constructed, which shakes scientific foundations and religious beliefs. It is claimed that the kind of questions we ask, the kind of explanations we seek and the criteria of rationality we use are all socially and culturally formed. This would mean that science exists in a specific social, historical and intellectual context. For a long time, people considered science as objective, rational and based on solid observational evidence, whereas religion as subjective, parochial and emotional.[46] With the emergence of the sociology of science, this idea is fading away. Sarojini Henry notes that when we speak about the social construction of science, it does not mean that science is merely a sociologically constructed form of knowledge without any reference to the actual 'reality'. It means to say that the earlier notion of an objective and value-free science is no more valid. Scientific research is also subject to dogma and clinging to old theories. Scientific theories are theory-laden, not theory-free. Scientists are now talking less of definite laws but more of probability, less determinism, more of hypothetical theories, less of truth and more of models and metaphors.[47]

---

44 *Ibid.*, p. 959.

45 *Ibid.*

46 Sarojini Henry, *The Encounter of Faith and Science in Inter-Religious Dialogue*, p. 46.

47 *Ibid.*

Concluding Remarks

Science can err. It has erred. It is presumptuous to claim that scientific theories, discoveries, and laws are absolutely reliable and free from error. We have seen that science is not free from the influence of society, religion, and personal inclination and emotion of scientific researchers, making scientific research subjective at least partially. It is now accepted widely that the early notion of science as value-free, objective, rational, and scientific discoveries as based on solid observational evidence is increasingly difficult to hold on to. Thus, it is foolish to hold on to scientific knowledge as the only valid knowledge, infallible and absolutely true for all time. Both science and religion as human activities are the product of human beings and, by nature, limited. It is wrong to insist on the absolute validity of one over the other. Both should be taken together as complementing rather than competing, enriching one another rather than encroaching, having a dialogical relationship as both are attempts to unearth the inexhaustible reality of God and his creation.

Chapter 7

Models of Science and Religion Dialogue

The term 'science and religion dialogue' refers to the whole concept of the relationship between science and religion. According to Gaymon Bennett, 'science and religion dialogue' is the shorthand for a diverse, complex and rapidly expanding series of questions, issues and insights concerning the relationship between science and religion. Dialogue between science and religion is necessarily multi-disciplinary and inter-disciplinary, and it involves multiple religious traditions, and sometimes it is interreligious.[1] I attempt to give various models of dialogue between science and religion proposed by some renounced scholars in this field. We have the famous Ian Barbour's four models, Ted Peter's models for science and religion dialogue, Michael Stenmark's model and finally, Indian contributions to science and religion dialogue.

1. Ian Barbour's Four Model of Science and Religion Dialogue

Ian Graeme Barbour (1923 –2013), a well-known scholar in Science and Religion dialogue, was born in Beijing to a Scottish father and American mother who both taught at Yanjing University. He spent his childhood in China, the United States, and England. He received his Ph.D in physics from the University of Chicago in 1950 and earned the Bachelor of Divinity degree from Yale University in 1956, and taught at Carleton College in Northfield, Minnesota. He was at the forefront of dialogue between science and religion, and his academic contribution in this field is tremendous. His four models of interaction between science and religion

1 Gaymon Bennett, "Introduction" in *Bridging Science and Religion*, edited by Ted Peters and Gaymon Bennett, (Minneapolis: Fortress Press, 2003), p. 4.

are considered as one of the best explanations of the historical interface of science and religion.

According to Ian Barbour, there are four main opinions or four models, the so-called 'Ian Barbour's Typology' of relating science and religion. They are - Conflict, Independence, Dialogue and Integration, and I will explain them one by one.

1.1. Conflict

The historical evidence of conflict between science and religion is seen in Galileo's case and the case of Darwin's evolution theory. The nature and degree of conflict between these two were quite different, but they are probably the best example of the conflict between science and religion. Till today this warfare image is quite common. According to Barbour, a conflict between science and religion is due to two reasons – *Scientific materialism* and *Biblical literalism.* **Scientific materialists,** who are the intellectual heirs of the French Enlightenment, the empiricism of David Hume and the evolutionary naturalism, have two beliefs – *first*, the scientific method is the only reliable path to knowledge; and, *second*, the matter is the fundamental reality in the universe. The first is an epistemological assertion about the characteristics of inquiry and knowledge, and the second is a *metaphysical* or ontological assertion about the characteristics of reality. The conflict happened due to the assertion of Scientific materialism that religious beliefs are not acceptable because religion lacks public data, experimental testing, and criteria of evaluation. Science alone is objective, open-minded, universal, cumulative, and progressive. Religious traditions, by contrast, are subjective, closed-minded, parochial, uncritical, and resistant to change. *Logical positivism* asserted that scientific discourse provides the norm for all meaningful language. It was said that the only meaningful statements are empirical propositions verifiable by sense data. Statements in ethics, metaphysics, and religion were said to be neither true nor false, but meaningless pseudo-statements, expressions of emotion or preference devoid of cognitive significance.[2]

At another end of the pole, we have **Biblical literalism** emerged as the product of literal interpretation of the Bible. Biblical literalists represented mainly by Christian fundamentalist groups, have maintained that scripture is inerrant throughout. These groups of Christian not only take the Bible literally but also as a basis for the defence of traditional values in a time of moral disintegration. They fought against the teaching of evolution theory in schools because it is contrary to scripture.[3] The fundamental problem, according to Barbour, lies in fragmented and specialized higher education. Scientists are not exposed to the history and philosophy of science, nor do they have any reflection on the relation of science to

---

2 Ian G. Barbour, *Religion and Science: Historical and Contemporary Issues*, (San Francisco: HarperSanFrancisco, 1990), pp. 77-78.

3 *Ibid.*, pp. 82-83.

society, to ethics, or to religious thought. Likewise, the clergy has little familiarity with science and is hesitant to discuss controversial subjects from the pulpit.[4] As long as this is the case, conflict is bound to happen.

1.2. Independence

This model views science and religion as totally independent and autonomous, and thus, conflict is avoided. The proponents of this idea maintain that science and religion have their own distinctive domains and particular methods and go in their own unique way without disturbing the other. Proponents of this view include - evangelical Christians who see science and religion as essentially independent spheres of human life; neo-orthodox Christians who hold that theology and science should not interfere with one another; existentialists with their emphasis on subjective knowledge. Langdon Gilkey makes the following distinctions: while science seeks to explain objective data, religion asks about the existence of order in the world and experiences of our inner life; while science asks objective *how* questions, religion asks personal *why* questions; while the basis of authority in science is logical coherence and experimental proof, the final authority in religion is God and revelation.[5] These are attempts to prove that science and religion are two separate things that work in a different realm and with a separate method.

Again, in support of this model, the followers of *Independence* point out the difference in language between science and religion. Scientific language is used primarily for prediction and control. For example, a common scientific language – theory - is a useful tool for summarizing data, correlating regularities and producing technological applications. In contrast, religious literature speaks about religious experiences of different types - guilt, fear, forgiveness, brokenness and wholeness, peace, unity, Enlightenment, etc. These activities and experiences have little to do with science.[6] Thus, with this model, conflict is averted, neither is there meaningful interaction between science and religion.

1.3. Dialogue

According to Barbour, the *Dialogue* model is a diverse group of views that go beyond the *Independence* model but portrays relationships between science and religion that are not as close or as direct as those in the *Integration* model. Science and religion are not without interaction; they rather help each other to move ahead. History tells us how Christianity contributed to the development of science. A number of well-known theologians support science-religion dialogue. Wolfhart Pannenberg maintains that theologians like scientists can use universal rational criteria in examining religious beliefs. A well-known Roman Catholic theologian

4 *Ibid.*, p. 84.

5 *Ibid.*, pp. 84-86.

6 *Ibid.*, p. 87.

Karl Rahner holds that, though the methods and contents of science and religion are independent, there are important points of contact and correlations between them. Another Roman Catholic scholar, David Tracy, sees a religious dimension in science. The works of philosophers of science like Thomas Kuhn, Michael Polanyi, etc., reduced the sharp contrast between science which is portrayed as *objective* and religion, portrayed as *subjective*. They help us see that science is not as objective or religion as subjective, as it is claimed. Several authors suggest the presence of methodological parallels between science and religion. The physicist and theologian John Polkinghorne suggests that both science and religion are theory-laden and depend on a personal judgment in research, and Holmes Rolston, the well-known philosopher, says that religious beliefs interpret and correlate experience just like science interprets and correlates experimental data.[7]

Kuhn also argues that dialogue between science and religion happens in the form of nature-centred spirituality, which believes in the imminence of the divine in nature. Scholars in this area speak about the sacredness of nature - seeing God in nature, realizing divinity within us and in nature; the parallel between holism and quantum physics; parallels between the experience of unity in the Eastern religions and the unity of the world as described by quantum physics, and so on.[8] Therefore, according to Kuhn, there is some sort of dialogue between the two, interactions at several levels between science and religion which we see undeniably in the course of history.

1.4. Integration

This model holds that it is possible to have a more direct and closer relationship between science and religion. Scholars who adhere to this group maintain that some sort of integration between the content of theology and the content of science is achievable. According to Ian Barbour, there are three versions of *Integration* – natural theology, theology of nature, and systematic synthesis. *Natural theology* claims that the existence of God can be inferred from the evidence of design in nature, of which science has made us more aware. In a *theology of nature,* the main source of theology is outside science, but scientific theories may affect the reformulation of certain doctrines, such as the doctrine of creation and human nature. In a *systematic synthesis*, both science and religion contribute to the development of inclusive metaphysics, such as that of process philosophy.[9]

Without rejecting what is good in the *Independence* model, Barbour tries to develop the *Dialogue* position concerning methodology and the *Integration* thesis concerning the doctrine of creation and human nature.

---

7 See *Ibid.*, pp. 90-94.

8 *Ibid.*, pp. 95-97.

9 *Ibid.*, p. 98.

2. Ted Peter's Model of Interaction between Science and Religion

Ted F. Peters (b. 1941) is a Lutheran theologian and presently a Professor of Systematic Theology at Pacific Lutheran Theological Seminary. He received his Master of Divinity from Trinity Lutheran Seminary and his Ph.D from the University of Chicago. He has written and edited a number of books in the area of science and religion. According to him, there are eight ways of relating science and theology as discussed below; out of these, the first four are known as 'warfare models', and the remaining four are 'non-warfare models.'

2.1. Scientism

Known also as 'naturalism' or 'secular humanism', scientism is an ideology built upon the assumption that only one reality exists, that is, the material world. Further, science provides the only trustworthy method for gaining knowledge about this material reality. Science has an exhaustive monopoly on knowledge. Religion provides only pseudo-knowledge, a false impression about nonexistent fiction. Thus, said the British philosopher Bertrand Russell: "what science cannot tell us, mankind cannot know." Fred Hoyle, an astronomer, also said that the Jewish and Christian religions have become outdated by modern science. Dialogue between science and religion is out of the question; scientism wishes to see the elimination of its enemy, i.e., religion.[10]

2.2. Scientific Imperialism

This model is slightly different from scientism; it seeks to conquer the territory of theology rather than trying to eliminate its enemy. While scientism is atheistic, scientific imperialism is theistic but claims that knowledge of the divine comes from science rather than revelation. It is considered that science is competent enough to tackle serious religious questions. The combination of quantum theory, Big Bang and thermo-dynamics can provide better explanations than Christianity for the resurrection of the dead. It even tries to put theology as a branch of physics.[11]

2.3. Ecclesiastical Authoritarianism

Some leaders in the Roman Catholic tradition perceived science as a threat to the church, and they tried to put it under the control of ecclesiastical authority, which, according to them, is founded on God's revelation. However, the Second Vatican Council dropped this idea and authorized that natural science should be

10 Ted Peters, "Theology and Natural Science", in *The Modern Theologians: An Introduction to Christian Theology in the Twentieth Century*, (Cambridge, Massachusetts: Blackwell Publishers, 1997), p. 650.

11 *Ibid.*, pp. 650.

free from ecclesiastical authority. Pope John Paul II was responsible for fostering dialogue between theology and natural science.[12]

2.4. Scientific Creationism

Also known as 'creation science' and is the grandchild of Christian fundamentalism which emphasizes biblical authoritarianism. The Creation scientists assume that biblical truth and scientific truth belong to the same domain. Creationists, many of whom are practising scientists, consider themselves as soldiers within the science army. Scientific creationists typically affirm: - (a) creation of the world out of nothing, (b) the insufficiency of mutation and natural selection to explain the process of evolution, (c) the stability of existing species and impossibility of one species evolving out of another, (d) separate ancestry for apes and humans, (e) catastrophism to explain certain geological formations, and (v) the relatively recent formation of the earth to about six to ten thousand years ago.[13]

2.5. The Two-language Theory

According to this model, science speaks one language - the language of facts and religion speaks another language - the language of values. They have their own sovereign territory. Speaking in terms of the two-language theory, Albert Einstein said that science could only ascertain what *is*, but not what *should be.* In contrast, religion deals only with an evaluation of human thought and action. Each language is restricted to its respective territory. Ted Peters cautions us that the two-language theory should not be confused with the classical *two books model* where it is perceived that revelation regarding God can be read from two books – *the book of nature* and *the book of scripture.* In this case, both books are meant to read the same thing – the works of God, whereas in the two-language theory, we are heading towards two different directions – either towards God or towards the world.[14]

2.6. Hypothetical Consonance

The term 'hypothetical Consonance' suggests that there are areas of correspondence, connection or relevance between the understandings of nature as conceived by natural science and various religious traditions. According to Ted Peters, 'consonance' comes in various forms. In its 'committed form,' it implies virtual accord or harmony. In its 'provisional' form, it functions as a hypothesis and is known as '*Hypothetical Consonance.*' Hypothetical consonance begins with the assumption that science and religion are trying to make sense of a single reality. In other words, science and religion both pursue the truth about the same reality. Though their methods and routes may vary, should we not consider them

12 *Ibid.*, p. 651.

13 *Ibid.*, p. 651.

14 *Ibid.*, pp. 651-652.

as travelling companions? Therefore, science and religion can engage in common research programmes, confirm and disconfirm claims together. Hypothetical consonance is a disposition toward dialogue. It is a commitment to the inherent fruitfulness of dialogue. It is this disposition, this commitment, that makes hypothetical consonance attractive.[15]

The central hypothesis of *hypothetical consonance* is that there can be only one shared domain of truth regarding the created world, and science at its best and faith at its best both humble themselves before truth. Therefore, one can trust that consonance will eventually emerge. This model leads to two forms of engagement between science and faith. One is *dialogue*, where scientists and theologians simply speak with one another without a preconceived goal regarding shared concerns in a common domain. Both partners assume that some level of consonance is possible, and they are pursuing it. The other is '*creative mutual interaction*', which is dialogue at a more advanced level. Here the scientists actually try to influence the theological agenda, and theologians actually try to propose fruitful paths for future scientific research. So, Ted Peters assumes the *hypothetical consonance* between science and religion and the possibility of creative mutual interaction between them.[16]

As the goal of hypothetical consonance is fruitful dialogue, it takes the following steps:- (a) Hypothetical consonance is not an attempt either by science or religion to prove or disprove one's own claims; (b) Hypothetical consonance does not require either science or religion to give up their intellectuality; (c) Hypothetical consonance avoids concluding that either science or religion has a lock on truth; (d) Hypothetical consonance keeps the relationship between science and religion from devolving into a turf war. Each may have exclusive claims about nature, but this need not result in cessation of dialogue between them; (e) Hypothetical consonance does not shy away from conflict. Science and religion will have points of disagreement, but hypothetical consonance treats conflict as a means to more fruitful engagement, leading to new insights.[17]

2.7. Ethical Overlap

This model especially stresses the recognized need on the part of theologians to show concern for ethical challenges posed by the environmental crisis. Ted Peters confesses that he is an advocate of hypothetical consonance, but also belongs to the ethical overlap group and believes that the ecological crisis poses a spiritual issue. An ethical vision to have a sustainable society that lives in harmony with its environment is the concern of everyone. So this model acknowledges that both

15 Gaymon Bennett, "Introduction" in *Bridging Science and Religion*, *Bridging Science and Religion*, edited by Ted Peters and Gaymon Bennett, (Minneapolis: Fortress Press, 2003), pp. 12-13. See also Ted Peters, "Theology and Natural Science", p. 652.

16 *Ibid.*, p. 13. See also Ted Peters, "Theology and Natural Science", p. 652.

17 *Ibid.*

religion and science have a common ethical concern – to make our planet a better place. Theologians usually take the doctrine of creation as the source to address ecological issues, but there is a need to appeal to eschatological redemption, that is, the new creation. The promise of new creation can provide a sense of direction in our attempt to bring about a sustainable society.[18]

2.8. New Age Spirituality

According to Ted Peters, the key to New Age spirituality is holism which attempts to overcome modern dualism, such as the split between science and religion, humanity and nature, male and female, etc. New Age spirituality attempts to achieve 'synthetic spiritualities' and seeks to construct a worldview that integrates and harmonizes science with religion. New Age physicists, Fritjof Capra and David Bohm, attempt to combine Hindu mysticism with physics. New Age spirituality seeks to cultivate awareness of the underlying and continually changing unity of reality.[19]

Of all these models, Ted Peters recommends 'hypothetical consonance' as the most viable model for relating science and theology. He feels that hypothetical consonance takes us beyond the limit of the two-language theory without initially violating the integrity of either natural science or Christian theology.[20]

3. Mikael Stenmark's Models of Science and Religion Relations

Mikael Stenmark (b. 1962) is the Dean of the Faculty of Theology and a Professor of Philosophy of Religion at the Department of Theology, Uppsala University, Sweden. He is a well-known scholar in science and religion relations and published several books and articles in this area. His book: *Rationality in Science, Religion and Everyday Life: Four Models of Rationality*, published in 1995, earned him a prestigious award – the John Templeton Foundation Prize.

3.1. Initial Proposal

In 2004 Michael Stenmark published a book – *How to Relate Science and Religion: A Multidimensional Model,*[21] where he suggests that there are five models or views on the relationship between science and religion. They are: the *independent view*, the *contact view*, the *monist view*, the *complete scientific expansionist view*, and the *complete religion expansionist view.* The *Independent view* holds that there is no overlap between science and religion, and it is not necessary also. On the other hand, the *Contact* view maintains that there is an overlap or interaction between science and religion, and it is also necessary to have such a contact. The *Monist*

18 *Ibid.*, p. 653.

19 *Ibid.*, pp. 653-654.

20 *Ibid.*

21 Mikael Stenmark, *How to Relate Science and Religion: Multidimensional Model,* (Grand Rapids, Michigan: William B. Eerdmans Publishing Company, 2004).

view holds that there is or should be a union of domains of science and religion. The *Complete scientific expansionist view* is an attempt to expand the realm of science into the territory of religion, and the *Complete religion expansionist view* may be understood as an expansion of the domain of religion into the field of science.[22] However, the last two could be classified as either a version of the *Contact view* or a version of the *Monist view*.[23]

3.2. Four Models of Science and Religion Interface

Some years after the publication of his book - *How to Relate Science and Religion*, Mikael Stenmark came out with a typology that is more or less the same as the typology he had given in his book. Having surveyed books and articles published on science and religion in the past twenty years, he concluded that there are *four models* of science and religion relations:

3.2.1. Irreconcilability Model

This view suggests that science and religion are in severe tension and direct conflict with each other. It is not possible to embrace both; we have to choose one. It is a simple fact that science and religion cannot be reconciled whilst still maintaining their respective identities, the distinctive features that characterize them as science or as religion, and not some other human activity. Science and religion are incompatible. They compete on the same turf, and in the end, one will emerge victoriously.[24] What Francis Crick, a Nobel laureate, has said represents suitably this model: "Not only do the beliefs of most popular religions contradict each other but, by scientific standards, they are based on evidence so flimsy that only an act of blind faith can make

them acceptable." John Worrall, a philosopher of science, also puts it bluntly: Science and religion are in irreconcilable conflict… There is no way in which you can be both properly scientifically minded and a true religious believer."[25]

3.2.2. Reconciliation Model

The very opposite to the Irreconcilability model is the one that emphasizes the compatibility of science and religion. It is called the Reconcilability model, which holds that science and religion can be combined or reconciled while maintaining

22 *Ibid.*, pp. 9, 251, 258, 259.

23 *Ibid.*, p. 258.

24 Mikael Stenmark, "Ways of relating science and religion" *The Cambridge Companion to Science and Religion* edited by Peter Harrison, (Cambridge: Cambridge University Press 2010, pp. 278-279. See also Mikael Stenmark, "Religion and Science", in Chad Meister and Paul Copan (eds.), *The Routledge Companion to Philosophy of Religion* (London: Routledge, 2007), pp. 692–701.

25 Cited in Mikael Stenmark, "Ways of relating science and religion," p. 279.

their respective identities and distinctive features.[26] A famous geneticist Francis Collin represents well this model when he says, "In my view, there is no conflict in being a rigorous scientist and a person who believes in a God who takes a personal interest in each one of us . . . I will argue that these perspectives not only can coexist within one person but can do so in a fashion that enriches and enlightens the human experience."[27] According to Stenmark, the Reconciliation model presupposes some kind of overlap or contact between the two practices. This is why he sometimes referred to this model as the **contact view**.[28]

Contact view or Reconciliation model can be subdivided further – one such division is a division into *weak contact view* and *strong contact view*. A *weak contact view* is defined as the view that merely minor reformations or changes of either science or religion are called for in the area of contact. Proponents of the *weak contact view* maintain that substantial reformulation of religion will seldom be called for. A *strong contact view* is a view that more substantial reformulations or changes of either science or religion are called for in the area of contact. Proponents of the *strong contact view*, on the other hand, claim that substantial reformulation of religious aims, methods, or beliefs/doctrines will frequently be called for.[29] Again, contact view may be divided into two groups – the *science-priority contact view,* which states that when there is a conflict in the contact area of science and religion, then a reformulation or change of religion is called for unless there are excellent reasons to believe otherwise. Another one is the *religion-priority contact view* which states that when there is a conflict in the contact area of science and religion, then a reformulation or change of science is called for unless there are excellent reasons to believe otherwise.[30]

Stenmark brings about the Reconciliation model's further classification, saying that two sub-models of the reconciliation model may be recognized. The first one is called the *reformative view,* which states that science can change, undermine or cause religious reformulation in the area of contact, or vice versa. The second one is called the *supportive view,* which maintains that science can support, reinforce or confirm religion in the area of contact, or vice versa. The *reformative view* believes that science and religion can be reconciled if one or both of them changes or reformulates their position in one way or the other. On the other hand, the *supportive view* holds that science and religion can be reconciled, not because one or both of them can change its content without losing its identity, but because they can actually support or confirm each other in one way or another.[31]

26 *Ibid.*

27 Cited in *Ibid.*

28 *Ibid.*

29 Mikael Stenmark, "Religion and Science", p. 788.

30 *Ibid.*

31 *Ibid.*, pp. 281, 282, 285.

The reconciliation model can be further classified into four models – the conservative reconciliation model, the traditional reconciliation model, the liberal reconciliation model and the postmodern or constructivist reconciliation model. The *conservative reconciliation model,* where conservative Christians are the proponents, holds that it is primarily science that needs to change its content and methods. Johnson, Dembski and Alvin Plantinga are the most vocal proponents of this model. The *traditional reconciliation model* opines that science might need to change some of its content, whereas Christianity certainly needs to change some but not most of its traditional content. Alister McGrath, Nancey Murphy, Polkinghorne and Francis Collins can be put under this model. The *liberal reconciliation model* maintains that science has more or less nothing to change; it is fine as it is; instead, Christianity needs to change most of its traditional content. Barbour, Drees, Kaufman, Peacocke and Sallie McFague advocate this model to varying degrees. The postmodern or constructivist reconciliation model maintains that neither science nor Christianity is acceptable as it is; instead, both need to change radically. Scholars such as Nietzsche, Derrida, Foucault and Rorty, and philosophers and sociologists of science such as Thomas Kuhn, Barry Barnes, David Bloor and Sandra Harding can be put under this category.[32]

3.2.3. Independence Model

Just like the reconcilability model, the Independence model also takes science and religion as compatible. According to this model, science and religion are compatible because they are two completely different but legitimate practices with no overlap.[33] Stenmark says that Stephen Jay Gould is one well-known proponent of the independence model. According to him, the net or magisterium of science covers the empirical realm trying to find out what the universe is made of and why it works this way. On the other hand, the magisterium of religion extends over questions of ultimate meaning and moral value. He concludes that these two magisterial do not overlap. Science and religion each have their specific domain and characteristic methods, and each can be justified on its own terms.[34]

3.2.4. Replacement Model

The fourth model, according to Mikael Stenmark, is the replacement model, which proposes that science could replace religion today or in the near future. It maintains that the domain of science can be expanded so that science might become our new religion. Perhaps the best-known advocate of this view is biologist Edward O. Wilson. The idea behind this is that religions are full of falsehood and superstition that they have to be destroyed and replaced with science.[35]

32 *Ibid.*, pp. 288-289.

33 Mikael Stenmark, "Ways of relating science and religion," p. 279.

34 *Ibid.*

35 *Ibid.*

From the above discussion, it can be inferred that for Stenmark, the reconciliation model is the most viable model for relating science and religion today. It rejects conflict thesis and independent model and sternly opposes the notion that science and religion are irreconcilable. This model opens room for mutual learning and enrichment, where it also advocates humility for both science and religion.

4. Indian Christian Attempts at Science and Religion Dialogue

The relationship between science and religion we have discussed so far is centred on the Western worlds – mainly Europe and America. But the problem is touching every people all over the world. There are several issues in the field of genetic science and developmental science that confront Indian people. So, Indian Christians can no longer ignore the gravity of the issue. Among the Indian Christians, Roman Catholics are far ahead of Protestant Christians in dealing with the relationship between science and religion. A number of Catholic theologians are deeply and seriously involved in the dialogue between science and religion. In some of their Institutions, they have science and religion studies. Jnana Deepa Vidyapeeth (Pontifical Institute of Philosophy and Religion), Pune is one such Institute that gives effort to the study of the interaction between science and religion. At the initiative of Jnana-Deepa Vidyapeeth, the 'Association of Science, Society and Religion' was formed in 1998 to foster a creative dialogue between science and religion, and it aims to conduct various programmes and hold conferences to promote healthy interaction between science and religion from Indian perspectives. Since its formation, it has actively coordinated activities like seminars, workshops, lectures, essay writing, and competitions promoting healthy interaction "science and religion."[36]

I will pick up two such philosophers of science as their pioneering works in science and religion dialogue are monumental.

4.1. Job Kohzhamthadam's Contribution to Science and Religion Dialogue

One of the best known among Indian Christians in science and religion dialogue is Job Kozhamthadam (b. 1945), who serves as a professor of Philosophy of science in the Jnana Deepa Vidyapeeth (Pontifical Institute of Philosophy and Religion), Pune. He has written and edited a number of books and published numerous articles in the area of science and religion. His whole idea in science and religion dialogue can be summarized as 'Constructive Collaboration.' He says that science and religion should not be adversaries attacking each other. But they can and should be comrades collaborating in a common cause. A correct and unbiased understanding of the nature and ideals of science and religion will reveal that the

36 See the official website for a detailed information of Association of Science, Society and Religion at *https://sites.google.com/a/jdv.edu.in/assr-india/*.

relationship between the two should be one of constructive collaboration aimed at satisfying the human quest for explanation and understanding and helping develop humans total and integrated persons.[37]

According to Kozhamthadam, fruitful dialogue between science and religion is rooted in two basic exigencies of the human person: the quest for knowledge and the quest for realizing or developing one's full potentialities. Knowledge is power; thirst for knowledge is an all-pervasive one. Human beings are continually seeking explanations, and there is an insatiable desire to know more and more. We want to know the *how* and the *why* of things. "This exigency drives humankind to launch out into all avenues and accept knowledge from all corners."[38] Secondly, human exigency is directed at developing oneself into a totally integrated person. We want to grow, to become better or to attain higher.[39] Human beings have material and non-material dimensions. They have emotional as well as rational needs. Valid knowledge can come not only from well-performed experiments but also from the testimony of reliable persons. Some human experiences are subjective, some unique to a person, some common to many persons. The total development will require paying attention to all these aspects and taking in elements from all the divergent sources. Such a development cannot be achieved by science alone. This makes dialogue and collaboration between science and religion inevitable.[40] Quoting the famous scientist Einstein, who says, "Science without religion is lame, religion without science is blind," Kozhanthadam maintains that constructive interaction between science and religion must be most welcomed.[41]

4.1.1. Possibility of Constructive Collaboration

Even though philosophers like Auguste Comte, David Hume and logical positivists could not see the possibility of science-religion dialogue,[42] Job Kozhamtham believes that *constructive collaboration* between science and religion is possible due to the following reasons:-

Firstly, science and religion are fully integrated in the beginning. The separation and antagonism came about mainly because of unjustified and mistaken claims about science by certain over-enthusiastic devotees of it on the one hand, and because of similar mistaken claims, inadequately founded beliefs, and a closed attitude on the part of certain votaries of religion. Several developments in

37 Job Kozhamthadam, "Science and Religion; Contenders or Collaborators", in *Vidyajoyti Journal of Theological Reflection*, (Vol. 52, No. 8, August, 1988), p. 364.

38 *Ibid.*, p. 368.

39 *Ibid.*

40 *Ibid.*, p. 369.

41 Job Kozhamthadam, "Towards a Constructive Interaction between Science and Religion," in *Vidyajoti Journal of Theological Reflection*, (Vol. 54, No. 12, December, 1990), p. 622.

42 *Ibid.*

theoretical science and in the history of philosophy of science as well as in religion removed several serious blocks from the path of positive collaboration.[43]

Secondly, towards the beginning of the twentieth century, the claims made by mechanical philosophy, supporters of positivism and scientism collapsed as these claims were based on misplaced hopes rather than on reality. For example, mechanical philosophy could not adequately explain many biological phenomena like sensation, irritability and reproduction. It could not explain several aspects of electromagnetism. The claim of science that it was solidly founded on the observable, whereas religion lacks such basis, also suffered a great setback because the theory of relativity and quantum mechanics fundamentally depend on several factors inaccessible to direct observation. For instance, the abstract 4-dimensional continuum plays a crucial role in the theory of General Relativity. Quantum mechanics reveals that the fundamental element of matter is not directly observable like ordinary particles. Again, while the supporters of scientism claim the unlimited accuracy and complete objectivity of scientific knowledge, Quantum mechanics, especially its principle of indeterminacy, dealt a death blow to these claims.[44]

Thirdly, developments in the history and philosophy of science have also contributed towards changing the traditional understanding of science as purely objective, reliable and based on observational facts. The works of Paul Feyerabend, Norwood Hanson, Thomas Kuhn, Larry Laudan, etc., brought about a 'demythologization' of science. They established the fact that science is not free from external influence, and science is not theory-free but theory-laden. According to Kozhamtham, these outstanding philosophers of science found out that scientific discoveries depend on several scientific and non-scientific factors like philosophical principles and that faith plays a pivotal role in science.[45]

Fourthly, Kozhamtham also points out that just like science, there had been a lot of change in Christianity – many changes have come in the understanding and interpretation of the Bible and revelation. Pope John Paul II stated on May 9, 1983, "So we should rejoice together that the world of science and the Catholic Church has learned to go beyond those movements of conflict."[46]

4.1.2. Nature of the Interaction

Kozhamtham maintains that the dialogue envisaged between science and religion is that of respectful partnership founded on mutual understanding and acceptance. It is not a relationship of domination by either party, but relations that aim at unity and a collaborative interaction where the autonomy of each and the complementary nature of both are maintained. This collaborative and

43 Job Kozhamthadam, "Science and Religion; Contenders or Collaborators", p. 371.

44 *Ibid.*, p. 371-372.

45 *Ibid.*, pp. 373-374.

46 Ibid., p. 375.

constructive relationship is to be brought about in the spirit of mutual recognition, mutual understanding and mutual appreciation.[47]

4.1.3. Future Plan of Action

Kozhamtham outlines a future plan of action in science and religion dialogue and comes to the conclusion that there are three things we need to bear in mind:

Firstly, we need to realize that the issue of the interaction between science and religion is highly urgent. The time has come to take this seriously.

Secondly, we need to avoid a number of approaches. A 'retreat' approach which says that both science and religion are autonomous, self-sufficient, and hence mutually independent system; let neither meddle with the other's affair – this attitude cannot solve the problem. The 'retreat' approach is an insult to God because both science and religion are closely related to God. An attitude of inquisitiveness based on *humble ambition* is necessary for constructive collaboration. Humility and ambition have to be exercised – humility will guard it against any sense of self-complacency and makes it open to other disciplines; ambition will provide the energy, drive and motivation needed for such a venture.[48]

Thirdly, both scientists and religious people have their share of responsibility for dialogue. Scientists must be willing to take a realistic stand with regard to the power and limitation of science, and religious people must remain open to scientific developments.[49]

Kozhamtham's main contribution to the field of science and religion dialogue is his proposal for *constructive collaboration* between science and religion. Having sharply criticized what he called a 'retreat' approach where science and religion are considered as independent of one another as an insult to God, he sees the possibility of collaboration. But to collaborate constructively, both scientists and religious leaders should give up their claims and approach each other with positive minds, realizing the urgency of cooperation and dialogue.

4.2. Kuruvilla Pandukattu's Contribution to Science and Religion Dialogue

Another well-known scholar in the field of science and religion dialogue is Kuruvilla Pandikattu, (b. 1957), an Indian Jesuit priest and Professor of Philosophy, Science and Religion at Jnana-Deepa Vidyapeeth (JDV). He is also the Director of JDV Centre for Science-Religion Studies and Association of Science, Society and Religion, Pune. He has written many books and articles and has actively engaged in science-religion dialogue for the past twenty years.

---

47 Job Kozhamthadam, "Towards a Constructive Interaction between Science and Religion," p. 623.

48 Job Kozhamthadam, "Science and Religion; Contenders or Collaborators", pp. 376-377.

49 *Ibid.*, p. 377.

He identifies a few challenges faced by science-religion dialogue in the Indian context. The first challenge is to insist that the conflicts of science and religion are foreign, and there is no need for dialogue in India. Pandikattu asserts that dialogue is necessary, not because there is a division between science and religion, but for the sake of an enriching future for humans. The second challenge comes from those who claim that science has nothing to offer, which Indian religions have not discovered earlier. The third challenge comes from dualists who hold that science and religion are two independent domains that cannot interact with one another.[50] Going beyond these challenges, Pandikattu puts forward prospects of science and religion dialogue in the Indian context, as we shall see below.

Pandikattu is hopeful that dialogical interaction between science and religion will lead to a renewed vision of God, the world and humans. He sees the evil effects of the technological revolution. But to condemn technological development will not help; with a spiritual vision and openness, we need to evaluate and befriend technology without demonizing it.[51] According to Pandikattu, neither the scientific nor the religious domain can claim to be absolute, reducing the other to non-existence. Both can learn from each other to take each other seriously and respect both body and spirit. He suggests four important elements in science-religion dialogue: *admire*, *advise*, *admonish* and *advance*, and he also underlines four vital parts in the process of dialogue: *acknowledgement*, *accommodation*, *acceptance* and *affirmation* of each other. Pandikattu is positive to see as the end product of creative dialogue – religions that are purified and sciences with a human face. Scientific insights will purify the religions of various superstitions, and the insights from the spiritual traditions will help scientists to be responsible towards humans. As a result of flourished religion and advanced science, we will have an open and vibrant society.[52]

Concluding Remarks

There was a time when science and religion were perceived as in conflict. It was then believed that science speaks in terms of experimentally proven fact; religion depends on belief; while scientific laws are definite, determinate and reliable, religion operates on faith and values. The positivist atheistic philosophy and the nineteenth century's Scientism added to the assumption of conflict and an irreconcilable rift between science and religion. However, on a closer look, science and religion are not as incongruent as it has been proclaimed by some thinkers like William Draper and Andrew Dickson White and several atheistic rationalists of the nineteenth century. We may say that the historical instances of

50 Kuruvilla Pandikattu, "Science-Religion Dialogue in India; Creative Challenges and Enabling Possibilities," *Together Towards Tomorrow: Interfacing Science and Religion in India*, edited by Kuruvilla Pandikattu, (Pune: Association of Science, Society and Religion, 2006), p. 417-418.

51 *Ibid.*, pp. 418-419.

52 *Ibid.*, pp. 421-423.

conflict between science and religion were shallow and mainly due to incorrect or limited understanding of science and religion. A number of scientists who had deep Christian conviction, such as Copernicus, Kepler, Galileo, Newton, etc., thought that science and religion are not enemies. Advancement in philosophy and sociology of science, especially from the 1960s, brought to light the reality of science as a 'social construct' - giving rise to the idea that there is enough room for science and religion to relate with one another.

The social studies of science with its branches – postcolonial studies of science and the study of science from a feminist perspective – bring science and religion closer by exposing the 'myth' of the absoluteness of scientific truth and the perfection of scientific research. They conclude that science is theory-laden and not theory-free; scientific research is not always objective but also subjective. Science does not solely depend on observational and experimental data but is deeply influenced by social and religious convictions, tradition, and scientists' personal predispositions. It is now conceived that science and religion have so many commonalities that could pave the way for mutual interaction and enrichment. The conflict thesis is almost gone now; people are talking about the importance and necessity of integration, creative dialogue and positive interaction between science and religion.

Chapter 8

Some Issues in Science and Religion Relations

There are several issues in science and religion relations. Some of them have been discussed before. I pick up a few of these here, such as miracle, astrology and the God of the gap theory and consider their place in an overall discussion of science and religion relations.

1. Miracle and Science

In all religions, miracles happen though miracles are not considered as the primary focus of any religion. God is understood as controlling everything in the universe, seen and unseen, big and small. God is beyond the laws of nature, sovereign and uncontrolled by any physical forces. Therefore, a miracle is part and parcel of religion, and for any religious man or woman, it is not miraculous that a miracle happens. It is rather natural that there is a miracle in nature. However, it is not surprising that atheists, in general, do not believe in a miracle as they do not believe in the source of such a miracle. Looking at from this perspective, it is rather surprising that there are people even among the believers who do not believe in miracles!

1.1. What is a Miracle?

There may be various ways of defining and understanding miracles. One definition could be, "a miracle is an event caused by special Divine action that would not or could not have occurred merely through the regular course of events in nature."[1]

1 Steven Horst, "Miracles and Two Accounts of Scientific Laws," *Zygon,* Vol. 49, No. 2 (June 2014), p. 325.

David Hume, an enlightenment philosopher, famously defined a miracle as "a violation of the law of nature." Many Christian theologians would disagree with Hume's conception of a miracle. According to St. Augustine, one of the most important Christian theologians, the whole nature was God's miraculous work. A miracle is to be understood primarily in terms of its impact on the observer. For him, a miracle is an event that is difficult or unusual above the hope or power of those who wonder. He reasoned that as God controls nature, so miracles cannot be contrary to nature. Therefore, a miracle is an event contrary to our knowledge of nature.[2]

Over against Hume's understanding of miracle, Thomas Aquinas, another great theologian, agreed with Augustine that miracles are not contrary to nature. But rather than arguing, as did Augustine, that miracles are contrary to our knowledge of nature, he noted that in a miraculous event, God acts beside the order planted in nature.[3] This may imply that there were already God's laws for nature, but sometimes God acts beside that planted order, not actually contrary to the natural order.

Till the middle of the eighteenth century, it can be maintained that there was no significant debate about the place of a miracle in science. For example, the great philosopher and scientist Rene Descartes (1596-1650) and one of the best known scientists and theologians Sir Isaac Newton (1643-1727) have no reservation in believing miracles. Descartes maintained that as God is sovereign, he can change not only natural laws, but even the canons of logic.[4] Before the eighteenth century, Western science was by and large controlled by the Church, and most scientists were faithful church members. So, there was no significant debate on the possibility of a miracle, and people did not see enmity between science and a miracle.

1.2. The Denial of Miracle

The scepticism developed in the eighteenth century resulted in the questioning of Church authority, and the philosophical movements like Positivism of Auguste Comte (1798-1857) and Scientism widened the gap between science and religion. A great debate on miracles started in Europe with the publication in 1748 of David Hume's essay "Of Miracles," the Section X of his *Inquiry Concerning Human Understanding*. Here Hume argues against the possibility of miracles, which he defines as "a violation of the laws of nature."[5] According to him, science and miracle cannot go together as they are like day and night. Science has revealed

2 Peter Harrison, "Miracles, Early Modern Science, and Rational Religion," *Church History*, Vol. 75, No. 3 (Sep., 2006), pp. 495-496.

3 *Ibid.*, p. 497.

4 Steven Horst, "Miracles and Two Accounts of Scientific Laws," p. 324.

5 Tor Egil Førland, "Acts of God? Miracles and Scientific Explanation," *History and Theory*, Vol. 47, No. 4, (Dec., 2008), p. 487.

that the universe is governed by natural laws, and if one believes in the natural laws, there is no room for believing in a miracle that violates those laws.[6] David Hume maintains that "a man of good sense" cannot believe in the occurrence of miraculous events.[7]

A great German Lutheran theologian Rudolf Bultmann (1884-1976), is famous for his negation of the possibility and importance of miracles. He maintains that modern man/woman who accepts scientific view cannot believe that miraculous events occur. To do so, he or she would have to violate certain principles that form the very foundation of his or her way of thinking and understanding the world. Miracles, according to Bultmann, make no sense because they do not conform to the basic principles of a scientific view.[8] John Collins, thus, says, "According to Hume, Bultmann, and others, an event that does not appear to conform to natural law and that cannot be interpreted so as to conform it to natural law, can make no sense to modern man. If one cannot answer the questions, 'What caused this event? What are the temporal antecedents of this event?,' then the event is meaningless and therefore useless to modern man."[9]

There are certain principles by which the universe and everything in it are understood to have worked. The first one is called the *Principle of Causality,* which assumes that events in our world follow certain orderly causal sequences. One event follows another not only with regularity but with certainty. For example, if we push a chair on the floor, it will *always* move; if we drop a pen from our hand, it will *always* fall, will not remain in the air. It will not sometimes move and sometimes fall because certain causal laws determine the relationship between the variables - mass, force, and the like - that are involved in these events.[10] The second principle is known as the *Principle of Noncontradiction,* which says that something cannot be one thing and the opposite of that thing at the same time. Something cannot be both existent and nonexistent; cannot be both moving and motionless; cannot be both in a given place and not in that place, and so on.[11] Based on these principles, it can be argued that a miracle cannot happen without breaking these principles. So, if we believe in these principles, there is no room for believing in a miracle.

1.3. The Possibility of Miracle

There are two ways of viewing the occurrence of miracle – *one* is to take a stand as a religious believer to acknowledge that God is there and he is sovereign, He

6 Steven Horst, "Miracles and Two Accounts of Scientific Laws," p. 323.

7 John Collins, "Science and the Denial of the Miraculous: Another Look" in Perspectives *in Religious Studies,* Vol. 10, No. 1983, p. 123.

8 *Ibid.*, p. 124.

9 *Ibid.*, 125.

10 *Ibid.*

11 *Ibid.*, p. 127.

controls everything, He is the maker of laws of nature, He does what he likes, and very much can change the natural law. The *second* way of looking at miracles is to see it as many Christian theologians did that miracle can happen without violating the laws of nature.

1.3.1. Robert Lamer argues that God can produce a miracle without violating natural law. He says, "If a transcendent agent creates or annihilates a unit of mass/ energy, or if He simply causes some of these units to occupy a different position than they did formerly, then He changes the material conditions to which the laws of nature apply. He thereby produces an event that nature on its own would not have produced, but He breaks no laws of nature."[12] For example, "If God were to create *ex nihilo* a fertilized egg in the body of a virgin, no laws of nature would be broken, yet the usual course of nature would have been overridden in such a way as to produce an event nature would not otherwise have produced."[13]

1.3.2. A contemporary scientist Francis Collins maintains that miracle is possible if God is God as we understand. To a question - as a scientist, do you believe in miracles? He answers:

> If God is who God claims to be, and who I believe he is, then he is not explainable in natural terms. He is outside the natural world; outside of space and time. So if God chose to intervene from time to time in the natural world by allowing the occurrence of miraculous events, I don't see why that is an illogical possibility. Once one accepts that idea that there could be something outside the natural, then miracles also become possible.[14]

A miracle is possible, and there should be no tension with science due to the following reasons:

(a) What we call or rather know of as "the laws of nature" are not perfect. We know it. The geocentric cosmology, which was considered the true expression of the reality of cosmos for many centuries, was found to be wanting after Copernicus' heliocentric cosmology. Again, Copernicus' theory on planetary movement was not perfect and later on rectified by Kepler, who discovered that planets move in elliptical orbits and not in a circular path as was held by Copernicus and others. Likewise, Newton's laws were not perfect. His concepts of a fixed universe and unchanged time, etc., were rejected as false after the advance of the relativity theory of Einstein and the magnificent discovery of quantum mechanics. The list may go on and on. The fact is – the laws of nature

12 Robert A. Larmer, "Miracles, Physicalism, and the Laws of Nature," *Religious Studies* 44, 2008, p. 150.

13 *Ibid.*

14 Francis Collins in an interview with him, in https://www.pbs.org/wgbh/questionofgod/voices/collins.html.

we know are not perfect. They are changing and will be changed with more scientific discoveries. Therefore, to reject a miracle on the ground that it goes against our 'known' laws of nature is unacceptable because we really do not know whether such a miracle really goes against the real law of nature or not.

(b) God is God because He is above and beyond this physical world and all the laws therein. He is the author, controller and changer of the laws of the physical world. White is white not because of itself but because of God. The physical and chemical properties of elements are designed and controlled by God, and He can change them at any time. Unless God is like that, He does not deserve to be a God. God permits miracles to happen, and it may be against our known laws of nature, but it may not be against the laws of nature of God. This leads us to the next point.

(c) Miracle is a miracle for us because we see it as something violating the laws of nature and also something that could not occur by itself unless some inducement is there. But, for God, a miracle may be quite natural; it would not be a miracle because it does not violate his laws of nature.

Thus, we may conclude that miracle is possible without trespassing scientific truths, so there should not be any tension between miracle and science.

2. Astrology and Science

There has been a long discussion whether astrology can be considered science or not; or in other words, whether scientists can consider astrology as a correct means of knowing the physical world? Is there any relationship between science and astrology, or they are simply opposite to one another? We will consider such questions as these and attempt to give astrology its proper place in the whole discussion of science and religion.

The Dictionary defines astrology as the study of the movement and relative positions of celestial bodies that are thought to influence human beings and the natural world. It is a belief that the position of stars and planets during the birth of an individual affects a person's temperament, personality, life, and the natural world. So, by reading and observing the heavenly bodies, Astrologers are believed to predict the individuals' future and what will happen in the world. Since the scientific revolution in the sixteenth century, there has been unending question and debate concerning the place of Astrology in science or the relationship between science and astrology.

Astrology is an age-old practice which was originated in Chaldea thousands of years before Christ. It was an accepted practice for predicting natural phenomena and their impact on human beings. By 700 B.C., the Zodiac was established. The conquests of Alexander the Great brought astrology to Greece and to the Romans, where it gained much popularity, with some of the greatest Roman emperors, including Julius Caesar, deeply depended on it. Astrology was formally codified with the work of Ptolemy. In his celebrated work – *Tetrabiblos*, he described in great detail the powers of the sun, moon and planets, and their significance in people's lives. *Tetrabiblos* is still recognized as a fundamental textbook of astrology. For Ptolemy, there are two means of knowing the universe and the first and the more effective way of knowing and predicting the universe is astrology. The secondary means of prediction is that we use the 'natural character' of the aspects of the movement of heavenly bodies to investigate the changes they bring about in that which they surround. He said that the second method is possible because of the manifest effects of the sun, moon and planets on the earth, for example, on weather and the tides.[15]

Astrology was very much part of the learning of the classical world. There were Chairs of Astrology at some universities, including those of Rome, Bologna and Salamanca. It was believed that astrology could offer an explanation of the universe in terms of mathematical computations based on observational data.[16]

During the scientific revolution in Europe, occult practices such as astrology and alchemy flourished with new science. A great scientist, Kepler was known to have a deep interest in astrology and even practised it himself. Until the middle of the seventeenth century, astrology was popular both among intellectuals and the general public. In general, it was accepted as one means of predicting and knowing the universe and human's destiny.[17]

It can be assumed that scientists had no qualms in recognizing astrology as a valuable tool to know the workings of the universe until the middle of the seventeenth century. Peter Wright's argument may be worth quoting here:

> It is impossible to find an adequate body of evidence for regarding astrology and science as conflicting intellectual systems. Up to the mid-seventeenth century, the vast majority of men of science seem to have accepted the basic postulates of astrology, however strongly critical they may have been of its practitioners. Many would probably have shared Bacon's view that the subject needed to be reformed, not abolished.[18]

However, from the end of the seventeenth century, not only theologians but also men of science came out in strong criticism against astrology. In the twentieth

15 Paul R. Thagard, "Why Astrology is a Pseudoscience," *PSA: Proceedings of the Biennial Meeting of the Philosophy of Science Association*, Vol. 1978, Volume One: Contributed Papers (1978), p. 224.

16 Peter Wright, "Astrology and Science in Seventeenth-Century England," *Social Studies of Science*, (Vol. 5, No. 4, Nov., 1975), p. 403.

17 Paul R. Thagard, "Why Astrology is a Pseudoscience," p. 224.

18 Peter Wright, "Astrology and Science in Seventeenth-Century England," p. 410.

century, Karl Popper is one of the well-known critics of astrology. His definition of true science as that which can be potentially falsifiable ruled out astrology as science because it is not falsifiable. From the eighteenth century till the middle of the twentieth century, astrology declined greatly, mainly due to the rise of rationalism and scientism. However, since the middle of the twentieth century, astrology has gained momentum in popularity.

Thus, the latter half of the 20th Century has seen a rise in the popularity of astrology again. This may be due to a general swing of interest toward the occult, particularly among the Western youths. A number of authors have attempted to ascribe a scientific basis to astrology in the light of modern scientific discoveries.[19] Today, many people believe in astrology, where they are somehow convinced that the position and movement of heavenly bodies – planets and stars deeply affected and impacted their lives.

Nowadays, many people are firmly attached to astrology and believe in the power of its prediction. For instance, Lynn Thorndike argues that astrology is the best scientific mean for a weather forecast. "The most scientific form of weather prediction was astrological, and an abundant literature on the subject, derived from India as well as from the Arabic, instructed one how to forecast rain, winds, and changes of temperature from the movements of the planets - direct, retrograde or stationary - through the twelve signs of the zodiac and the twenty-eight mansions of the moon."[20] However, in spite of this, astrology is becoming more and more unpopular among scientists. Lawrence E. Jerome may represent the general opinion of scientists in the twentieth-first century when he says,

> Astrology is neither a science nor an art but rather a system of magic divination based on ancient superstitions and the principle of correspondences. There can be no scientific validity in the methods, predictions or supposed 'influences' of astrology, almost by definition. It originated as a magical system and the passage of some 6000 years has not altered its status… Astrology, as we have seen, is based on magical correspondences and not on any possible physical influences by celestial bodies. Astrology can never be made 'scientific', essentially by definition; it belongs to the superstitious past and there it should remain.[21]

Today astrology is quite popular, especially in India. Many people depend on it for several things. Our discussion leads us to conclude that it cannot be considered as science or having relationship with science. It is more of religious occult practice.

---

19 Lawrence E. Jerome, "On Astrology and Modern Science: A Critical Analysis," *Leonardo*, Vol. 6, No. 2 (Spring, 1973), p. 121.

20 Lynn Thorndike, "The True Place of Astrology in the History of Science," *Isis* , Sep., 1955, Vol. 46, No. 3 (Sep., 1955), p. 274.

21 Lawrence E. Jerome, "On Astrology and Modern Science: A Critical Analysis," pp. 121, 128.

3. God of the Gap

The term "God of the gaps" is a perspective in which gaps in scientific knowledge are taken to be evidence or proof of God's existence. "God of the gaps" argument says that wherever a gap in scientific knowledge exists, there is evidence of divine intervention. Thus, the phrase *God of the gaps* refers to attempts to use statements about divine intervention in the physical world to fill in the 'gaps' in scientific knowledge and explanation. It is the attempt to introduce God as an explanatory hypothesis on the level of efficient causality to make up for limitations in current scientific understanding. The approach has been criticized because, eventually, scientific discoveries close the gap, making the appeal to divine explanation irrelevant and unnecessary.[22] Let me try to give a simple explanation - There is some feature of the world that science cannot explain. Christians or those who believe in God rush to claim that this feature can only be explained by God. This is called the "God of the gaps" theory. But, if science later produces a probable scientific explanation to this feature, the God who filled the gap is no longer needed and is pushed out of the system. This is the danger of applying God of the gaps theory.

Charles A. Coulson was regarded as the first one who used this phrase in a sense it is used now in relation to science and religion discussion. The phrase appeared in his book - *Science and Christian Belief,* published in 1955. However, the term "God of the gaps" appeared long before him in some other writings. For example, In his *Letters and Papers from Prison,* German theologian, Dietrich Bonhoeffer in correspondence from May 25, 1944, observes in response to Carl F. von Weizsacker's *The World-view of Physics* that:

> Weizsacker's book . . . brought home to me how wrong it is to use God as a stopgap for the incompleteness of our knowledge. For the frontiers of knowledge are inevitably being pushed back further and further, which means that you only think of God as a stop-gap. He also is being pushed back further and further, and is in more or less continuous retreat. We should find God in what we do know, not in what we don't . . .[23]

With this statement, Bonhoeffer connects the fallacy of the God-of-the-Gaps in physical science with the fallacy of the God-of-the-Gaps in all of life.[24]

When there is a physical phenomenon that scientists could not explain, or there is no scientific explanation to it, or scientific knowledge is limited and cannot explain such phenomena, then, theologically, it is explained as the work of

---

22 *https://www.encyclopedia.com/education/encyclopedias-almanacs-transcripts-and-maps/god-gaps* (17.08.2021).

23 *Letters and Papers from Prison,* pp. 190-191, quoted in *Ibid.*

24 Richard H. Bube, "Man come of age: Bonhoeffer's response to the god-of-the-gaps," *Journal of the Evangelical Theological Society*, (14 No. 4 Fall 1971), p. 206.

God. Thus, by doing so, God is put in the gap of scientific knowledge. The great scientist and theologian Isaac Newton also used this approach. In the *General Scholium*, a sort of epilogue to his celebrated work - *Mathematical Principles of Natural Philosophy*, known as *The Principia*, Isaac Newton wrote:[25]

> This most elegant system of the sun, planets, and comets could not have arisen without the design and dominion of an intelligent and powerful being. And if the fixed stars are the centers of similar systems, they will all be constructed according to a similar design and subject to the dominion of the One ... And so that the system of the fixed stars will not fall upon one another as a result of their gravity, he has placed them at immense distances from one another.

By this time, Newton or the scientific community was not fully aware of the workings of the solar system and the stars. So, for him, God fills the gap with his intervention by placing the fixed stars at immense distances from one another so that their gravity will not make them fall upon one another. However, a French mathematician and physicist, Laplace (1749 – 1827), solved the problem which Newton could not – why fixed stars will not fall upon one another. He explained in detail his discovery to Napoleon. After listening to him, Napoleon asked him: Where God fits into his mathematical calculation, and Laplace's famous reply was: "Sir, I have no need of that hypothesis." Byron Jennings writes: "Newton had needed that hypothesis, i.e. God, to make the solar system work. Newton believed that the planetary orbits were unstable and unless God intervened periodically, the planets would wander off into space. Newton had not done the mathematical analysis sufficiently completely. Laplace rectified the problem. Newton also had no model for the origin of the solar system. Laplace eliminated these two gaps that Newton had God fill."[26] This reveals the danger of using God as the one who fills the gap in scientific knowledge because, more and more scientific discoveries and increase in scientific knowledge will decrease the gap and finally push God out of the system.

Richard H. Bube, Professor of Material and Electrical Engineering Sciences, Stanford University, comments:

> Newton invoked the God-of-the-Gaps when certain irregularities in the motion of the planets could not be explained by his concurrent theory of gravitation; since the mechanics of the theory of gravity could not explain this irregularity, Newton concluded that it must be a direct manifestation of the intervention of God. Newton was wrong;

25 Marcelo Gleiser, "What The 'God Of The Gaps' Teaches Us About Science?" in https://www.npr.org/sections/13.7/2015/04/08/398227737/what-the-god-of-the-gaps-teaches-us-about-science (17.08.2021).

26 Byron Jennings, "There is No Need for God as a Hypothesis" in https://www.quantumdiaries.org/2011/09/16/there-is-no-need-for-god-as-a-hypothesis/ (17.08.2021).

> subsequent analysis of the details of the planetary system provided a natural mechanism for these irregularities. An evidence for the activity of God was lost.[27]

Though God did not appear in Laplace's mathematical calculation of how stars and planets work, that does not mean that God is not there or has no role in it. God is very much active in the whole working of the universe and every part therein. The danger is to limit God's work in some particular scientific problem as the proponent of the God of the gap theory did.

One of the most renounced scholars in Science and Religion, Ian Barbour, criticizes the 'God of the gap' theory saying that it is not necessary. He says,

> The "God of the gaps" was as unnecessary in biology after Darwin as it had been in physics after Laplace. Adaptive changes could be accounted for by random variation and natural selection *without involving divine intervention. We have Darwin to thank for finally making it clear that God is neither a secondary cause operating on the same level as natural forces nor a means for filling gaps in the scientific account.*[28]

Today, most Christian theologians recognize the fallacy of the "God of the Gaps" argument. "They emphasize the importance of seeing God in all phenomena, the natural as much as the supernatural, and of recognizing that the very existence of the material universe depends moment-by-moment upon the sustaining activity of God."[29] They see that such advocacy results in less and less evidence for the existence and activity of God, resulting from more and more knowledge of His creation with scientific discoveries.

---

27 Richard H. Bube, "Man Come of Age: Bonhoeffer's Response to the God-of-the-Gaps," p. 207.

28 Ian G. Barbour, *Religion and Science: Historical and Contemporary Issues* San Francisco: HarperSanFrancisco, 1997), p. 73.

29 Richard H. Bube, "Man come of Age: Bonhoeffer's Response to the God-of-the-Gaps," p. 207.

Chapter 9

Ethical Issues in the Genetic Sciences

When science enters the realm of genetic engineering, it produces such magnificent and, at the same time, controversial results that lots of questions are asked concerning its ethical, moral and religious correctness. There is huge technical potential in biotechnology, such as DNA sequencing, cloning, DNA hybridization, large scale production of specific proteins, ELISA enzyme assays, and monoclonal antibodies.[1] This huge potential also brings about serious ethical and theological questions - how far we should go in this area? Is it right to alter the natural processes of reproduction? Is it right to alter God's creation individuality? Can we change the identity of a particular organism, animal or plant by means of genetic engineering? Is it alright to create organs or new species with biotechnology? If we do, is it amount to playing God? If so, can or should we play God? These and many more questions are asked in the field of genetic sciences. I will discuss in brief the various issues pertaining to ethical questions on science – pointing out the promises of these new sciences and trying to bring to light the ethical and theological problems they enhanced.

1. The Problem of 'Playing God'

The phrase 'playing God' refers to acting as if we are in total control of something or taking the role of God in doing and deciding things for others. For instance, the act of playing God may include deciding who is to live or die in a situation where not everyone can be saved. According to Ted Peters, the phrase 'playing God' can have at least three overlapping meanings. The *first* meaning has to do

1 John R. Jungck, "Unlimited Questions in Genetic Engineering", *The American Biology Teacher*, (Vol. 46, No. 8, Special Focus: Genetic Engineering, Part 2, Nov. - Dec., 1984), p. 429.

with learning God's awesome secrets. It refers to the sense of awe rising up from new discoveries into the depths of life. Science and its accompanying technology are shedding light down into the hitherto dark and secretive caverns of human reality. Mysteries are being revealed, and we, the revealers, sense that we are on the threshold of acquiring 'Godlike' powers. It is a natural sense of taking pride in the revelatory power of science that leads us to think we are gaining godlike powers.[2]

The *second* meaning of 'playing God' has to do with the actual wielding of power over life and death. This applies to medical doctors working in the clinical setting with emergency surgery. The patient feels helpless. The life of a patient seems to depend on the attention and skill of the surgeon who stands between the patient and death. The doctor is the only door to life. Regardless of whether or not doctors feel they are omnipotent in this situation, the patients impute it to them. The medical meaning of 'playing God' has two assumptions – the first assumption is that decisions regarding life and death belong to God. The second assumption is that a human being with the power of life and death is thought of in a godlike role. This godlike role may make a physician proud and put himself or herself in danger of violating divinely appointed limits.[3]

A *third* meaning of 'playing God' is the use of science to alter life and influence human evolution. "Playing God" in this case means that we, at least the scientists among us, are substituting ourselves for God in determining what human nature will be. It refers to placing ourselves where God and only God belongs. Developments in genetic sciences give scientists the ability to alter DNA and perhaps alter the essence of a human being. Genetic engineering is the primary area of science that provokes fears of playing God. Yet, such fears also arise in nuclear physics and ecology.[4]

The possibility and fear of 'playing God' as we go further in biotechnology gives rise to the question of bioethics.

2. Bioethics

Bioethics is the part of ethics that concerns medicine and biological research. It is basically the study of controversial issues in biological sciences and medicine that were brought about by advancements in these fields. 'Bioethics' also has been used to describe the investigation and a study of ways in which decisions in medicine and science touch upon our health and lives and upon our society and environment. It is concerned with questions about basic human values such as the right to life and health, the rightness or wrongness of certain developments in healthcare institutions, life technology, medicine, health professions, and the

2 Ted Peters, *Playing God? Genetic Determinism and Human Freedom*, (New York: Routledge, 2003), p. 11.

3 *Ibid.*, pp. 11-12.

4 *Ibid.*, p. 12.

responsibility of society for the life and health of its members.[5] Thus, we may say that bioethics is the systematic study of the moral dimensions of the life sciences and healthcare to determine whether a particular decision and conduct in medicine and biological science is ethically right or wrong.

There are several ethical issues in relation to medical practices. One such issue is the use of an artificial respiratory system. Respirators were originally invented for people who were expected to recover and be able to breathe on their own. Within a short period of time, they began to be used on people in various situations. For example, to keep premature babies survive who would have died in earlier decades. Many of these babies go on to have normal, healthy lives, but many face a lifetime of severe disabilities and serious health complications. Thus, this system – giving artificial respiration, gives rise to many questions - Ought life to be preserved regardless of the nature or quality of that life? Should people who are permanently and irreversibly unconscious be kept alive indefinitely? And if there are times when life should not be preserved, who should be authorized to make these decisions? During the 1960s, these questions began to be debated at academic conferences and in scholarly journals, giving birth to the field of bioethics.[6]

The term 'bioethics' was coined in the early 1970s by biologists who brought to the public's attention two pressing issues: the need to maintain the planet's ecology, on which all life depends, and the implications of advances in life sciences toward manipulating human nature. In his book, *Bioethics: Bridge to the Future*, published in 1971, Van Rensselaer Potter focused on the growing human ability to change nature, including human nature, and the implications of this for our global future. Although the term 'bioethics' has referred almost exclusively to problems in biomedicine, in recent years, the field has covered the wider context provided by the life scientists of the early 1970s, including their environmental and public health concerns. While bioethics has been interdisciplinary since its inception, theology played a foundational role in its creation, and it continues to have a profound influence today. Three theologians, in particular, were instrumental in the birth of bioethics: Joseph Fletcher, an Episcopal minister; Paul Ramsey, a Methodist minister; and Richard McCormick, a Jesuit moral theologian. At its inception, the central issues in bioethics were researching human subjects, genetics, organ transplantation, death and dying, and reproduction.[7]

5 http://www.bioethics.org.au/Resources/Resource%20Topics/Bioethics%20Default.html (29.01.2017)

6 Bonnie Steinbock (ed.), *The Oxford Handbook of Bioethics*, (Oxford: Oxford University Press, 2007), pp. 2-3.

7 *Ibid.*, p. 3. Cf. Stephen G. Post, "Introduction" in *Encyclopedia of Ethics*, Stephen G. Post (ed.), (New York: Macmillan Reference USA), p. xi.

3. Genetic Engineering

Genetic engineering, which is also known as 'recombinant DNA technology' is the purposeful rearrangement of the genetic information of an organism.[8] Genetic engineering deals with the elementary language of life, the letters and words by which cells translate their genetic code, inherited from their predecessors, into the daily biochemical business of life. They will pass that same message on to their own inheritor.[9] It is a set of technologies used to change the genetic makeup of cells, including the transfer of genes within and across species boundaries to produce improved or new organisms. The techniques involve sophisticated manipulations of genetic material and other biologically important chemicals. Genes are the chemical blueprints that determine an organism's traits or character. Moving genes from one organism to another transfers those traits or characters, producing the new or improved or different organism. With the help of genetic engineering, it is possible to produce organisms with desired gene combinations that do not or could not occur in nature or by natural means. The genetic engineer can isolate a gene from any organism - plant, animal, or microorganism. Since the first genetic engineering experiment done in 1971, this technology has grown very fast, and within a few decades, high success has been achieved in this field, of course, amidst a number of debates and controversies concerning its ethical and moral implications.

3.1. The Difference between Genetic Engineering and Traditional Breeding

The way genetic engineering works towards producing novel organisms is different from classical plant and animal breeding, which operates through selection across many generations for traits of interest. While genetic engineering manually moves genes from one organism to another, traditional breeding moves genes through mating or crossing the organisms in hopes of obtaining offspring with the desired combination of traits. Classical breeding operates on traits, only indirectly selecting genes, whereas biotechnology targets genes, attempting to influence traits. The potential of biotechnology is to rapidly accelerate the rate of progress and efficiency of breeding.[10] Again, traditional breeding is also less precise than genetic engineering. In classical breeding, half of the genes from each parent are passed on to the offspring. This may include many undesirable genes

8 Winston J. Brill, "Genetic Engineering Applied to Agriculture: Opportunities and Concerns", *American Journal of Agricultural Economics*, (Vol. 68, No. 5, Proceedings Issue, Dec., 1986), p. 1081.

9 Thomas H. Murray, "Ethical Issues in Genetic Engineering", *Social Research*, (Vol. 52, No. 3, Bioethics, Autumn 1985), p. 471.

10 Harshada Kulkarni, *et al.*, "Genetic Engineering: A Question of Ethics", *Research Journal of Chemical and Environmental Sciences*, (Vol. 2, No. 6, December 2014), p. 1.

for traits that are not wanted in the new organism. Genetic engineering, however, allows for the movement of a single or a few genes, which give an accurate result.[11]

We know that nature can produce organisms with new gene combinations through sexual reproduction. A brown cow bred to a yellow cow may produce a calf of a completely new colour. But reproductive mechanisms limit the number of new combinations. Cows must breed with other cows. If we want a purple colour cow, we need to breed a cow with another having purple genes and only then it would be possible to produce a purple colour cow. A genetic engineer has no such restriction. If purple genes are available anywhere in nature, for example, in a sea urchin or an iris, those genes could be used in attempts to produce purple cows. This unprecedented ability to shuffle genes means that genetic engineers can create gene combinations that would never be found in nature.[12]

3.2. Applications of Genetic Engineering

Advances in biotechnology have broadened the range of agricultural, medical, and food possibilities. With the help of genetic engineering, we are able to produce or will be able to produce soon stronger crops that are able to resist disease, pests, and weeds; plants and animals that have been genetically engineered to produce better fruits or twice as much milk; germ-line therapies that, if done, could eliminate perhaps thousands of inherited diseases - such modem scourges as breast cancer, cystic fibrosis, Huntington's chorea, and Alzheimer's disease.[13] Genetic engineering has been used in agriculture quite extensively. In fact, this is the area where genetic engineering has reached the furthest developed stage. Genetic engineering in animals and humans has been lagging far behind in comparison with it. We already have produced genetically modified foods that are available in the market.

The development of genetic engineering in the agricultural sector is such that plants and crops are engineered to express resistance to herbicides and specific pests. Scientists promised that genetically modified plants would have a better texture, more flavour and higher nutritional value than wild varieties of the same crops. There are also plants engineered to last longer on the shelf, appear fresher for longer and survive the shipping process in better condition. Better yielding seeds are produced by means of genetic engineering, and these are used in the green revolution to increase food production. Also, in the agricultural sector, research is being conducted to modify certain insects to attack the predators of

11 N. A. "What is Genetic Engineering and How Does it Work" in http://agbiosafety.unl.edu/basic_genetics.shtml (23.01.2017).

12 Harshada Kulkarni, *et al.*, "Genetic Engineering: A Question of Ethics", p. 1.

13 See Isaac Rabino, "Ethical Debates in Genetic Engineering: U.S. Scientists' Attitudes on Patenting, Germ-Line Research, Food Labeling, and Agri-Biotech Issues", *Politics and the Life Sciences*, (Vol. 17, No. 2, Sep., 1998), p. 147.

specific crops. Therefore, fewer amounts of pesticides will have to be applied to the crops, allowing for better environmental and human health.[14]

Genetic engineering gives us surprising results in the animal also. In 1996 Dolly, a sheep cloned from the udder cell of another sheep, was born in Scotland. In 2001 the surrogate mother, a cow named Bessie, gave birth to Noah, the gaur, an endangered Asian ox, but it died after two days due to some infections. Pets, including dogs, cats, and even a bull, have been cloned. Pigs, implanted with human genes, grow organs for human transplant that will not be rejected by their recipients. The gene responsible for spider web silk has been engineered into goats. Scientists believe that species can be protected by cloning the endangered animal and even bringing back those already extinct.

Genetic engineering on humans has also already produced a good result. Human insulin produced by genetically engineered bacteria currently is sold to people with diabetes who are allergic to the standard animal insulin. New vaccines for human health have been developed. These vaccines are not only more effective, but they are safer than ones in current use. Genetic engineering has also given us some very sensitive and specific diagnostic tools for various virus, bacterial, and fungal diseases, as well as genetic diseases.[15] After the human genome project was successfully done in 2003, the prospect of human genetic engineering is wider but with more and more severe consequences on the horizon.

3.3. Ethical and Theological Issues in Genetic Engineering

With advancement and promises in genetic engineering come serious concerns, worries and threats. Isaac Rabino highlights some of the concerns and questions connected with genetic engineering:- Is bioengineered food safe? What will the interaction of genetically engineered species do to the environment? Will resistant crops threaten natural diversity? What will be the effects in succeeding generations of germ-line therapy? Will human germ-line research open the door to eugenics? Can one person or company patent - or in effect, own - genes or portions of genes?[16]

The ethical issues raised by genetic engineering may be put into three categories: *First*, there are worries about the risks to public health and environmental integrity now and in the future, among them fears of Andromeda-likes trains of microbes, agricultural releases of deliberately redesigned organisms, and biological warfare.[17] There is a fear of a public health disaster if some genetically super-powered microorganism be accidentally released onto an unsuspecting public. Another concern is that since the beginnings of genetic engineering research, one of the most horrible possibilities imagined was the

14 Harshada Kulkarni, *et al.*, "Genetic Engineering: A Question of Ethics", p. 2.

15 Winston J. Brill, "Genetic Engineering Applied to Agriculture", p. 1082.

16 Isaac Rabino, "Ethical Debates in Genetic Engineering", p. 147.

17 Thomas H. Murray, "Ethical Issues in Genetic Engineering", p. 472.

deliberate creation of disease-causing organisms or the melding of disease-causing genes with a previously harmless microbe. What if, for example, we could insert the gene from poisonous bacteria into omnipresent bacteria like Escherichia coli? The concern remains that, should the powerful techniques of genetic engineering be turned to biological warfare, they could result in the purposeful, not accidental, creation of an Andromeda-strain-like organism.[18] There are more serious concerns when genetic engineering is applied to creating humans, for example, in the form of a clone. We will discuss this in a separate section.

Second, there are concerns about the privatization and commercialization of genetic engineering, including the question of justice in patenting, the autonomy and freedom of the university which are conducting research, and the ownership of life forms. Patenting is one of the most celebrated issues associated with genetic engineering. Opinion remains divided on the wisdom of permitting patenting of life forms themselves rather than of the processes by which they are developed, which has been less controversial. By permitting life forms to be patented, something that is importantly 'public' is being made 'private.' Again, it is felt that giving exclusive ownership of the thing produced through genetic engineering to an individual or company is unjust because public money is used for research in genetic engineering, whereas the outcome goes to the private sector. Still, another concern raised was in the field of academics. Universities where research is done are controlled by Industry that funded the research work. By doing so, there is a shift in research priorities away from issues to which industry is indifferent to or hostile and towards topics likely to be useful to the industry.[19] What is important for human beings and the environment is not necessarily the priority in research but what is beneficial for Industry. In other words, what sells well in the market gets priority in academic research, and universities are quite helpless to set their own priorities.

Third, there are issues surrounding the use of gene therapy in humans. Much of the debate about human gene therapy has centered on the question of whether deliberately altering a person's genes constitutes amorally forbidden tampering with life. Because of this, scientists are charged with 'playing God'. Separately and in collaboration, a number of religious leaders and theologians expressed concerns about the genetic manipulation of a human being. For instance, religious leaders wrote to the then US President Jimmy Carter in June, 1980 signed by the General Secretaries of National Council of Churches, America, the Synagogue Council of America, and the U.S. Catholic Conference expressing their reservation for germ-line research. There was also a document circulated by Jeremy Rifkin signed

18 *Ibid.*, pp. 475, 477.

19 See *Ibid.*, pp. 475, 479-482.

by sixty-one religious leaders, social activists, authors, theologians, and scientists, expressing their concerns for the genetic manipulation of a human being.[20]

Research in human gene therapy, or technically called *human germ-line research,* is an attempt where genes are modified and make the altered genes pass from one generation to the next to do away with the defect in the genes. The purpose is to cure diseases and eliminate them for future generations. Apart from what has been cited above, the World Council of Churches way back in 1979 expressed its reservation and called attention to the ethics of germ-line research. In March of 1998, a group of eminent molecular biologists and geneticists met in Los Angeles, USA, to discuss how, why, and when germ-line genetic engineering should proceed. Those who oppose germ-line research advance a number of reasons against it that deserve serious consideration. Firstly, they see germ-line therapy as unethical and germ-line as something sacred that human beings should not involve in its alternation. They do not believe that nature makes a mistake and hold that some things are best left to develop as intended by nature. It is unethical to involve in the business of defining the genetic characteristics of a race. They said that doing germ-line research is like 'playing God', which we should not do. Secondly, many express concerns about 'unpredictable', 'unknown' long term side effects on individuals or the species and lack of total confidence in researchers' abilities to foresee all possibilities. Even scientists feel that while the potential is tremendous, there is too much threat for unexpected harm.[21]

Celia Deane-Drummond advances three categories of response to genetic engineering: Public responses, Theological responses and Ethical responses.[22] *Public responses* include the fear about the idea that genetic engineering amounted to a 'messing about with nature', and the commitment that what is present in nature and untouched by human interference is good. It is also felt that genetic engineering destroys the uniqueness of the human being among creation when human genes are transferred to animals. At the same time, genetic engineering also shows no respect for animals and the environment either. It is strongly felt that genetic engineering is only to meet human's greed and profit. *Theologically* it is pointed out that God's love for all creation demands respect for the interest of all creatures. Human motivation to develop new varieties and transgenic species need to be carefully scrutinized. The promise of genetic engineering to make a better future: disease-free human, etc., is tempered by the realization of human sinfulness and the need for the redemptive initiative of God. *Ethical issues* on genetic engineering include the anthropocentrism of biotechnology – it is done for the benefit of human beings alone, where the wider impact of genetic engineering

20 *Ibid.*, p. 485.

21 Isaac Rabino, "Ethical Debates in Genetic Engineering", p. 153-154.

22 See Celia Deane-Drummond, "Biotechnology: A New Challenge to Theology and Ethics", in Christopher Southgate, et al., *God, Humanity and the Cosmos: S Companion to the Science-Religion Debate*, (London: T&T Clark International, 2005), pp. 370-386.

leads to anxiety that it is to the detriment of life and the planet as a whole. The key to environmental ethics is 'respect for the natural world', and genetic engineering destroys this very respect. Human beings, animals and plants are all part of a biotic community mutually depending on each other. However, in genetic engineering, there is a tendency to treat animals and plants as mere commodities and become objects of exploitation. This would result in environmental degradation.

4. Human Genome Project (HGP)

Human biological life can be compared to a book, we may say, 'book of life' where information is written by means of genes. Genes are primarily responsible for determining how humans will be, their characters, how they carry their essential functions, etc. These genes are carried in DNA by chromosomes. The human cell has 23 pairs of chromosomes, some 25,000 genes and over 3 billion chemical units. The Human Genome Project (HGP) identifies the order or sequence of these chemical units and maps their locations in the 23 pairs of chromosomes.[23] DNA, or deoxyribonucleic acid, is the hereditary material in humans and almost all other organisms. Most of the DNA molecules are packaged into thread-like structures called chromosomes which are present in the cell nucleus. Some DNA molecules are also present in the mitochondria of the cell. The information in DNA is stored as a code made up of four chemical bases: adenine (A), guanine (G), cytosine (C), and thymine (T). They come in predictable pairs facing each other: A plus T or C plus G, no other combinations.

The HGP was the international, collaborative research program whose goal was to complete mapping and understanding all the genes of human beings. All our genes together are known as our "genome." The HGP was the natural culmination of the history of genetics research.[24] The main purpose of the project is to determine "the precise location and molecular details of all of the genes and interconnecting segments that make up the human chromosomes." Since genes control "the activities of the cells and hence those of the entire organism, such knowledge would be an extraordinarily powerful tool to explore what are now unfathomable mysteries of human development and disease."[25]

HGP was officially launched in the United States on October 1, 1990, as a fifteen-year programme to map and sequence the complete set of human chromosomes. Countries like United Kingdom, France, Germany, Japan, and China also participated. The Human Genome Project was completed in April, 2003, 2 years ahead of its original schedule. The work of the HGP has allowed

23 Job Kozhamthadam, "The Genome Revolution and the Science-Religion Dialogue", in *Vidyajoti Journal of Theological Reflection*, (Vol. 65, No. 2, February, 2001), p. 90.

24 https://www.genome.gov/12011238/an-overview-of-the-human-genome-project/ (30.01.2017).

25 Thomas F. Lee, *The Human Genome Project: Cracking the Genetic Code of Life*, (New York: Springer Science + Business Media, LLC, 1991), p. 1.

researchers to begin to understand nature's complete genetic blueprint for building a human being. As researchers learn more about the functions of genes and proteins, this knowledge will have a major impact in the fields of medicine, biotechnology, and the life sciences. Thus, the HGP was one of the greatest explorations in history - an inward voyage of discovery rather than an outward exploration of the planet or the cosmos.

It has been found out that Human DNA is largely junk - that is, 98.6 per cent does not code for proteins. Half of the junk DNA consists of is repeated sequences of various types, most of which are parasitic elements inherited from our distant evolutionary past. Only 1.1 per cent to 1.4 per cent constitutes sequences that code for proteins and that function as genes.[26]

4.1. The Goal of HGP

The HGP has specific goals to reach, and they are as follows:[27]

- To determine the sequences of the 3 billion chemical base pairs of nucleotides that comprise the DNA chains in our forty-six (23 pairs) chromosomes.
- To investigate the nature, structure, function and interaction of the genes, genomic elements and genomes of humans and relevant pathogenic and model organisms.
- To study the relationship between genetic variation and the environment in the origins and characteristics of human populations and the causes, diagnoses, treatments, and prevention of disease.
- To store this information in databases and to improve tools for data analysis.
- To transfer related technologies to the private sector and address the ethical, legal, and social issues that may arise from the project.

It was thought that there were around 100,000 genes in human beings, but after the whole process of mapping was completed, it was found out that there are about 20,000 to 25,000 protein-encoding genes in the human genome. This is much less than expected and confusing when we compare with a yeast cell that has 6,000 genes, or with a fly with 13,000 genes, a worm with some 26,000 genes, and a rice cell with fifty thousand genes. Ted Peters thus comments, "... no longer could human uniqueness or complexity or even distinctiveness be lodged in the number of genes... perhaps what is distinctively human could be found not in the genes themselves but in the multiple proteins and the complexity of

26 Ted Peters, *Playing God?*, p. 5.

27 Bensu Karahalil, "Pharmacogenomics and Toxicogenomics in Food Chemicals", in, *Advances in Food Biochemistry* edited by Fatih Yildiz (London: CRC Press, Taylor & Francis Group, 2010), p. 483.

protein production. Culturally, DNA began to lose some of its magic, some of its association with human essence."[28]

HGP was definitely a unique scientific research project that helped us know the inner working of human beings. Job Kozhamthadam, a well known Indian Christian philosopher of science, remarks that the completion of HGP was "a most valuable gift by science to humanity, a most fitting new millennium gift."[29] Some compare it to the discovery of the wheel or discovery of the antibiotics and with the splitting of the atom, while for others, this achievement was as important as landing on the moon. The then President of USA, Bill Clinton, remarked that this achievement unlocked the secret language in which God created life. James Watson, a renowned scientist who co-discovered the double-helix structure of DNA and was the first director of the HGP remarked: "We have the book and now we've got to learn how to read it."[30] This comment indicates that the completion of HGP and the knowledge gained from this research is not sufficient unless there is an adequate follow-up programme. The findings and records of HGP will definitely help scientists and researchers in genetics sciences solve a number of human health problems – to do away with our health deficiencies and make human beings and other organisms stronger and more productive.

4.2. Ethical Issues Connected with HGP

The ethical issues raised by the HGP can be grouped into two general categories. In the first category, we have the impact of genetic engineering. The map of the human genome provides information that will allow us to diagnose and eventually treat many diseases. This map will also enable us to determine the genetic basis of numerous physical and psychological traits, which raises the possibility of altering those traits through genetic intervention. The future generations may not share their predecessors' views about the desirability of the traits that have been bequeathed to them. They may be grateful when they learn that we deprive them of genes associated with horrible diseases, but they may feel limited by our choices regarding their physical, cognitive, or emotional traits. In short, there is a danger that social-historical trends and biases could place genetic limitations on future generations.[31]

The second general category consists of ethical questions pertaining to the acquisition and use of genetic information. Once we pinpoint the genetic basis for diseases and other phenotypic traits, what parameters should be set for the acquisition and use of genetic information? The key issue to be considered here is the use of genetic screening. Screening for diseases with the due consent of a

28 Ted Peters, *Playing God?*, p. 5.

29 Job Kozhamthadam, "The Genome Revolution and the Science-Religion Dialogue", p. 85.

30 *Ibid.*

31 Marion L. Carroll and Jay Ciaffa, "The Human Genome Project: A Scientific and Ethical Overview", in http://www.actionbioscience.org/genomics/carroll_ciaffa.html (03.02.2017).

patient or a legal proxy is generally viewed as ethically permissible, but even this form of screening can create some significant ethical challenges. The knowledge that one is or may be affected by serious disease can create difficult situations for both patients and their families.[32]

James Bernat, a Neurologist, wrote about the ethical implications of HGP, highlighting important procedures to follow while using genetic testing. First, it is a physician's duty to be knowledgeable about genetic testing, like the types and availability of genetic testing for diagnosis, screening, preventive testing, and predictive testing of genetic disease. Physicians further need to understand the meaning of a positive or negative test and its implication for their patients. Secondly, patients should be informed about the implications of their test results and should have the opportunity to receive psychological and genetic counselling as part of the testing program. Their consent should be taken into consideration. As the misuse of information represents a serious ethical problem, physicians should protect patient confidentiality. In fact, over half of US states have enacted laws restricting or prohibiting health insurers from using patients' genetic information in pricing, issuing, or structuring health insurance since 1991.[33]

As it is said: "With great power comes great responsibility" – our knowledge of human self, our ability to read 'the book of life', our access to the secrets of human life and characters – the great and marvellous power of the human genome project unveiled before us, demands greater responsibility. The information we receive from the HGP is vital and, at the same time easy to misuse. It is our responsibility to use wisely and prudently; otherwise, it may destroy human life, the very thing it endeavours to protect.

5. Stem Cells Research

Stem Cells are particular types of cells that are distinguished from other cell types by two important characteristics - *First,* they are unspecialized cells capable of renewing themselves through cell division, sometimes even after long periods of inactivity. *Second,* under certain physiologic or experimental conditions, they can be induced to become tissue - or organ-specific cells with special functions. In other words, they have a remarkable potential to develop into many different cell types in the body during early life and growth.

Depending on their ability to reproduce, stem cells can be divided into four types. The *first* one is called *totipotent* (totally potent) stem cells which are capable of forming every type of body cell. Each *totipotent* cell could replicate and differentiate and become a human being. *Secondly,* we have *pluripotent* stem cells, which can develop into any of the three major tissue types: endoderm (interior gut lining), mesoderm (muscle, bone, blood), and ectoderm (epidermal tissues

32 *Ibid.*

33 James L. Bernat, "The Human Genome Project Raises Ethical Issues that Deserve Our Attention", *Neurology Today,* (Volume 1 - Issue 2, July/August 2001), p. 4.

and nervous system). *Pluripotent* stem cells can eventually specialize in any bodily tissue, but they cannot develop into human beings. The *third* one is *oligopotent* stem cells which have the ability to differentiate into a few cells only. The *fourth* one is *unipotent* or specific stem cells committed to making only one type of tissue. Hematopoietic stem cells, for example, are responsible for all types of blood cells but no other tissue types. These renew themselves, yet they specialize in the tissue they produce.[34]

Again, based on their sources, stem cells are divided into two - *Embryonic stem cells* that come from the embryos formed during the blastocyst phase of embryonic development and *adult stem cells* which are derived from the adult tissue.

The embryonic stem cells are derived from the embryos of humans or other animals. Since 1998 scientists have had the possibility of studying human embryonic stem cells in the laboratory. When an egg is fertilized, it begins a series of cell divisions that generates a small population of thoroughly totipotent cells. We can harvest any one of these cells, and we can collect, study, and use them in the very early embryo to produce new embryos or stem cells in the laboratory. After about a week, several hundred cells form a ball called a *blastocyst*. The ball consists of an outer layer of cells and an inner layer that we can tease out by breaking open the outer layer. Now, this inner layer, called the inner cell mass, contains stem cells that have the ability to grow and divide into a colony of cells on a Petri dish. It was James Thompson, at the University of Wisconsin, USA, who for the first time broke open a human embryo, teased out these cells of the inner cell mass, and spread them out on a Petri plate. He was able to find a rare instance where one of the cells of the inner cell mass divided and divided again to produce a clone.[35]

5.1. Potential Value of Stem Cells Research

Stem cells research is believed to hold promise for treating and curing devastating conditions such as Parkinson's disease, Alzheimer's disease, diabetes, spinal cord injury, heart problems, and many other illnesses. Ted Peters lists the positive aspects of stem cells research for human health - Stem cell research is valuable especially for the improvement of transplantation therapy and toward lengthening a person's life. Stem cells would be of enormous value for providing cardiomyocytes to renew heart muscle to prevent congestive heart failure. Hematopoietic stem cells can be used for producing healthy blood in the bone marrow to resist infection by the HIV virus and to treat AIDS and possibly sickle cell anaemia; cultivating endothelial cells to reline blood vessels as a treatment for atherosclerosis, angina, and stroke due to arterial

34 See Ted Peters, *Playing God?*, pp. 174-175.

35 Randy Schekman and Marjorie Shultz, "Stem Cell Research: Opportunities and Challenges", in *Bulletin of the American Academy of Arts and Sciences*, (Vol. 59, No. 3, Spring, 2006), p. 18.

insufficiency; rejuvenating islet cells in the pancreas to produce natural insulin to fight diabetes; renewing of neurons in the brain to treat Parkinson's disease and victims of stroke; growing of fibroblast and keratinocyte cells to heal skin in the treatment of burns; and giving of chondrocytes or cartilage cells to treat osteoarthritis or rheumatoid arthritis.[36]

5.2. Stem Cells Controversy

Stem cell research meets with stern opposition. The main critique of this research is that it required the destruction of a human embryo of blastocyst stage (some four days after fertilization). That is, a fertilized egg was not given a chance to develop into a fully-developed human. The core of this debate - similar to debates about abortion, for example - centers on the question, "When does life begin?" Many assert that life begins at conception when the egg is fertilized. It is often argued that the embryo deserves the same status as any other full-grown human. Therefore, destroying it (removing the blastocyst to extract stem cells) is akin to murder. People also take issue with the creation of chimaeras. A chimaera is an organism that has both human and animal cells or tissues. In stem cell research, human cells are often inserted into animals (like mice or rats) and allowed to develop. This creates the opportunity for researchers to see what happens when stem cells are implanted. Many people, however, object to the creation of an organism that is 'part human.' The stem cell debate has risen to the highest level of courts in several countries.[37]

The International Stem Cell Forum conducted a study of regulatory approaches to human embryonic stem cell research in 50 countries. The following trends emerged: A small number of countries prohibit all embryonic stem cell research. Most countries permit in-vitro research with an embryo with no mention of stem cells, limiting the creation of stem cell lines to surplus in-vitro fertilization embryos under certain conditions or limiting research to imported cell lines. Seven countries explicitly permit the creation of an embryo for research purposes. All 50 countries studied prohibited human reproductive cloning.[38] Production of embryonic stem cell is illegal in Austria, Denmark, France, Germany, and Ireland but permitted in the USA, Finland, Greece, the Netherlands, Sweden, and the UK. In the United States, it is not illegal to work with or create embryonic stem cells.

International Society for Stem Cell Research (ISSCR), another vibrant organization, made guidelines for stem cell research. The ISSCR guidelines prohibit - (a) all experiments that lack a compelling scientific rationale or raise strong shared ethical concerns - in particular, human reproductive cloning; (b) in

36 Ted Peters, *Playing God?*, pp. 176-177.

37 "What are Stem Cells?" in http://www.medicalnewstoday.com/info/stem_cell (30.01.2017).

38 International Stem Cell Forum Ethics Working Party, "Ethics Issues in Stem Cell Research" in *Science, New Series*, (Vol. 312, No. 5772, Apr. 21, 2006), p. 366.

vitro culture of human embryos beyond 14 days or the formation of the primitive embryonic streak; and (c) the interbreeding of animals likely to harbour human gametes.[39]

India is tightening regulations on human embryonic stem cells research within the country as well as possible international projects that might involve embryonic material from India. There is fear and concern that India could emerge as a major source of embryonic stem cells as there is almost no public or religious debate on abortion, which is legal up to twenty weeks of pregnancy and done in a massive way across India. A national bioethics panel, set up by India's department of biotechnology, has drafted new guidelines for human genomics research that also cover rules for the collection and use of embryonic stem cells. According to the guidelines, scientists may harvest human embryos for research before day 14 of gestation with the informed consent of the donor. All projects would have to be approved by the national bioethics panel, and researchers would have to share any commercial benefits that emerge from embryonic stem cell lines with the donor.[40]

Senior officials say that the new rules draw on existing ethical guidelines from the Indian Council of Medical Research but that they will be enforceable. Two Indian research centres are among the ten worldwide named by the US National Institutes of Health as holding human stem cell lines that are eligible for US federal research funds. Reliance Life Science Research, Mumbai is one of the two. Government officials have said they may need to regulate in-vitro fertilisation clinics that are potential sources of embryonic stem cells.[41]

6. Cloning

When we say 'cloning' what's come to our minds most of the time is 'reproducing the exact copy of a person in a laboratory.' There is a general opinion that if we clone a person, the cloned person will look exactly like the person cloned. This shows our limited understanding of the whole technology of cloning. There are different types of cloning. But for most of us, 'cloning' is connected solely with 'reproductive cloning', where cloning is done to produce the entire individual. We have more or less no idea about another important type of cloning, that is, 'therapeutic cloning', where cloning technology is used for replacing or repairing damaged tissues or organs.

6.1. What is Cloning?

Cloning is the production of identical genetic copies of a donor cell or individual. Clones exist naturally when a cell or an organism reproduces asexually (e.g.,

39 George O. Daley, *et al.*, "The ISSCR Guidelines for Human Embryonic Stem Cell Research", *Science, New Series,* (Vol. 315, No. 5812, Feb. 2, 2007), p. 603.

40 Ganapati Mudur, "India To Tighten Rules On Human Embryonic Stem Cells Research", in *BMJ: British Medical Journal,* (Vol. 323, No. 7312, Sept. 8, 2001), p. 530.

41 *Ibid.*

mitosis, binary fission, budding, etc.) or when two genetically identical individuals are produced naturally. But the term cloning is rarely used to describe these methods. Today, the term 'clone' typically is construed to represent a genetically identical copy of a cell, tissue, organ, or individual created by deliberate human effort.[42] DNA cloning technology is also used in genetic engineering, such as transgenic technology - where DNA from one species is inserted into another. Transgenic animals are created most often for the purposes of studying the disease. By inserting disease-causing DNA into the animal models, scientists are able to experiment on animals rather than humans in their efforts to find effective treatments and cures. In addition, by using transgenic technology, extremely rare human or animal diseases can be produced in a sufficient number of animal subjects for study and experimentation, rather than relying only on naturally occurring cases as subjects.[43]

6.2. Types of Cloning

There are various types of cloning, but we will explain the two main types here – *therapeutic cloning* and *reproductive cloning.*

6.2.1. Therapeutic Cloning

Efforts are being made to clone cells for therapeutic purposes and are generally referred to by the terms *therapeutic cloning* or *biomedical cloning.* The main purpose and goal of therapeutic cloning is to produce cells, tissues, or organs that would be a perfect match for their recipient, into whom they would be transplanted in order to treat or cure diseases. In therapeutic cloning, the nucleus of an egg cell is removed and replaced by the nucleus of a body cell from the intended recipient. This process is referred to as 'somatic cell nuclear transfer'. Then, the egg is permitted to grow to the embryo stage from which embryonic stem cells - potentially able to develop into any type of cell - may be extracted. This process, in turn, destroys the embryo. The stem cells can then be exposed to cells of the desired type for transplant, develop into the desired cells/tissues/organs, and be used for medical transplantation purposes. In 2002, the first successful transplantation of cloned kidney-like organs in cows was documented. In January 2006, embryonic stem cells were used to successfully treat sickle cell anaemia in mice, correcting the genetic mutation that causes the life-threatening disease.[44]

6.2.2. Reproductive Cloning

Cloning a complete organism or cloning to produce the whole individual is generally referred to as *reproductive cloning.* Reproductive cloning aims to produce

---

42 Roxanne Greitz Miller, "Cloning: A Critical Analysis of Myths and Media", *Science Scope*, (Vol. 29, No. 6, Genetics, MARCH 2006), p. 71.

43 *Ibid.*

44 *Ibid.*, p. 72.

a new individual that is an exact genetic copy of the donor. The first successfully cloned animal produced from an adult cell was Dolly, a sheep born in 1996. Since then, several animals, including cows, mice, goats, rabbits, pigs, a deer, a cat, a horse, a mule, and a few recently extinct or endangered species, have been cloned. Thus far, the greatest achievement in cloning was reached when an Afghan hound dog named Snuppy was born in 2005 in South Korea. This resulted from years of research and 1000 attempts to clone a dog by a research team.[45]

Ian Wilmut and his colleagues at the Roslin Institute in Edinburgh, Scotland, produced a cloned Dolly. Wilmut devised a cloning procedure, patented it, announced it to the press on February 22, 1997. The Roslin team removed cells from the udder of a pregnant ewe, placed them in a culture, and starved them of serum nutrients for a week until the cells became quiescent. Then, they took an unfertilized egg, or oocyte, from another ewe and removed the nucleus. When removing the nucleus with the DNA, they left the remaining cytoplasm intact. The scientists then placed the quiescent cell next to the oocyte, and then they introduced pulses of electric current. The gentle electric shock caused the cells to fuse, and the oocyte cytoplasm accepted the quiescent DNA. Normal cell division took place, and after six days of cell division, the merged embryo was implanted into the uterus of the surrogate ewe and brought through pregnancy to birth on July 5, 1996. The newborn lamb was named Dolly.[46] Dolly lived 6.5 years and died in 2003. It has to be noted here that after more than 200 times attempts, the Roslin could make eight ewes to give birth. Seven of these newborn lambs died shortly after birth. Dolly is the only one to survive.

Though scientists claim that it is possible to clone a human being, there is no such incident mainly due to the opposition – no country in the world allows human cloning. According to Walter Glannon, some of the possible uses of cloning technology in humans include: (a) 'replacing' a loved one who is dying or has died; (b) producing an individual with specially designed physical or cognitive traits; (c) providing a child for an infertile couple, when all other reproductive alternatives have been exhausted; (d) producing a child for a lesbian or gay couple; (e) preventing genetic diseases in people by genetic intervention at the embryonic stage of development and (f) growing tissues or organs for transplantation.[47] Some of these seem to be less controversial, whereas others are greatly controversial.

45 *Ibid.*

46 Ted Peters, *Playing God?*, p. 161.

47 Walter Glannon, "The Ethics of Human Cloning", *Public Affairs Quarterly*, (Vol. 12, No. 3, Jul., 1998), pp. 287-288.

6.3. Myths and Facts about Cloning

There are a number of 'myths' circulating in connection with cloning. The media, especially cinema and science fiction, are spreading these myths. I will present these myths and facts about cloning in the form of a table as follows:-[48]

	Myths	Facts
1	Cloned individuals (such as animals) are grown in a laboratory.	Cloned individuals are gestated within surrogate animals
2	Cloned individuals are the age of the donor when they are produced.	Cloned animals are born as infants, the same as any other animal. Therefore, they are behind the host in age accordingly (e.g., a sheep cloned at age five will have a clone five years younger), there is no technology to increase the growth rate of clones.
3	Cloned human individuals are produced in order to serve as the source of transplant organs for the donor.	Whole-organ cloning is still in experimental stages, but it does not involve growing the organ or tissue within human clones for transfer to the donor humans.
4	Clones have the memory of the host and act the same as the host.	The idea that cells, or in this case, a DNA sample, have the memory of the donor - is widely disputed by scientists. While a clone is genetically identical to the donor, a significant percentage of personality and behaviour is caused by environment and experience and not by one's DNA
5	Cloning extinct prehistoric species is possible.	DNA used in cloning must be extremely well preserved; it is likely that very few, if any, prehistoric sources will be successfully cloned. However, more recently extinct species may be cloned; work is currently underway with a few species that have recently become extinct and had well-preserved DNA available, as well as a closely related species able to serve as the surrogate mother
6	Cloning is a relatively easy process, inexpensive and highly successful.	Cloning is an extremely difficult process; it typically takes hundreds - if not thousands - of attempts before a successful clone (cell or animal) is produced, and the scientific process to do so takes a number of years. Moreover, the process is very expensive.

48 This table is prepared from Roxanne Greitz Miller, "Cloning: A Critical Analysis of Myths and Media", pp.73-74.

6.4. Ethical and Theological Concerns

Cloning raised lots of questions in the mind of people. Many people, Churches, Christian organizations, and the government came out with a strong condemnation of cloning and demanded its ban. Few examples may be cited here –

In 1997 a *Time* magazine poll asked, "Is it against God's will to clone human beings?" 74% answered 'Yes', and 19% 'No.' This reveals the general opinion of people concerning cloning. "Stop Cloning Around" was the title of a *Christianity Today* editorial, and a *Christian Century* editorial said that "cloning a person would violate that person's freedom to establish her own identity." The Christian Life Commission of the Southern Baptist Convention issued a resolution on March 6, 1997, titled "Against Human Cloning." The United Methodist Genetic Science Task Force followed suit on May 9, 1997, recommending that the U.S. President ban the practice before it gets started. 'Don't fool with Mother Nature' and 'You shouldn't play God' are some of the popular slogans against cloning.[49]

In 1997, a press release issued by the Church of Scotland said that cloning human beings would be ethically unacceptable as a matter of principle because it would violate the uniqueness of human life, which God has given to each of us and to no one else. The Roman Catholic Church also opposed cloning for reproduction. Roman Catholic spokespersons repeatedly appeal to the church commitment: human life and hence human dignity begin at the time of egg fertilization. Fertilization should take place in a natural way, not by artificial or technological manipulation. Cloning represents an unnatural method of procreation, and the creation of embryos slated for destruction is akin to abortion.[50]

Gilbert Meilaender, a Lutheran ethicist, voices his concern for protecting the dignity of the child. What a child needs, he presumes, are two loving parents who procreated sexually. He maintains,

> To say that a child ought to spring from the sexual union of a man and a woman (indeed, more precisely but unnecessarily for our purposes here, from the union of husband and wife) is not just to utter a moral rule. It is to see the child not simply as a project at which we aim in order to meet our needs and desires but as a gift. The child replicates neither father nor mother - and that genetic independence is a sign that parental nurture is ordered toward the independence of the next generation. Cloning would alter that mystery of our humanity in incalculable and irreparable ways.[51]

There is no consensus idea among the countries as to how far cloning should be allowed. Many countries dislike both types of cloning – *therapeutic*

---

49 Ted Peters, *Playing God?*, p. 160.

50 See *Ibid.*, pp. 163, 167.

51 Quoted in *Ibid.*, p. 169.

and *reproductive,* whereas some countries allow therapeutic cloning but ban reproductive cloning.

In the UN Sixth (Legal) Committee in the month of November 2014, the U. S. delegation worked vigorously in support of the Costa Rican draft, which was co-sponsored by sixty-three countries. The Costa Rican proposal recommended a complete ban on both reproductive and therapeutic cloning. This was vehemently opposed by Belgium, the United Kingdom, and other states whose competing resolutions proposed banning reproductive cloning but allowing member countries to make their own decisions on therapeutic cloning. The committee remained sharply divided regarding therapeutic cloning.[52]

In the last week of February 2005, the 'United Nations Declaration on Human Cloning' was passed. It contains the following points:[53]

(a) Member States are called upon to prohibit any attempts to create human life through cloning processes and any research intended to achieve that aim;
(b) Member States are called upon to ensure that, in the application of life science, human dignity is respected in all circumstances and, in particular, that women are not exploited;
(c) Member States are also called upon to adopt and implement national legislation to bring in to effect paragraphs (a) and (b) above;
(d) Member States are further called upon to adopt the measures necessary to prohibit applications of genetic engineering techniques that may be contrary to human dignity.

The resolution was passed with 71 members in favour, 35 against, and 43 abstentions. Belgium, which had argued in favour of allowing therapeutic cloning, said it would not be bound by a text approved by such a narrow vote. Richard Gardner, chairman of the working group on stem cell research and cloning at the Royal Society, said that the declaration would have no effect on research into therapeutic cloning in the United Kingdom.[54]

The European Parliament passed a resolution on March 13, 1997, which says that the cloning of human beings cannot under any circumstances be justified or tolerated by any society because it is a serious violation of fundamental human rights and is contrary to the principle of equality of human beings as it permits a eugenic and racist selection of the human race, it offends against human dignity, and it requires experimentation on humans. Each individual has a right to his

---

52 "Efforts to Ban Human Cloning Source", *The American Journal of International Law*, (Vol. 99, No. 1, Jan., 2005), p. 266.

53 *Ibid.*

54 Susan Mayor, "UN Committee Approves Declaration On Human Cloning", *BMJ: British Medical Journal,* (Vol. 330, No. 7490, Mar. 5, 2005), p. 496.

or her own genetic identity, and that human cloning is and must continue to be prohibited.[55]

In 1997 the then Director-General of the World Health Organisation (WHO), Hiroshi Nakajima, in a Press release, said, "WHO considers the use of cloning for the replication of human individuals to be ethically unacceptable as it would violate some of the basic principles which govern medically assisted procreation. These include respect for the dignity of the human being and protection of the security of human genetic material."[56] In line with this statement, in its Fiftieth World Health Assembly, the WHO passed a resolution to affirm that the use of cloning for the replication of human individuals is ethically unacceptable and contrary to human integrity and morality.[57]

Concluding Remarks

The increase in scientific knowledge and advancement enhance tremendous progress and development in the field of biotechnology. With the growth in genetic engineering, scientists are now capable of creating organs and even individuals. Now scientists can produce plants that could produce their own pesticides and weed killers; they have the ability to select the gender of animals by manipulating the cells that produce eggs and sperm; they can transfer genes from one species to another to produce new species. A number of cloned animals were already born. Scientists can make animals of one species gestate and give birth to an animal of a different species! They have genetically modified rice to contain high amounts of vitamin A by transferring daffodil and bacteria genes into the rice's genome. Pigs, implanted with human genes, grow organs for human transplant that will not be rejected by their recipients. The gene responsible for spider web silk has been engineered into goats; genes from a fish are engineered into a tomato to breed a tomato that is resistant to cold, and so on.

With great power comes great responsibility; our great power to manipulate genes - transferring genes from one individual to another, power of germ-line therapy, power of therapeutic and reproductive cloning, etc. – raise several ethical and theological questions. Unless we learn to draw a line, a limit to exercise our scientific power, we may fall into the sin of 'playing God.' Genetic engineering is definitely helpful, but at the same time dangerous unless we use it wisely, keeping in mind the theological and ethical implications.

55 John Harris, "'Goodbye Dolly?' The Ethics of Human Cloning", *Journal of Medical Ethics*, (Vol. 23, No. 6, Dec., 1997), p. 354.

56 Cited in *Ibid.*

57 *Ibid.*

Chapter 10

Violence of Science

That science brings tremendous development to human society and helps human beings in numerous ways is a fact which no one would deny. But, the various developments science has brought to the world are not without problems. Developmental projects like the building of big dams, nuclear power plants, green revolution in agriculture, etc., always have severe negative consequences that threaten the life and very existence of human beings and the environment. Tragedies, accidents and destruction that science and technologies have brought to humans and the environment, which I call here as 'violence of science.' is no longer to be ignored by the students of science and religion. A few such prominent cases where science and technology become the source of violence and tragedy are discussed below.

1. Dams

Jawaharlal Nehru, the first Prime Minister of India, declared as he inaugurated Bhakra Nangal Dam that "Dams are the temple of modern India." It seems he imagined that the construction of large dams would solve many problems of India – It would generate electricity, provide water for irrigation to farmers, supply water to households and industries, provide inland water transport facilities, would reduce and regulate floods, and provide recreational space, fishing and boating, and so on. So, it is no wonder that Nehru praised dams and even asked people who suffered because of them to endure them patiently, for they suffer in the interest of the country. However, the construction of dams is not altogether a positive phenomenon; it has severe negative effects on people and the environment.

According to the survey made by the World Commission on Dams 2000, there are more than 45,000 large dams and half of the world's rivers are obstructed by these dams. By the year 2000, dams generated 19 per cent of the world's electricity supply and irrigated over 30 per cent of the 271 million hectares irrigated worldwide. However, it is reported that dams displaced over 40 million people worldwide apart from the environmental havoc they created.[1] With more than 5000 large dams, India is the third-largest dam builder in the world, preceded by the USA and China.

1.1. Dams for Development

As highlighted above, building dams is considered inevitable if we are thinking of developing a country with its people. The blessing of dams may be reiterated as below:

(a) Dams are built for the generation of electric power, which is much needed for the development of the country. It is almost impossible to live without electric power, and the constructions of nuclear electric power plants have their own demerits, so the building of dams for electricity is inevitable.

(b) Dams are useful for controlling and regulating devastating floods. As it could regulate the river's flow by collecting large water bodies and releasing them as the need arise, dams are the most effective means of flood control.

(c) We need water for so many things. Dams are useful to supply water for domestic and industrial purposes. As most of our Indian rivers are rain-fed rivers, they almost dry up in the summer season. We need a water reservoir that would supply water for drinking and other purposes. Most Indian big and small cities depend on these big dams for water supply.

(d) India is an agricultural country that depends so much on monsoon rains. However, there is hardly enough rain to water agricultural crops during the summer months and even sometimes in rainy seasons. We need a regular water supply in our fields - dams are the source of water for irrigation.

(e) Dams also provide us with suitable recreational places, and they also act as tourist attractions that generate revenue for the government as well as income for the local people. Some dams and reservoirs are used for fishing, boating and sports and other recreational activities.

(f) Dams provide water transportation which is always the cheapest mode of transport. The poorer section of society is believed to have benefited from this.

---

1 Esther Duflo and Rohini Pande, "Dams", *The Quarterly Journal of Economics*, (Vol. 122, No. 2, May, 2007), p. 601.

1.2. Negative Impacts of Dams

Dams, especially large dams, have great potentialities as well as devastating effects. People, land and the environment suffer immensely due to the construction of big dams. Some of the negative impacts of big dams may be highlighted as follows:

1.2.1. Impacts on Human Beings

The construction of large dams results in the inundation of vast land. Vast Inhabited lands were submerged by water that uprooted people from their land, forcing them to leave their villages. The loss is tremendous. For those tribals and Adivasis who are mainly the victims of displacement due to dams, it is not only loss of their village, land and source of income; it is loss of almost everything. Land for the tribal is a holy sanctuary, a temple where they worship God, a sacred place animated by spirits.[2] The importance of land/earth for the tribals is never better illustrated than the belief that divine beings make their dwelling on the land, in the land and beneath the earth. Mountains, rivers, trees, rocks, and forests are all hosting various spirits and divine beings. Among the Tribals, it is widespread to consider God as using nature like hills, rocks and cliffs, rivers, and forests. Many hills are considered sacred as they have supernatural or divine connections with God. Rocks, cliffs, etc., are regarded as divine tutelary objects; they are regarded as God's servants or agents through which God reveals himself. Rivers are considered sacred as they are the channels by which God empowers the people and blesses them.

The land symbolises the unity of all living creatures, including the spirits and the Supreme Being. The misuse of the land implies chaos among creatures. It is like killing one's own mother because the land is considered as a mother. Many tribes in India have myths that say that they were born out of the earth or their forefathers emerged from stones. The land holds not only the clan, village and tribe as one, but it also unites the Supreme Being, spirits, ancestors and creation as one family. So, for the Tribals, the whole universe is a religious universe. Rocks and boulders, trees and rivers are not just empty objects, but religious objects; the voices and songs of animals speak of a religious language.[3]

When dams water inundated the land, rivers, mountains, rocks, forests, and sacred grove, the tribals lost their culture, religion, and most importantly, their God. Because for the tribals, God and land and everything in it are inseparably related. Destruction of land directly corresponds to the destruction of the relationship between humans and God because it is equivalent to the destruction of the immanence of God or rather the destruction of the divine presence. It has to be remembered here that when these peoples are displaced and given another

---

2 K. Thanzauva, *Transforming Theology: A Theological Basis for Social Transformation*, (Bangalore: Asian Trading Corporations, 2002), p. 218.

3 A. Wati Longchar, "Tribal Theology: Nature and Method and Perspective" in *Journal of Tribal study*, (Vol. 5, No. 1, January-June, 2001), pp. 9-10.

settlement, no amount of compensation would really compensate their loss; no money can buy back the things they lost. That is why the Hmar, a tribe in Manipur, when opposing the Tpaimuk dam, expressed that they can live without power, but they cannot live without their land. They say, "For the Hmar people, the land is part of us. We are sustained by what it provides. We can say that we are the land… Our rich culture, tradition, history, language and memory flow in these rivers. We cannot allow the rivers to be disturbed."[4]

Satyajit Singh observes that the rehabilitation of displaced people is one of the least satisfactory aspects of reservoir projects. The government believes in giving cash compensation for land and houses submerged. It does not envisage a plan for compensating the loss of employment or disruption of livelihood other than from ownership of land. The landless labourers, marginal farmers, sharecroppers, tenant cultivators, artisans, cattle grazers, fisherfolk, etc., who depend on the regions natural resources are not compensated for their loss. The relocation plan aims to satisfy only the elite, and that too marginally, who own land. Even this meagre plan is not implemented satisfactorily. There is evidence of widespread corruption and delay in payment of compensation which is usually below the market rate. Where land is provided for relocation, it is of an inferior variety or not productive at all. At times forests are cut to provide resettlement sites. No effort is made to recreate the village as it was in the old site. Neither is any effort made to minimize the loss of essentials of social, cultural and spiritual value.[5]

Cash compensation is paid in a lump sum without any advice to the displaced people regarding proper investment or channelising it towards a new livelihood. Farmers who have learnt nothing but the agriculture technique are thus unable to decide upon a new occupation. Once provided the cash, they fall prey to the consumerist attitude, which made them buy a motorcycle, a bicycle, a transistor, nowadays television, and the like. Cash compensation runs out in no time.[6] Rashmi Shrivastava expresses the need for sensitivity on the part of the government in relocating the affected people; she says,

> There can be no doubt that getting uprooted is not a happy experience. The human problem arising out of displacement of such a populace requires great sensitivity, empathetic approach towards planning and execution of their rehabilitation and resettlement. Their traditional identity and relationship with their social and physical environment suffer as village communities get delinked from traditional sources of

4 Vibha Arora and Ngamjahao Kipgen, "'We can live without power, but we can't live without our land': Indigenous Hmar Oppose the Tipaimukh Dam in Manipur", *Sociological Bulletin*, (Vol. 61, No. 1, January-April 2012), p.113.

5 Satyajit K. Singh, "Evaluating Large Dams in India", *Economic and Political Weekly*, (Vol. 25, No. 11, Mar. 17, 1990), p. 568.

6 *Ibid.*

livelihood, affecting community life and causing social problems. The traditional tribal leaders do not seem to have involved in the process of rehabilitation. Their symbiotic relationship with their habitat's cultural and religious significance needs to be taken into account while recreating harmonious environment at the new relocation site to avoid psychological insecurity.[7]

1.2.2. Impacts on Environment

The environmental impact of large dams is tremendous, and a detailed study is not intended here. I am going to highlight a few of the important impacts of dams on the environment.

(a) Construction of big dam causes a vast area of land to come under water. Trees, herbs, animals, organisms of various types are destroyed instantly. Not only these, archaeological and historical places of great value that are rare with exceptional beauties and values disappear after lying under the reservoir. Animal, birds, livings creatures lost their home. Among these flora and fauna destroyed by dams, rare, endangered and endemic species are often the victim, resulting in the extinction of some animal and plant species.

(b) Rivers are made to flow. Blocking the river and making it accumulate in one place is not natural, and if it is done, disaster befalls nature. When a flowing river is forcibly stopped and accumulated in one place, the chemical content of water, water temperature, dissolved oxygen content, and the physical properties of a reservoir are all changed. As a free-flowing river ecosystem is changed to artificial slack-water reservoir habitat, many aquatic animals and organisms suffer and die as the atmosphere is no longer suitable for living.

(c) The migrating fish are one of the most severely affected species; the wall of the dam blocks their way, which is a great blow to their reproduction as most of these migrating fish come from marine water to rivers for laying eggs. In some cases and with some species, the dam completely separates spawning habitats from rearing habitats.

(d) The dam also traps sediments, which are essential for maintaining physical processes and habitats downstream of the dam. The alteration of a river's flow and sediment transport downstream of a dam often causes the greatest sustained environmental impacts. Life in and around a river evolves and is conditioned on the timing and quantities of river flow. Disrupted and altered water flows can be as severe as completely de-watering river reaches and the life they contain. Even subtle changes

7 Rashmi Shrivastava, "Environmental Stewardship and Sustainable Development: A Study of the Role of Government in Rehabilitation of Persons Affected by Sardar Sarovar Dam in India", *The Indian Journal of Political Science*, (Vol. 68, No. 3, JULY - SEPT., 2007), p. 504.

in the quantity and timing of water flow impact aquatic and riparian life, which can unravel the ecological web of a river system.[8]

(e) Normal passing ways of territorial animals are hindered since the dam works as a barrier resulting in a chaotic life.

It is high time to consider whether we should go ahead with the construction of big dams or not. Should we ask those who are affected to suffer in the interest of the country as our first Prime Minister Nehru did years ago, or should we seek to find suitable alternative solutions to lessen the sufferings of the environment and peoples – the poor, the weak and marginalized who are the worst affected peoples when big dams are constructed. One suggestion that seems to be eco-friendly and pro-peoples is to build several small dams. China has gone far ahead in constructing small dams. According to Satyajit Singh, China has over 88,000 small hydropower stations with an installed capacity of about 8,500 MW. Arguing in favour of small hydel projects, Singh states, "Small hydel schemes require a drop of about ten metres only, they require less capital, there are lower distribution costs, and transmission losses are negligible. Moreover, as production is small, it meets local requirements and plays an important role in the overall development of the people of the rural areas."[9] With its numerous fast-flowing rivers, India has huge potential of building small, less devastating but useful dams. This type of project will cause no big hazard to the people and environment but will be beneficial to both the local poor peoples and the environment.

2. Green Revolution

Green revolution is the name given to the science-based transformation of the so-called 'Third World' agriculture. In India, Punjab was its most celebrated success.[10] The Green Revolution in India began in the 1960s by introducing high-yield crop varieties and applying modern agricultural techniques that increased food production. It began when high-yielding wheat was introduced to India in 1963 by American agronomist Norman Borlaug, who is known as 'the Father of the Green Revolution.' As a result of the Green Revolution, food production increased manifold, which was basically because of the use of high-yielding varieties of seeds coupled with the application of fertilizers, proper irrigation facilities, and modern farming methods. The Green Revolution from the middle of the 1960s changed India's food production drastically, and India became one of the leading food-producing nations in the world.

However, due to the rise in the use of chemical pesticides and fertilisers, there were many negative effects on the soil and the land. Vandana Shiva notes

8 "Environmental Impacts of Dams", in https://www.internationalrivers.org/environmental-impacts-of-dams (06.02.2017).

9 Satyajit K. Singh, "Evaluating Large Dams in India", p. 571.

10 Vandana Shiva, *The Violence of the Green Revolution: Third World Agriculture, Ecology, and Politics*, (London: Zed Books Ltd., 1993), p.19.

that Punjab is neither a land of prosperity nor peace after two decades of the Green Revolution, and it is a region riddled with discontent and violence. Instead of abundance, Punjab has been left with diseased soils, pest-infested crops, waterlogged desert and indebted and discontented farmers.[11] We will look at some of the positive contributions of the Green Revolution and then come to the negative aspects of the Green Revolution.

2.1. Positive Result of Green Revolution

That India became one of the leading food producers in the world because of Green Revolution was a fact that is beyond contestation. An increase in productivity is the primary aim of the Green Revolution, and it was quite successful in this area. The Green Revolution in India resulted in a record grain output of 131 million tons in 1978-79, and this established India as one of the world's biggest agricultural producers. The Green Revolution is credited not only with producing more food but also for creating plenty of jobs both for agricultural workers as well as industrial workers by creating related facilities such as factories and hydroelectric power stations. Thus, many people are benefited from the Green Revolution.

There were four basic elements in the method of the Green Revolution. *Firstly,* to produce more, more land needs to be used; so with Green Revolution, more and more land is under cultivation. The expansion of farming areas gives more production. *Secondly,* the practice of 'double-cropping in the existing farmland' is another important feature of the Green Revolution. Instead of one crop season per year, the decision was made to have two crop seasons per year. Double-cropping is possible due to irrigation and the mechanization of farming. Dams were built for irrigation purposes so that there could be enough water supplies during the dry season. *Thirdly,* the success of the Green Revolution is largely credited to the using of seeds with improved genetics. Apart from seeds imported from outside, the Indian Council for Agricultural Research developed new strains of high yield variety seeds, mainly wheat, rice, millet and corn. *Fourthly,* as these 'high-yielding seeds' go well with fertilizers and pesticides, the green revolution in India is also characterized by the heavy use of fertilizers and pesticides, thereby making some of the unfertile lands into cultivable fields.

2.2. Negative Impact of Green Revolution

The Green Revolution has several negative effects ranging from soil toxicity, huge loss of water to high expenditure, environmental degradation, and poverty to millions of farmers. Some of the prominent negative impacts of the Green Revolution may be given as follows:

11 Vandana Shiva, *The Violence of Green Revolution*, p. 19.

(a) Vandana Shiva observes that the science and technology of the Green Revolution excluded poor regions and poor people as well as sustainable options. As Green Revolution is based on 'building on the best', it has nothing to offer to the poor and a region of scarcity.[12]

(b) The crop and varietal diversity of indigenous agriculture was replaced by a narrow genetic base and monocultures. The focus was on internationally traded grains and a strategy of eliminating mixed and rotational cropping and diverse varieties by varietal simplicity. While the new varieties reduced diversity, they increased resource use of water and chemical inputs such as pesticides and fertilizers.[13]

(c) Green Revolution technology required heavy investments in fertilizers, pesticides, seed, water and energy. Intensive agriculture generated severe ecological destruction, created new kinds of scarcity and vulnerability. Thus, the green revolution introduced new constraints on agriculture by wasting and destroying land, water resources, and crop diversity.[14] According to some investigators, as fertilizers and pesticides are in great demand for the success of the Green Revolution, increases of 100 per cent or more in fertilizers and 600 per cent or more in pesticides have been necessary. Not only must the farmers finance a high input of agricultural chemicals to maintain their yield, but they must learn. Without proper applications in terms of amounts, timing, and synchronization with watering procedures, the chemicals can be rendered useless or possibly detrimental to crop production. These chemicals are a source of major environmental contamination.[15]

(d) The shift from indigenous varieties of seeds to the Green Revolution varieties involved a shift from a farming system controlled by peasants to one controlled by agri-chemical and seed corporations and international agricultural research centres. As the seeds are no longer local products that the farmers generated by themselves, they have to spend a huge amount of money purchasing the costly seeds. Farmers have to take credit from banks to buy them. James Metress observes that the farmer must have ready capital to invest in his operation or be able to obtain sufficient credit. Seed producers and distributors, agricultural chemicals, storage facilities, farm equipment manufacturers, and banking services are as vital as the seeds themselves. This shows that for

12 Vandana Shiva, *The Violence of the Green Revolution*, p. 45.

13 *Ibid.*, pp. 45-46.

14 Vandana Shiva, *The Vandana Shiva Reader*, (Kentucky: The University Press of Kentucky, 2014), p. 31.

15 James F. Metress, "The Myth of the Green Revolution", *Social Science*, (Vol. 51, No. 2, SPRING 1976), p. 92.

the success of the Green Revolution, there are many important things behind it.[16]

(e) The Green Revolution is also dependent on the intensive application of the latest developments in modern agricultural technology, which is not altogether positive. Irrigation is essential to the success of the new seeds. Without irrigation, the 'miracle grains' are no better than the local varieties. Unfortunately, the intensive use of irrigation has many drawbacks. In some areas, irrigation has already led to lowered water tables due to well drilling. Furthermore, increased salinity of the soil and reduced water flow in rivers have resulted in cutbacks in hydroelectric allocations, which affect both pumping for irrigation and the production of chemical fertilizers.[17]

(f) Another significant consequence of the Green Revolution, according to P. N. Junankar, is the increasing inequality in rural India. As the high-yielding varieties of crops require a regular supply of irrigation and fairly large amounts of fertilizers, the advantage has been biased towards the large farms. Since the new varieties are profitable, there would be an increase in capitalist farming, an attempt by landlords to evict their tenants and cultivate the land with hired labour, and an attempt by large farmers to buy out small farmers as far as the land ceiling legislation will allow.[18] So, the Green Revolution favours the rich and capable farmers while marginalizing small farms and the poor peasants.

The agriculturists, economists and agronomists have preached the 'good news' of the Green Revolution as the saviour of agriculture in many countries. It is considered all over the world as the best way of increasing agricultural products. Consequently, Norman Borlaug, who initiated this movement and thus known as 'the father of the Green Revolution' was awarded Noble Peace Prize in 1970. He is credited with saving over a billion people from starvation. However, the increased use of chemical fertilizers, pesticides, irrigations and genetic-based monocultures with high-yielding new seeds are all harmful to the land, rivers and people. While the rich farmers who can afford to swing with the oscillation of the Green Revolution are getting the benefits double and triple fold, the poor and the peasant are left with devastating poverty, debts and frustration.

---

16 *Ibid.*, p. 93.

17 *Ibid.*, p. 92.

18 P. N. Junankar, "Green Revolution and Inequality", *Economic and Political Weekly*, (Vol. 10, No. 13, Mar. 29, 1975), p. A-15.

3. Patenting and Bio-piracy

Another burning issue brought about by modern scientific development is the issue of private ownership of biological resources.

3.1. Patent

A patent is an exclusive right granted by a government to an inventor to manufacture, use, or sell an invention for a certain number of years. It is a grant made by a government that confers upon the creator the sole right to make, use, and sell the invention for a set period of time. Patents on biodiversity imply that corporations who own the patent get exclusive rights to produce and distribute seeds, livestock, and medicine. This establishes monopolies on food and health, makes it illegal for farmers to save and exchange seeds, and prevents decentralized, pluralistic economies for food and medicine production.[19]

The United States patent law grants the holder a twenty-year monopoly in exchange for a detailed disclosure of the invention. It also gives the holder the "right to exclude others from making, using, offering for sale, or selling the invention throughout the United States or importing the invention into the United States."[20] The danger of Patenting for the non-patent holders is that it is a tool of power and control over technology and people because it confers property rights that influence how, where, by whom, and at what cost new technologies are used.[21]

Wangari Maathai notes that patenting living material is also called 'bio-piracy' because corporations get genetic material from the farmers and local communities, constantly developing new combinations and characteristics. This practice is harmful to environment as well as human beings. On the other hand, the old tradition has increased biodiversity, productivity and innovation over the centuries, without using genetic engineering technology or claiming private ownership of such resources, which are considered a common heritage.[22]

3.2. Bio-piracy

Bio-piracy is a situation where indigenous knowledge of nature, originating with indigenous people, is used by others for profit, without permission from and with little or no compensation or recognition to the indigenous people

19 Vandana Shiva, "Vandana Shiva: Controversy over Biopiracy in India & Developing World" in *https://www.organicconsumers.org/news/vandana-shiva-controversy-over-biopiracy-india-developing-world* (11.02.2017).

20 John Reid, "Biopiracy: The Struggle for Traditional Knowledge Rights", *American Indian Law Review,* (Vol. 34, No. 1, 2009-2010), p. 81.

21 Eda Kranakis, "Patents and Power: European Patent-System Integration in the Context of Globalization", *Technology and Culture,* (Vol. 48, No. 4, Oct., 2007), p. 689.

22 Wangari Maathai, "The Link between Patenting of Life Forms, Genetic Engineering & Food Insecurity", *Review of African Political Economy,* (Vol. 25, No. 77, September, 1998), p. 527.

themselves. Developed countries exploit developing countries genetic resources and indigenous communities traditional knowledge in the name of patents on the inventions derived from those genetic resources. This leads to bio-piracy.[23] "Bio-piracy refers to the use of intellectual property systems to legitimize the exclusive ownership and control over biological resources and biological products and processes that have been used over centuries in non-industrialized culture."[24]

John Reid observes:[25]

> Biopiracy occurs when genetic resources and traditional knowledge is taken from biodiverse developing countries without permission. This knowledge is then used to patent related inventions without sharing the resulting commercial profits. The original holder of the knowledge receives no gains from the use and is likely barred from obtaining a patent.
>
> Without formal legal protection for indigenous communities, biopiracy is often a shortcut to massive profits without having to provide fair compensation to the original sources of the information.

3.3. Patent and Bio-piracy Controversy

In recent years there have been several cases of bio-piracy by means of a patent. The following are some of the famous cases:-

Firstly, Eli Lilly was one of the first drug companies to be accused of bio-piracy. Eli Lilly developed two drugs from rosy periwinkle, found on the island-nation of Madagascar. These drugs were *vinblastine* and *vincristine*, which are used to treat Hodgkin's disease and childhood leukaemia, respectively. Eli Lilly earned about $ 100 million from the sale of these drugs, and neither Madagascar nor the indigenous inhabitants obtained any royalties. Moreover, a drug to treat malaria was recently being developed from the same plant, making the case more serious.[26]

Secondly, another famous example is the Neem tree. Neem has been used in India for several purposes, both medicinal and cosmetics, from time immoral. In 1993, a Company in the USA filed a patent application for the use of Neem in the United States and the European Union. The patent application claimed an oil extract of the tree could be used as an insecticide and fungicide.[27] The patent was granted by the European Patent Office to the United States Department of

23 Suvarna Pandey, "Biopiracy Related to Traditional Knowledge & Patenting Issues", in *http://birac.nic.in/webcontent/dib.pdf* (11.02.2017).

24 *http://www.countercurrents.org/bhargava140709.htm* (11.02.2017).

25 John Reid, "Biopiracy: The Struggle for Traditional Knowledge Rights", pp. 79-80.

26 *Ibid.*, p. 88.

27 *Ibid.*, p. 89.

Agriculture and the chemical multinational, W. R. Grace, in 1995. Due to heavy opposition from India, the European Patent Office revoked the patent in 2000. But the revocation was appealed and in March, 2005 Patent Office in Munich, Germany, finally ruled against the revocation plea.[28] However, it was upheld in the United States.

Thirdly, probably the most famous example of bio-piracy is the United States patent issued for turmeric. The Indian Council for Scientific and Industrial Research opposed the patent based on lack of novelty because turmeric has been used in India for years. The patent was eventually revoked, but not until the Indian government spent nearly $6 million fighting the patents for turmeric and neem-based medicines.[29]

Fourthly, the Basmati rice controversy is another important case. Ricetec, a Texan seed breeding company, collected some specimens of the Basmati rice plants from India and Pakistan. Then cross-bred those with some high-yielding varieties and claimed that it had produced a new rice variety. They sold this by the name 'Texmati' and 'Kasmati.' Later on, they dropped those pretensions and sold their rice as 'Basmati' and have patented their product in the US.[30]

Calling bio-piracy through patents as the 'second coming of Columbus,' Vandana Shiva observes:

> Through patents and genetic engineering, new colonies are being carved out. The land, the forests, the rivers, the oceans, and the atmosphere have all been colonized, eroded, and polluted. Capital now has to look for new colonies to invade and exploit for its further accumulation. These new colonies are in my view the interior spaces of the body of women, plants and animals. Resistance to biopiracy is a resistance to the ultimate colonization of life itself – of the future of evolution as well as future of non-Western traditions of relating to and knowing nature. It is a struggle to protect the freedom of diverse species to evolve. It is a struggle to protect the freedom of diverse cultures to evolve. It is a struggle to conserve both culture and biological diversity.[31]

The basic issue in bio-piracy and patenting of biological products is that knowledge and genetic resources belonging to a region, community or country is stolen or privatized. Often justice is violated when the patent holder unfairly profited from the patent without sharing the profit with the original owner.

---

28 *The Hindu*, 9 March, 2005.

29 John Reid, "Biopiracy: The Struggle for Traditional Knowledge Rights", p. 90.

30 Biplab Dasgupta, "Patent Lies and Latent Danger: A Study of the Political Economy of Patent in India", *Economic and Political Weekly*, (Vol. 34, No. 16/17, Apr. 17-30, 1999), p. 985.

31 Vandana Shiva, *Biopiracy: The Plunder of Nature and Knowledge*, (New Delhi: Natraj Publishers, 2012), p. 5.

As the patent holder used the patented material for business and money-making enterprises with large production, depletion of biodiversity leading to the ecological crisis is the inevitable outcome of the whole process. As loss of biodiversity is irreversible, the loss generated by bio-piracy and patenting is tremendous, affecting the indigenous people and the environment at large.

4. Nuclear Power Plants

A nuclear power plant is a type of power station that generates electricity using heat from nuclear reactions which take place within a reactor. The plant also has machines that remove heat from the reactor to operate a steam turbine and generator to make electricity. Electricity made by nuclear power plants is called nuclear power.

As of 2016, India has seven nuclear power plants with 21 nuclear reactors in operation, having an installed capacity of 6780 MW and six more reactors are under construction and are expected to generate an additional 4,300 MW. The USA has the largest number of nuclear power plants, followed by France and Japan. U.S. electricity from nuclear energy in 2015 was 19.5 per cent, with 797.2 billion kilowatt-hours generated. There are 99 operating reactors. Nuclear plants made up the largest percentage of the electricity generated in 2015 in seven states of the United States. As of 2016, 30 countries worldwide are operating 450 nuclear reactors for electricity generation, and 60 new nuclear plants are under construction in 15 countries. Nuclear power plants provided 10.9 per cent of the world's electricity production in 2012. In 2015, 13 countries relied on nuclear energy to supply at least one-quarter of their total electricity.

4.1. Nuclear Power Plant Disasters

Though Nuclear power plants are important for producing electricity, there is much opposition due to their potential danger to the environment and human beings. There have already been three big nuclear power plant disasters in the world that increased fear in people's minds. I will discuss these three accidents in brief.

4.1.1. Three Mile Nuclear Power Plant Accident

The Three Mile Island nuclear power plant was situated on an island near Harrisburg, Pennsylvania, in the USA. It has two pressurized water reactors with a thermal power output of 2700 MW. In 1979 a cooling malfunction caused part of the core to melt in the number 2 reactor leading to its destruction. As a result of this, some radioactive gas was released a couple of days after the accident but fortunately not enough to cause serious harm to the environment or local residents.

Comprehensive investigations and assessments by several well-respected organizations have concluded that in spite of serious damage to the reactor, the actual release had negligible effects on the physical health of individuals or the environment. However, removing the damaged fuel and other clean-up activities at the Three Mile power plant took 14 years with an expenditure of about 1000 million US dollars. Adding the loss of the reactor and some other costs, it is reasonable to assume that the total costs of the number 2 reactor accident lie in the range 5,000-10,000 million US dollars.[32]

Though there was no report of injury or serious health effects from the Three Mile Island Nuclear plant accident, it was enough to warn the government to be more careful in starting a new nuclear power plant and instil fear and anxiety in the minds of the people. Since this incident, there has been much reduction in the building of Nuclear power plants in the USA.

4.1.2. Chernobyl Nuclear Plant Disaster

The most devastating nuclear power plant disaster happened when the Chernobyl power plant, situated 120 km North of Kiev, the capital of Ukraine, exploded on 26 April 1986. The consequent reactor fire, which lasted for 10 days, resulted in an unprecedented release of radioactive material from a nuclear reactor and adverse consequences for the public and the environment.

The large amounts of radioactivity released caused severe ground contamination in the vicinity of the plant. Also, substantial amounts of radioactivity were lifted high up in the atmosphere and transported all over Europe, producing significant local ground contamination depending on wind and precipitation factors. Two members of the Plant staff were killed directly by the explosion. About 134 emergency workers were exposed to doses high enough to result in acute radiation syndrome, causing the death of 28 of these workers in 1986, whereas 19 more died between 1987 and 2004 of various causes that may or may not be directly attributable to radiation exposure. By 2005, close to 7,000 thyroid cancers, some 15 with lethal outcomes, were diagnosed in population groups exposed to intake of radioactive iodine in the first few months after the accident. Most of the thyroid cancers are probably attributable to the accident, and the numbers are expected to increase.[33]

The resulting contamination of the environment with radioactive material caused the evacuation of more than 1,00,000 people from the affected region during 1986 and the relocation after 1986 of another 2,00,000 people from Belarus, the Russian Federation and Ukraine. Some five million people continue to live in areas contaminated by the accident.[34] The Chernobyl accident was very

32 Lars Högberg, "Root Causes and Impacts of Severe Accidents at Large Nuclear Power Plants", *Ambio*, (Vol. 42, No. 3, APRIL 2013), p. 272.

33 *Ibid.*, p. 257.

34 See the 'Forward' to *Environmental Consequences of the Chernobyl Accident and their Remediation: Twenty Years of Experience*: *Report of the Chernobyl Forum Expert Group 'Environment'* (Vienna: International Atomic Energy Agency, 2006).

costly. Total costs over the first 25 years since the Chernobyl accident have been estimated to lie in the range of 2,50,000 - 5,00,000 million US dollars. Much of site clean-up, such as removal and safe storage of the damaged core and other recovery work still remains to be done.[35] Around 8,00,000 ha of agricultural land was removed from service, and timber production halted in around 7,00,000 hectares of forest due to the high uptake of cesium in the wood. Numerous adverse effects were observed mainly in high exposure areas within about 30 km from the reactor. Such effects included:[36]

- Increased mortality of coniferous plants, soil invertebrates, and mammals;
- Reproductive losses in plants and animals;
- Genetic effects in both somatic and germ cells in plants as well as animals.

The tragic accident at Chernobyl has had a chilling effect on the prospects for nuclear power. In response to the accident, major political parties in England, Germany, and Italy have adopted positions against the further development of nuclear power. In Sweden, a commission is considering how soon the country's 12 plants can be closed down. The opposition has also intensified in the United States, where the nuclear power industry is at a standstill: no new plants have been ordered since 1978. More than 100 plants, some of them near completion, have been cancelled.[37]

4.1.3. Fukushima Daiichi Nuclear Power Station Disaster

The Fukushima Daiichi Nuclear Power Station is located on the east coast of Japan, about 250 km to the north of Tokyo. There are six boiling water reactors on the site, all taken into operation during the 1970s. Unit one had a rated thermal power output of 1380 MW, units two - five 2380 MW each, and unit six 3290 MW. On March 11, 2011, a magnitude 9 earthquake occurred with an epicentre in the sea about 200 km to the northwest of the Fukushima Daiichi station. The tsunami generated by the earthquake hit the plant with wave heights that temporarily inundated the station up to about 14 m above sea level, whereas the reactors were designed to withstand wave heights of 5.7 m. As a result, the lower floors of the reactor and turbine buildings were flooded with saltwater, causing failure of the emergency diesel and much other power distribution and

35 Lars Högberg, "Root Causes and Impacts of Severe Accidents at Large Nuclear Power Plants", p. 276.

36 *Ibid.*

37 Barry Commoner, "Nuclear Power for the Third World: Bane or Blessing?", *World Policy Journal,* (Vol. 4, No. 2, Spring, 1987), p. 231.

instrumentation and control equipment as well as causing other damage. The end result was that cooling of the reactor cores in units 1-3 was lost.[38]

Large amounts of hydrogen and fission products were released to the containment. The containments developed leaks due to overpressure and other possible mechanisms. The leakage of hydrogen caused violent explosions destroying the upper parts of the reactor buildings in units 1, 3, and 4. Substantial amounts of fission products escaped into the environment. In combination with rainy weather, the airborne releases of radioactivity caused substantial ground contamination, especially in a plume extending some 40 km to the northwest of the plant. It is estimated that as much as 1800 km sq. of land has contamination levels resulting in a potentially cumulative radiation dose of 5 millisieverts.[39]

About 1,50,000 people have been evacuated from the contaminated zones, mainly within a radius of 20 km from the plant. Evacuation of hospitals faced difficulties, and it has been estimated that some 60 patients died from complications related to the evacuation.[40] Before the accident, 54 reactors supplied about 30% of the electricity in Japan. A number of reactors on the east coast were shut down automatically due to the earthquake. As a safety measure, the Japanese government directed all the nuclear power plants to shut down. None were permitted to restart until they got safety reviews and local political approval. By the beginning of May 2012, all Japanese power reactors were shut down.[41]

In connection with the safety of the nuclear power plants, Lars Hogberg notes that the importance of maintaining high global standards of safety management and safety culture cannot be emphasized enough. All three severe accidents discussed above had their root causes in system deficiencies indicative of poor safety management and poor safety culture in both the nuclear industry and government authorities. Unless there is an effective and perpetual global search for such deficiencies by industry, governments and international organizations, and appropriate actions are taken, the likelihood of a future severe accident somewhere in the world cannot be ruled out in the near future.[42]

4.2. Opposition to Nuclear Power Plants in India

Like many other countries, the construction of nuclear power plants met with strong opposition from the local people as well as social activists in India. The accidents of nuclear power plants around the world increase the fear and anxiety of the people. There are cases where the local people successfully resisted the

38 Lars Högberg, "Root Causes and Impacts of Severe Accidents at Large Nuclear Power Plants", pp. 277-278.

39 *Ibid.*, pp. 278-279.

40 *Ibid.*, p. 281.

41 *Ibid.*, p. 281-282.

42 *Ibid.*, p. 283.

construction of nuclear power plants. There was a proposal to build nuclear power plants at Peringome near Kannur and another in Bhoothathankettu Ernakulam district, Kerala. These two proposals were withdrawn following protests from local residents. It was a government school teacher and the then General Convenor of anti-nuclear power project protests, N. Subramanian, who led the protest movement against the construction of nuclear power plant at Peringome. The project was finally withdrawn in 1991. The protest movement against Kudankulam Nuclear Power Plant is the strongest and the most enduring. In 2011 a Public Interest Litigation (PIL) was filed with the Supreme Court asking for nuclear power development to be delayed until safety concerns were independently assessed. However, in May 2013, the apex court ruled in favour of the construction of the power plant, saying that the court was satisfied with the safety measures and that the nuclear power plant was built considering the larger public interest. Indian churches and Christian organizations, namely, the Church of South India, the Catholic Bishops Conference of India, the National Council of Churches in India, etc., were at the forefront in the protest movement against Kudankulam nuclear power plant. In spite of such strong protests, the government went ahead with the construction and Unit 1 was inaugurated in 2014.

5. Bhopal Gas Tragedy

One of the most destructive violence of science was witnessed in the case of the Bhopal gas tragedy in 1984. On the catastrophic night of Dec 2-3, 1984, a gas leak from the Union Carbide India Limited (UCIL) plant in Bhopal, Madhya Pradesh, resulted in the worst industrial disaster the world has ever witnessed. About 40 tons of highly poisonous methyl isocyanide gas was accidentally released from Union Carbide's Bhopal plant, which spread throughout the city. The result was a nightmare beyond words can explain! On the 3rd December 1984 morning, while it still was dark, the residents of Bhopal awoke to clouds of suffocating gas, and they began running desperately through the dark streets, victims arrived at hospitals, breathless and blind. The lungs, brain, eyes, muscles, as well as gastrointestinal, neurological, reproductive and immune systems of those who survived, were severely affected. When the sun rose, the magnitude of the devastation was revealed! Dead bodies of humans and animals blocked the street, leaves turned black, and a smell of burning chilli peppers lingered in the air!

The Bhopal Gas Tragedy was a catastrophe that has no parallel in the world's industrial history. About 5 lakh people living near the plant were directly affected. About 15,000 people died, according to the official record. However, NGOs claim that more than 35,000 have lost their lives to date, and over 5 lakhs survivors still suffer from various ailments and disabilities, and no one can say that future generations will be free from the continuing effect.

After 17 years, in July 2001, Supreme Court ordered that I-cards be issued to gas victims and permanent cards given to those who need lifelong medical aid. In June 2010, seven ex-employees, including the former UCIL Chairman, Warren Anderson, were convicted of causing death by negligence and sentenced to two years imprisonment. Anderson died on 29 September, 2014.[43]

The investigation conducted by a team from the Union Carbide Corporation (UCC) concluded that a large volume of water had been introduced into the tank of methyl isocyanide. This caused a chemical reaction that forced the pressure release valve to open and allowed the gas to leak. The investigation conducted by UCC also suggests that only an employee with the appropriate skills and knowledge of the site could have tampered with the tank. An independent investigation by the engineering consulting firm Arthur D. Little, Inc. determined that the water could only have been introduced into the tank deliberately since process safety systems - in place and operational - would have prevented water from entering the tank by accident.[44] However, other sources testified that the safety system was badly maintained. It is assumed that it was possible for the water to leak into the tank due to bad maintenance and leaking valves. UCC was reported to have admitted that most of the safety systems were not functioning on the night of the accident.[45]

Concluding Remarks

Science is useful; scientific discoveries and modern technological developments are directed towards developing and advancing human beings. However, science also brings so much violence and devastation to humans, animals and the environment. Scientific developments which are meant for the development of human beings, such as dams, nuclear power plants, green revolution and creation of new species of crops, medicine, etc. have adverse consequences to human beings and the environment where the poor, the helpless animals and multitudes of organisms are the primary victims. The construction of large dams destroyed many biodiversities, plant and animal lives, displaced millions of people without proper rehabilitation, and left countless landless and homeless – cultural and religious loss is incalculable. The green revolution, though increased crop production, left infested land, poorer soil and poorer poor. Nuclear power plants have already created havoc due to their accidental-prone reality, and many developed countries have already stopped building a new nuclear power plants. The advancement in genetic science brought privatization and commercialization

43 See the *Times of India* report in *http://timesofindia.indiatimes.com/event/Bhopal-gas-tragedy/articleshow/55053059.cms* (18.02.2017).

44 "Cause of the Bhopal Tragedy" published by Union Carbide Corporation, in *http://www.bhopal.com/Cause-of-Bhopal-Tragedy* (18.02.2017).

45 Ingrid Eckerman, *The Bhopal Saga: Causes and Consequences of the World's Largest Industrial Disaster,* (Hyderabad: Universities Press, 2005), p. 41.

of scientific developments where a number of such inventions had gone to private ownership through patenting and bio-piracy.

Adequate measures need to be taken to ensure that these scientific developments do not cause unnecessary harm and should not be a threat to any form of life. As the government is primarily responsible for what we call 'violence of science,' it should ensure the safety and rights of the people as well as the environment when such developmental projects are to be initiated. If the welfare of the marginalized people – the poor and the powerless, and the oppressed animals and plants – the primary victims of the violence of science, are taken into consideration when a decision is taken for any developmental work, much of the violence of science would be reduced if not averted.

Chapter 11

Social Studies of Science Feminist and Postcolonial Perspectives

Social Studies of Science is a new discipline in the studies of science. It is basically the study of the various social dimensions of scientific and technological developments. It deals with the relationship between science and society. At the same time, it is a critique of the dominant male-dominated Eurocentric sciences. Social studies of science also examine the effects of science and scientific developments on the marginalized, the poor, and the environment. Here we will look at two important components of social studies of science, such as Feminist critiques of science and the postcolonial studies of science.

1. Feminist Critique of Science

The feminist discussion of science is part of the whole feminist movement, done within the walls of feminist discourse. Scholarship on feminist critique on science emerged in the 1960s and developed slowly and got momentum in the 1970s and, we may say, matured only in the 1980s. However, till today not many feminists are active in the discussion on women and science. I may use the term 'feminists of science' for those engaged in the discussion on science from a feminist perspective. Feminists of science raise various questions concerning the androcentric nature of science and scientific research - issues such as women's access to science studies, job opportunities for women in scientific institutions and laboratories, silence on female contributions in science, androcentric biases in the selection of research areas and topics, exclusion of women in scientific activities, negative portrayal of women in sciences, overall male biases in scientific research, the overstressing of objective research in science, and the like. They seem confident that women's contributions to science studies could bring transformation in science and scientific research.

There are many good things science brought to women: safer and less painful childbirth and lower infant mortality rates, labour-saving conveniences for the home like washing machines, frozen foods, and non-iron fabrics, the exposure and criticism of unhelpful superstitions and prejudices, and so on.[1] However, feminists of science are not happy about science and how scientific development took place, indicating that the relationship between science and women is far from cordial. They feel that modern science is androcentric with all its biases in favour of men neglecting women and women issues. The various levels and forms of the feminist critique of science may be discussed as follows:

1.1. Exclusion of Women in Science

The exclusion of women in science takes the various forms of denying women with scientific talents to access to universities and other scientific learning centres, denying them all but menial research roles with inadequate workspace and equipment and pay, and denying them membership in prestigious scientific academies and professional organizations. More recently, this exclusion has taken subtler forms: restrictive admissions quotas for undergraduate and graduate women students, less financial assistance for women students, little authority or the possibility of advancement, exclusion from the most important scientific meetings and collaborations and information networks, restricted access to prestigious scientific academies, and, of course, such newer phenomena as sexual harassment. These exclusions result in women occupying the lower and middle ranks of science for years yet still have not managed to pierce the upper scientific strata in anything beyond token numbers.[2] Feminist scholars have documented practices of exclusion that effectively discourage women from participating in many scientific disciplines. Many of these works discuss explicit forms of discrimination, such as differentials in pay and employment status, sexual harassment, and the failure of scientific communities to acknowledge important work by women scientists; other studies focus on more subtle barriers, such as gender roles, the masculine cultures of science and technology, and female under-representation in women's interest in pursuing scientific and technical careers. The feminist scholarship also addresses the exclusion of women's concerns in

1 Janet A. Kourany, "Towards a Female-Friendly Philosophy of Science," *PSA: Proceedings of the Biennial Meeting of the Philosophy of Science Association*, (Vol. 1992, Volume Two: Symposia and Invited Papers, 1992), p. 320.

2 *Ibid.*

science and technology and ways in which this might be rectified through new pedagogical, research, and assessment approaches.[3]

Right from the beginning of the movement, the feminists of science have sought means and ways to include more information about women in the science curriculum and make science studies more attractive to women. They try to inject issues like women's health, the history of women in science, etc., into the curriculum of science studies.[4] Despite these obstacles, some women have developed strong interests in and made important contributions to scientific and technological development as professional scientists, technologists and amateur scientists and popularizers of science.[5]

1.2. Discrimination of Women in Science Job

According to the report of a survey done by the National Science Foundation, USA, on 'Women and Minorities in Science and Engineering' in 1986, though women's participation is seen at every level and employment sector, women still face lower salaries at all levels, lower rates of tenure and promotion, and higher rates of unemployment in all fields.[6]

1.3. The Androcentric Biases in Science

Helen Longino, one of the leading feminists of science, points out that feminists, in and out of science, often condemn masculine bias in the sciences from the vantage point of commitment to a value-free science. Androcentric bias, once identified, can then be seen as a violation of the rules, as 'bad" science.[7] Feminists maintain that male bias in science has affected scientific theories and the interpretation of data. One example is the assumption by Darwin and his successors that competition and struggle are the main forces in natural selection. This assumption seems to have reflected the bias of a male-dominated culture, which valued competition. The language about scarcity, competition and the survival of the fittest served the interests of nineteenth-century capitalist societies but produced an incomplete and distorted understanding of nature. Instead, they urge the use of such concepts as plenitude and cooperation. Only much later was it recognized that cooperation and symbiosis are often crucial in evolutionary

3 Emma Whelan, "Politics by Other Means: Feminism and Mainstream Science Studies", *The Canadian Journal of Sociology*, (Vol. 26, No. 4 Autumn, 2001), p. 539.

4 Sue V. Rosser, "Feminist Scholarship in the Sciences: Where Are We Now and When Can We Expect a Theoretical Breakthrough?" in *Feminism and Science*, edited by Nancy Tuana, (Bloomington: Indiana University Press, 1989), p. 4.

5 Emma Whelan, "Politics by Other Means: Feminism and Mainstream Science Studies", p. 539.

6 Sue V. Rosser, "Feminist Scholarship in the Sciences...", p. 5.

7 Helen E. Longino, "Can There Be A Feminist Science?" *Hypatia*, (Vol. 2, No. 3, Feminism & Science, 1, Autumn, 1987), p. 60.

survival. Again, more blatant examples of gender bias are evident in studies on the biological basis of sex differences, such as claims that there is a neurological difference between the sexes in brain lateralization. This accounts for the purportedly innate superiority of males in mathematics and spatial visualization.[8]

According to Emily Martin, the male bias in science is seen in the way science textbooks explain human reproductive organs. Female reproductive physiology is depicted negatively, whereas male reproductive physiology is explained in positive terms. Menstruation is viewed as a failure – as the debris of the uterine lining, the result of necrosis, or dead tissue. Praising the strength of male reproductive physiology, medical textbooks acclaim, instead of taking it as wasteful, the great number of sperms – several hundred million sperms – that the normal human male can manufacture per day. Androcentric reading is seen when these medical textbooks compare between male and female reproductive physiologies – 'Whereas the female sheds only a single gamete each month, the seminiferous tubes produce hundreds of millions of sperms each day.' Emily Martin laments that while these authors marvel at the greatness of male reproductive physiology, none of these texts expresses such intense enthusiasm for any female processes.[9]

Helen Longino holds that a feminist perspective can contribute to objectivity in science by facilitating the critique of auxiliary hypotheses and by suggesting alternative ones. For example, it has often been said that 'man the hunter' was the key to the evolution of the earliest humans from primates and hominids. Male hunting would have encouraged tool use, upright posture, and mental capacities. But did not women use similar capacities as gatherers and nurturers? Longino maintains that science reflects gender-related preferences in the choice of problems, models, and concepts in our culture, which affect the content and practice of science.[10]

Another source of radical critiques is the psychoanalytic theory claiming that a growing girl achieves selfhood by identifying with her mother, while a growing boy does so by separating himself from his mother. This leads men to value separation, independence, objectivity, and power, the attitudes typical of contemporary science while dependence characterized womanhood.[11]

---

8 Ian G. Barbour, *Religion and Science: Historical and Contemporary Issue,* (New York: Harper One, 1997), p. 148.

9 Emily Martin, "The Egg and the Sperm: How Science has Contributed a Romance Based on Stereotypical Male-Female Roles", in *Feminism and Science* edited by Evelyn Fox Keller and Helen E. Longino, (Oxford: Oxford University Press, 1996, p. 104.

10 Helen Longino, "Scientific Objectivity and Feminist Theorizing," *Liberal Education*, (No. 67, 1981), 187-95, cited in Ian Barbour, *Religion and Science*, p. 148.

11 Ian Barbour, *Religion and Science*, p. 149.

1.4. Western Dualism and Male-Science Superiority

The feminists consider the pervasive Western dualism as one of the reasons for women inferior status in science. Some of these dualisms are mind and body, reason and emotion, objectivity and subjectivity, domination and submission, impersonal and personal, power and love. In each case, the first term has been identified in the Western culture as male, the second as female. The problem comes when these first terms are taken to characterize science: mind, reason, objectivity, domination, impersonality, power. Science is stereotypically male, and nature is referred to in female images.[12]

1.5. Lack of Recognition of Women's Contribution in Science

Feminists criticize science as tending to leave women largely invisible in its knowledge and research. It is alleged that medical researchers have often failed to include females in animal studies in basic research as well as in clinical research unless the research centred on controlling the production of children.[13] Evelyn Fox Keller, one of the well-known feminists of science, points out that the predominance of men in science has led to a bias in the choice and definition of problems with which scientists have concerned themselves. She gives a few examples: contraception has not been given enough scientific attention for testing and experimenting, only male rats are used as female rats have a four-day cycle that complicates experiments.[14] This has led to drugs not being adequately tested for women patients before being marketed and a lack of information about the etiology of some diseases in women. Again, research on conditions specific to females has received low priority, and research on diseases that affect both sexes has been primarily concerned with the predisposing factors for the disease in males, while very little research has been concerned with high-risk groups of females.[15]

Sue Rosser argues that though women were always part of science, many times, the works of women scientists have been credited to others, brushed aside and misunderstood, or classified as non-science. She cites a few examples where the works of women scientists have been curtailed in history. Though Catherine Green was the real inventor of the cotton gin, Eli Whitney was credited with the invention of cotton gin as he applied for the patent and was granted it. Rosalind Franklin, who made contributions to understanding the molecular structures of DNA, etc. was not recognized properly but brushed aside and undervalued. The groundbreaking work of Ellen Swallow in water, air and food purity, sanitation and industrial waste disposal was classified as home economics, seemingly because the

12 *Ibid.*

13 Janet A. Kourany, "Towards a Female-Friendly Philosophy of Science", p. 321.

14 Evelyn Fox Keller, "Feminism and Science" in *Feminism and Science* edited by Evelyn Fox Keller and Helen E. Longino, (Oxford: Oxford University Press, 1996), p. 29.

15 Janet A. Kourany, "Towards a Female-Friendly Philosophy of Science", p. 321.

work was done by a woman. The feminists of science call for the rediscovery of the names and contributions of the lost women of science in history. The historians of science have done amazing work on this issue. Few may be cited here – *The Lady Laureates: Women Who Have Won the Nobel Prize* by Olga Opfell (1978); *Women in Mathematics* by Lynn Osen (1974); *Women Scientists in America: Struggles and Strategies to 1940* by Margaret Rossiter (1982) many individual biographies on famous women figures such as, Marie Curie, Rosalind Franklin, Sophie German, Mary Somerville, and Sofia Kovalenskia have also emerged.[16]

Janet Kourany strongly suggests that the philosophy of science should investigate women's contributions to science; works of ordinary women scientists and that of the extraordinary ones should be both investigated. If this is done, the philosophy of science will help both men and women to appreciate women's unique contributions to science and will thereby help people to attain a conception of science that significantly relates to women as well as men. If the task of the philosophy of science is to characterize the logic of science, then one useful thing philosophers of science can do is to characterize the logic of women's science as well as that of men.[17]

1.6. Negative Portrayal of Women in Science

Another charge feminists have levelled against science is that it has portrayed women in negative terms. A favourite theme has been women's intellectual capacity. For example, in the seventeenth century, women's brains were considered too 'cold' and 'soft' to sustain rigorous thought. In the late eighteenth century, the female cranial cavity was considered too small to hold a powerful brain. In the late nineteenth century, the exercise of women's brains was thought to shrivel their ovaries. Today, it is assumed that as women are controlled more by the left brain, they are emotional, inferior in mathematical skills.[18] Several feminists of science have critiqued the studies on brain lateralization, hormones and brain anatomy that attempt to link differences in male and female brains with behavioural traits such as visuo-spatial ability, verbal ability and aggression. They said that there are flaws in the whole process of investigation, and moreover, social factors should also be taken into consideration when one studies the functioning of the human brain.[19]

1.7. A Gender-Free Science

According to Keller and Longino, the early feminists sought a gender-free science by urging greater access for women in science education and research and by rediscovering the stories of women whose outstanding scientific accomplishments

16 Sue V. Rosser, "Feminist Scholarship in the Sciences…", pp. 4-5.

17 Janet A. Kourany, "Towards a Female-Friendly Philosophy of Science", p. 327.

18 *Ibid.*, p. 321.

19 Sue V. Rosser, "Feminist Scholarship in the Sciences…", p. 7.

had been forgotten or repressed. But today, feminists of science go further and have used the concept of gender to analyze the content and practice of science. They started seeking an alternative philosophy of embodied and socially, temporally, and spatially situated knowledge, stressing pluralism, community, and reflexivity.[20] Harding and Hintikka also express the necessity to root out sexist distortions and perversions in epistemology, metaphysics, methodology and the philosophy of science. Scientific knowledge, founded on masculine experience as understood by men, is thus only partial human experience only partially understood and distorted.[21] Evelyn Fox Keller has also criticized the androcentric bias in contemporary biological science and proposed to produce a 'liberated science' that is not a new science but a liberated one that takes into consideration the contribution of women, the need of women and the potential of women.

According to Lisa Stenmark, participants in science and religion are mostly white, male, privileged, and thus they carry the same biases as the pool of scientists whose work they analyze. She is also very critical of feminists who overly focus on categories such as 'white, male privilege' since it ignores the fact that women such as herself are part of the same social location. However, the real problem is not a social location but a commitment to the presuppositions of modernism. Stenmark urges scholars in science and religion to listen to the voices from the margins and turn to postmodernist views of knowledge as the relationship of head, hand and heart, honour the importance of diversity in a community, and adhere to participatory values.[22]

Feminists of science seek a *gender-free science* within the prevailing norms of scientific objectivity as well as beyond it, where the emphasis is given to *subjective research*. Male biases are to be rejected not simply because they are patriarchal but because they are 'bad science.' They can be corrected by a greater commitment to objectivity and openness to evidence. Some feminists, rejecting objectivity itself as a male ideology, go much further in advocating a new '*feminist science*' that emphasizes subjectivity in scientific research. If there can be no value neutrality in science, then one can only seek a differently gendered science, accepting the inevitability of relativism.[23] Sandra Harding calls this 'feminist science' as 'feminist postmodernism,' saying that it is skeptical about the possibility of value neutrality, rationality, and objectivity. She concludes, "It has been and should be moral and political beliefs that direct the development of both the intellectual and

20 Evelyn Fox Keller and Helen E. Longino, "Introduction", *Feminism and Science*, p. 9.

21 Harding and Hintikka, "Introduction", in *Discovering Reality: Feminist Perspectives on Epistemology, Metaphysics, Methodology, and Philosophy of Science* Edited by Sandra Harding and Merrill B. Hintikka (Dordrecht, Holland: D. Reidel Publishing Company, 1983), pp. ix-x.

22 Robert Russell, "Feminist Critiques of Science and Religion", in *http://www.counterbalance.org/rjr/femin1-body.html* (21.02.2017).

23 Ian Barbour, *Religion and Science*, p. 148.

social structures of science. The problematic concepts, theories, methodologies, interpretations of experiments, and uses have been and should be selected with moral and political goals in mind, not merely cognitive ones."[24]

Feminists of science, since the 1960s, have expressed their unhappiness with the ways science and scientific research have been done. They felt that modern science centered on European mentality is androcentric and oppressive to women. They raised issues like discrimination of women in science jobs, male biases in scientific research, lack of recognition of women's scientific works and also a negative portrayal of women in science. These feminists sought a gender-free science where the contribution of women, the need of women and the potential of women are honoured. Feminists of science assumed that subjectivity in scientific research might be an important contribution of women.

2. Postcolonial Studies of Science

Postcolonial studies of science involve two things – It is a critique of colonial-Eurocentric sciences from a postcolonial perspective. It is also a study of science from the so-called 'third world' perspective, or we may use it in a more recent term – the Global South. Modern science was manufactured and developed in Europe, and it has always been Eurocentric in its contents and methods. The postcolonial critique of science primarily addresses the issue of Eurocentrism of science.

2.1. Postcolonial Critique of Eurocentric Science

A postcolonial critique of science is primarily a critique of the influence of modern Western science on other cultures. Postcolonial critiques of science also fit within a broader framework of critiques of Eurocentrism, colonialism, and the construction of the non-West as 'other.' A number of scholars are involved in the postcolonial critique of science, namely, Chinua Achebe, Ashcroft, Griffiths and Tiffin, Homi Bhabha, Ashis Nandy, Ngugi Wa Thiong'O, Edward Said, Gayatri Spivak etc. The postcolonial critiques argue that Western science has resulted in partial and distorted accounts of nature and social relations within science. Modern science and technology has dislocated the so-called third world' societies, destroyed traditional cultures and played havoc with the environment of these nations. It has also replaced a way of knowing, which is multi-dimensional and based on the synthesis, in these societies, with a linear, clinical, inhuman and rationalist mode of thought.[25]

The emergence of postcolonial critique of science shows that the Western sciences are just one kind of culturally specific 'ethnoscience' among the many

24 Sandra Harding, *The Science Question in Feminism,* (Ithaca: Cornell University Press, 1986), p. 250.

25 Annette Greenall Gough, "Beyond Eurocentrism in Science Education Research", in *http://www.aare.edu.au/data/publications/1994/gouga94282.pdf* (03.03.2017).

that have existed. Many of the so-called 'Third World' authors envision and plan to develop fully modern sciences within the cultural legacies and progressive political tendencies of their own societies. It is not that Western sciences are to be reformed for 'Third World' uses; instead, other scientific traditions are to be 'edited' and strengthened to make them more effective for contemporary purposes. These critics are opposed not to science but to the worldwide dominance of only one ethnoscience and of one that inherently legitimates - perhaps even requires - imperialism against other scientific traditions, other cultures, other peoples and nature itself.[26]

The postcolonial critique of science is quite similar to the feminist critique of science. Both approaches criticize pretensions to universality and the dominating, exploitative and imperialist character and consequences of modem sciences. Both are concerned with creating less partial and distorted histories of how modern Western science arose and the earlier traditions it suppressed or stole. They are not anti-science, but they seek to foster better sciences that avoid the sins they criticize. However, the feminist ones are centered in gender analyses and primarily in Western ones. Similarly, the postcolonial ones are centered in analyses of European expansionism.[27]

According to Sandra Harding, Western science, which is simply 'science' for Eurocentrists, is conceptualized as fundamentally pure ideas, not as the culturally determinate institutions and practices that historians, sociologists and anthropologists report. Moreover, the indigenous people encountered are conceptualized as not capable of or as no longer producing any interesting ideas since they are thought to be fundamentally savages, simple peoples, or members of once advanced but now backward societies.[28] The postcolonial studies of science intend to address such a distortion of ideas in the realm of science.

2.2. Features of Postcolonial Studies of Science

Warwick Anderson maintains that a postcolonial perspective suggests fresh ways to study the changing political economies of capitalism and science, the mutual reorganization of the global and the local, the increasing transnational traffic of people, practices, technologies, and contemporary contests over intellectual property. He continues by saying that the postcolonial study of science and technology suggests a means of writing a history of the present, of coming to

26 Sandra Harding, "After Eurocentrism: Challenges for the Philosophy of Science", *PSA: Proceedings of the Biennial Meeting of the Philosophy of Science Association,* (Vol. 1992, Volume Two: Symposia and Invited Papers, 1992), p. 311.

27 *Ibid.*, p. 312.

28 Sandra Harding, "After Eurocentrism: Challenges for the Philosophy of Science", p. 312.

terms with the turbulence and uncertainty of contemporary global flows of knowledge and practice.[29]

According to Anderson, a postcolonial analysis thus offers us a chance of disturbing conventional accounts of so-called global technoscience, revealing and complicating the durable dichotomies produced under colonial regimes, which underpin many of its practices and hegemonic claims. These binaries still operate in terms of global/local, first-world/third-world, Western/Indigenous, modern/traditional, developed/underdeveloped, big-science/small-science, nuclear/non-nuclear, and even theory/practice. Attention to the complex border zone of hybridity and impurity should help us to understand how ideas about difference - racial (white/other), temporal (modern/traditional), class (elite/subaltern) - are enacted and disturbed in the performance of technoscience. A postcolonial perspective might show us how scientific and technological endeavours become sites for fabricating and linking local and global identities, as well as sites for disrupting and challenging the distinctions between global and local.[30]

Postcolonial science studies also address issues such as the rising corporate globalization, increased commodification of science, and further alienation and circulation of intellectual property and attempt to understand and engage with these transnational processes. Sandra Harding suggested relocating the projects of science and science studies that originate in the West on the more accurate historical map created by the new postcolonial studies. As Harding recognized, scholars in India, the Philippines, and elsewhere in what was called 'the Third World', had already been doing this for many years, but their work was virtually unknown in European and North American science studies circles.[31] Harding maintains that postcolonial accounts provide resources for more accurate and comprehensive scientific and technological thought. She asks for employing the category of the postcolonial strategically as a kind of instrument or method of detecting phenomena that otherwise are occluded. She emphasized the importance of local knowledge and called for more dynamic global histories, but her main goal is to strengthen modern scientific objectivity, remedying dysfunctional universality claims.[32]

According to Itty Abraham, for postcolonial science studies, China and India are playing a vital role because they set a sharply defined racial contrast to the West, and also because they are old enough and their civilization is also old enough to claim to offer alternative ways of being and knowing.[33] Abraham

29 Warwick Anderson, "Introduction: Postcolonial Technoscience", *Social Studies of Science*, (Vol. 32, No. 5/6, Oct. - Dec., 2002), pp. 643-644.

30 *Ibid.*, p. 644.

31 Warwick Anderson, "Introduction: Postcolonial Technoscience", p. 645.

32 *Ibid.*, p. 650.

33 Itty Abraham, "The Contradictory Spaces of Postcolonial Techno-Science", *Economic and Political Weekly*, (Vol. 41, No. 3, Jan. 21-27, 2006), p. 213.

highlighted the difficulties Indian scientists are facing as they attempt to play in the scientific playground of the world dominated by the Western world. *Firstly*, Scientists in the Global South always find it difficult to publish their work abroad due to prejudices against them and financial problems to pay the fees associated with the publication of their works abroad. Work being transmitted on an Indian institution's letterhead is often perceived as being of inferior quality and sometimes leads to Indian scientists waiting until they are abroad on a visit before publishing research conducted and completed in India. *Second* is the difficulty of establishing the priority and credibility of research conducted by non-western scientists, even when it is demonstrably important and scientifically rigorous.[34]

Concluding Remarks

Until the middle of the twentieth century, science was considered the house of experimentally proven facts, and the scientific approach was purely objective, value-free, and neutral. The science we talked about was also predominantly, if not exclusively, European science with its androcentric emphasis. The works of philosophers of science and sociologists of science in the 1960s challenged this Eurocentric and patriarchal, dominating science. These philosophers and sociologists of science argued that science was not as objective as it claimed to be; it was rather influenced by society and other factors. Science was considered value-laden and not value-free, which was never neutral. Scientific research was also always influenced by the surroundings – the existing scientific theories and laws as well as the personal predisposition of a scientist. It was in the context of this that social studies of science emerged.

Social studies of science may have several wings, but we discussed here its two important components – Postcolonial studies of science and Feminist critique of science. The postcolonial studies of science centered around two important issues: A critique of colonial-Eurocentric sciences from a postcolonial perspective; and doing science from the perspective of the so-called 'third world.' The feminist critique of science includes discussion on the exclusion and discrimination of women in science, the androcentric biases in science, male-science superiority, lack of recognition of women's contribution in science and the negative portrayal of women in science. To address these issues, the feminists of science propose a 'gender-free science' that will consider the contribution of women, the need of women, and the potential of women.

34 *Ibid.*, p. 214.

Concluding Remarks

Chapter 12

Theological Responses to Science and Religion Dialogue

The interface between science and religion sometimes creates conflict and misunderstanding. We need both science and religion in our daily life, and it is not possible or wise to embrace one and discard the other. As Christians, we cannot escape from the facts of science and scientific developments and new scientific knowledge that seem to have challenged our theological position. It is our responsibility to reflect and respond to science and religion interaction theologically so as to find means and ways to relate these two meaningfully. We need to develop new theological insights that can reduce the traditional conflict between science and religion because we find that our traditional Christian theology is, sometimes, inadequate. Therefore, we need to re-read and reformulate the classical Christian theologies and doctrines in the light of new scientific development and knowledge.

A number of theologies have been suggested that can bridge the gap between science and religion. These theologies are believed to have the potential to integrate science and religion. We will look at some of these here in brief – natural theology, theology of nature, Process theology, and Hefner's theological anthropology, which he calls 'theology of the created co-creators.'

1. Natural Theology

In Natural theology, the existence of God is inferred from the observed facts and experience apart from divine revelation. The source of theology is not scripture or revelation but scientific truth and evidence of design in nature. Famous Christian theologian Thomas Aquinas offers several versions of the cosmological argument for a First cause. He also presented the teleological argument for the orderliness and intelligibility of nature in general and the evidence of design in particular natural phenomena.[1] William Paley argued that coordination of many complex parts for a single function, such as vision in the case of the eye, testifies to an intelligent Designer. In the same vein, F. R. Tennant argued that nature is a unified system of mutually supporting structures that have led to a living organism and have provided the conditions for human moral and intellectual life. In Roman Catholic thought, natural theology is highly appreciated and is considered as a preparation for the truths of revealed theology.[2]

The most active discussions on natural theology in the West occurred during the late medieval period (roughly 1100–1400 C.E.) and the early modern period (1600–1800 C.E.). Natural theology is supported by the recent cosmological principle called 'the *Anthropic Principle*' where it is argued that the universe is 'fine-tuned' for the possibility of life and that there must be an intelligent designer that made the universe suitable for life. John Leslie, a philosopher, defends the *Anthropic Principle* as the evidence of design in nature. A well-known scientist Freedman Dyson says that the universe is an unexpectedly hospitable place for living creatures to make their home in. Though he does not think that the architecture of the universe proves the existence of God, but claims that the architecture of the universe is consistent with the hypothesis that the mind plays an essential role in its functioning. Hugh Montefiore, who was the Bishop of Kingston from 1970 to 1978 and Bishop of Birmingham from 1977 to 1987, also argues that there are many instances of design in the universe, including the Anthropic Principle.[3]

Amidst several oppositions due to its liberal nature, Natural theology has a great appeal in a world of religious pluralism. As it draws it resources from scientific data, this theology has no strict religious boundary.

A more modern view of natural theology suggests that reason does not so much seek to supply proof for the existence of God as to provide a coherent form drawn from the insights of religion to pull together the best of human knowledge from all areas of human activity. In this understanding, natural theology attempts to relate science, history, morality and the arts in an integrating vision of the place of humanity in the universe. This vision, integrating activity of reason, is religious to the extent it refers to an encompassing reality that is transcendent in power and value. Natural theology is thus not a prelude to faith but a general worldview within which faith can have an intelligible place.[4]

---

1 Ian G. Barbour, *Religion and Science: Historical and Contemporary Issues*, (New York; Harper Collins Publisher, 1997), pp. 98-99.

2 *Ibid*., p. 99.

3 *Ibid*., pp. 99-100.

4 "What Is Natural Theology?", in *http://www.giffordlectures.org/overview/natural-theology* (18.03.2017).

2. Theology of Nature

According to Ian Barbour, in the theology of nature, the primary sources of theology lie outside science, but scientific theories may affect the reformulation of certain doctrines, particularly the doctrines of creation and human nature.[5] A theology of nature starts from a religious tradition based on religious experience and historical revelation. But it holds that some traditional doctrines need to be reformulated in the light of current science. Here science and religion are considered to be relatively independent sources of ideas, but with some areas of overlap in their concerns. In particular, the doctrines of creation, providence, and human nature are affected by the findings of science. If religious beliefs are to be in harmony with scientific knowledge, some adjustments or modifications are called for. Our understanding of the general characteristics of nature will affect our models of God's relation to nature. Today, nature is understood to be a dynamic evolutionary process with a long history of emergent novelty, characterized throughout by chance and law. The natural order is ecological, interdependent, and multileveled. These characteristics will modify our representation of the relation of both God and humanity to non-human nature. This will, in turn, affect our attitudes toward nature and will have practical implications for environmental ethics. The problem of evil will also be viewed differently in an evolutionary rather than a static world. So, to reconcile the rift between science and religion, the theology of nature played an important role.[6]

Arthur Peacocke, a biochemist and theologian, suggests a reformulation of traditional beliefs in response to current science. He gives a chance a positive role in the whole process of creation and in the life of creatures. According to him, God creates through the whole process of law and chance, not by intervening in gaps in the process. God creates in and through the processes of the natural world that science unveils. He speaks of chance as God's radar sweeping through the range of possibilities and evoking the diverse potentialities of the natural system.[7] So, for Peacocke, science has disclosed the relationship between God and the natural world. Science, therefore, is an important and integral part of theology.

We also see a clear example of natural theology in the writings of Teilhard de Chardin, a French Jesuit priest. His celebrated book – *The Phenomenon of Man,* according to Barbour, is a synthesis of scientific ideas with religious ideas derived from Christian tradition and experience. In his other work, Teilhard speaks of continuing creation and a God immanent in an incomplete world. Barbour notes, "His vision of the final convergence to an 'Omega Point' is both a speculative

5 Ian G. Barbour, *Religion and Science*, p. 98.

6 *Ibid.*, pp.100-101.

7 *Ibid.*, p. 101.

extrapolation of evolutionary directionality and a distinctive interpretation of Christian eschatology."[8]

Concern for the preservation of our environment is one of the main themes in the theology of nature. It is a critique of classical Christian theology, which overstressed the transcendental aspect of God and its emphasis on the difference between human and non-human. Theology of nature has several components – *Firstly*, **Stewardship of nature** where it is understood that the land belongs to God, who created it and we, human beings, are only trustees or stewards responsible for the welfare of the land. *Secondly*, **Celebration of nature,** which goes beyond stewardship as it implies that nature is valuable in itself. Genesis clearly reveals the goodness of Creation and God's satisfaction in it, the covenant between Noah and God includes all creatures, psalms often refer to the value of nature, Job is overwhelmed by the majesty of natural phenomena. So, creation is to be celebrated. *Thirdly*, **A Sacramental View of Nature** where it is believed that God is present in nature. Nature is seen as the vehicle of God's grace, and it is in and through nature that God reveals Himself. Redemption of God is not seen as to rescue human beings but as the salvation of the whole creation. *Fourthly*, **the Holy Spirit in Nature** that talks about the presence of the Holy Spirit in nature – the Spirit of God was moving over the face of the water.[9]

The theology of nature, therefore, is a viable theology for reconciling science and religion due to its being rooted in the scripture and revelation and its concern for the created order. Moreover, it is not agitated against science but willing to modify some of the traditional doctrines in the light of new scientific discovery. Most importantly, in the theology of nature, science is considered as an important and integral component.

3. Process Theology

Process theology is the product of Process philosophy developed by Alfred North Whitehead (1861–1947). Charles Hartshorne (1897–2000) and John B. Cobb (b. 1925) are the two well-known process theologians. Whereas the term 'process theology' can refer to their philosophies in that they are philosophical theologies, it also refers to the works of a number of theologians, who are primarily Christians, who have employed these philosophies to interpret the doctrines of their religious traditions. According to Whitehead, religion and science are the two strongest general forces that influence us aside from bodily impulses. The basic intellectual problem of modernity is that these two forces - the force of our religious intuitions and the force of our impulse to accurate observation and logical deduction - now

8 *Ibid.*, p. 102.

9 *Ibid.*, pp. 102-103.

seem opposed to each other. The future course of history, Whitehead suggested, depends upon our decision regarding the relations between them.[10]

In trying to bridge the gap between science and religion, Whitehead emphatically rejected a supernatural, omnipotent God, but he maintains that no adequate, coherent system was possible without speaking of God. He described God as an actual entity, consciously responsive to the world and influencing it by means of values. Whitehead holds that God created our world not out of nothing but out of chaos by inducing new forms of order. The nature of the world, being eternal, is as necessary as the nature of God, which means that the relationship between God and the world is necessary, not arbitrary. Rather than being an exception to all metaphysical principles, God is their chief exemplification. God does exert influence in the world - in fact, in every event, from subatomic particles to human experience. But this divine influence is a regular aspect of the normal pattern of causality, not an exception thereto.[11]

According to Barbour, Process philosophy or theology is a promising candidate for building the bridge between science and religion today because it was itself formulated under the influence of both scientific and religious thought. In the Process view, reality, including God, is conceived as a dynamic web of interconnected events. Nature is characterized by change, chance, novelty, and order, incomplete but still coming into being.[12] Process thinkers understand God to be the source of novelty and order. Creation is a long and incomplete process. God is not the unrelated Absolute, the Unmoved Mover, but instead interacts reciprocally with the world, an influence on all events though never the sole cause of any event. Process metaphysics understands every new event to be jointly the product of the entity's past, its own action, and the action of God. Christian process theologians point out that the power of love, as exemplified in the cross, is precisely its ability to evoke a response while respecting the integrity of other beings. They also hold that divine immutability is not a characteristic of the biblical God, who is intimately involved with history.[13]

One of the hallmarks of process theology, as distinct from classical conceptions of God, has been its emphasis on the power of persuasion. Process thinkers like Whitehead, etc., reject the idea of divine omnipotence. God is understood as persuasive rather than controlling. Whitehead maintains that the discovery that God is a persuasive agency, not a coercive agency, is one of

10 David Ray Griffin, "Process philosophy and theology" in *The History of Science and Religion in the Western Tradition: An Encyclopedia*, edited by Gary B. Ferngren (New York: Garland Publishing, 2000), p. 245.

11 David Ray Griffin, "Process philosophy and theology", p. 247.

12 Ian G. Barbour, *Religion and Science*, p. 104.

13 .*Ibid.*

the greatest intellectual discoveries in the history of religion.[14] One of the most important Process theologians, Charles Hartshorne, understands God in two different ways – God as unchanging in purpose and character but changing in experience and relationship.[15]

The interest of process theologians in grounding their work explicitly in biblical scholarship is not so external or arbitrary. Many have adopted process theology precisely because it seems to support aspects of their biblically-shaped convictions rejected as false in most modern thought. For example, the biblical understanding of God as interacting with the world in love found clear and persuasive expression in Whitehead and Hartshorne. There is, then, nothing artificial about correlating this philosophical doctrine with the scripture from which it is derived.[16]

Ian Barbour conceives that these three theologies – Natural theology, theology of nature and process theology all contribute in one way or the other to integrate science and religion and bridge the gap between them. He concludes with the following note:

> I am in basic agreement with the 'Theology of Nature' position, coupled with a cautious use of process philosophy. Too much reliance on science in natural theology can lead to the neglect of the areas of experience that I consider most important religiously. As I see it, the center of the Christian life is an experience of reorientation, the healing of our brokenness in new wholeness, and the expression of a new relationship to God and to the neighbour.[17]

4. Theology of the Created Co-Creator

Philip Hefner (b. 1932), a professor emeritus of systematic theology at the Lutheran School of Theology at Chicago, tried to throw theological light that may be useful to pull science and religion together or much closer. He suggests 'a theology of the created co-creators' as a viable alternative theology that could address the problem of science and religion dialogue.

---

14 Nancy Frankenberry, "Some Problems in Process", *Religious Studies,* (Vol. 17, No. 2; Jun., 1981), p. 179.

15 Ian G. Barbour, *Religion and Science*, p. 104.

16 John B. Cobb, Jr., with David J. Lull and Barry A. Woodbridge, "Introduction: Process Thought and New Testament Exegesis", *Journal of the American Academy of Religion*, (Vol. 47, No. 1, Thematic Issue: New Testament Interpretation from a Process Perspective, Mar., 1979), p. 24.

17 Ian G. Barbour, *Religion and Science*, p. 105.

According to him, human beings are not only God's creation, but they are also co-creators. The core of Hefner's proposal for the theology of 'the created co-creator' is as follows:

> Human beings are God's created co-creators whose purpose is to be the agency, acting in freedom, to birth the future that is most wholesome for the nature that has birthed us – the nature that is not only our own genetic heritage, but also the entire human community and evolutionary and ecological reality in which and to which we belong. Exercising this agency is said to be God's will for humans.[18]

According to William Irons, this is a theological statement, not a scientific one, but it represents scientifically informed theology.[19]

From this core theological proposal arose a theological theory that has three elements:[20]

(i) God creates the human being to be a co-creator in the creation that God has brought into being and for which God has purposed.
(ii) The conditioning matrix that has produced the human being – the evolutionary process – is God's process of bringing into being a creature who represents the creation's zone of a new stage of freedom and who therefore is crucial for the emergence of free creation.
(iii) The freedom that marks the created co-creator and its culture is an instrumentality of God for enabling the creation to participate in the intentional fulfilment of God's purposes.

Again from this core, he draws out nine hypotheses which are as follows:[21]

Hypothesis 1: Integral to *Homo sapiens* and its evolutionary history are certain structures and processes, the requirements for whose functioning may be said to constitute, at least in a tentative way, goals and purposes for human life.

Hypothesis 2: The meaning and purpose of human beings are conceived in terms of their placement within natural processes and their contribution to these same processes.

Hypothesis 3: A concept of 'wholesomeness' is both unavoidable and useful as a criterion governing the behaviour of human beings within their natural ambience, as they consider what their contribution to nature should be.

18 Philip Hefner, *The Human Factor: Evolution, Culture and Religion*, (Minneapolis: Fortress Press, 1993), p. 27.

19 William Irons, "An Evolutionary Critique of the Created Co-creator Concept," *Zygon,* (Vol. 39, No. 4, December 20040), p. 773.

20 Philip Hefner, *The Human Factor*, p. 32.

21 See *Ibid.*, pp, 40- 49.

Hypothesis 4: Nature is the medium through which the world, including human beings, receives knowledge, as well as grace. If God is brought into the discussion, then nature is the medium of divine knowledge and grace.

Hypothesis 5: Freedom characterizes human existence as the condition in which humans have no choice but to act and to construct the narratives and symbols that contextualize that action. Such contextualization provides justification, explanation, and norms for guiding and assessing the action. This condition is intrinsic to the evolutionary process at the level of *Homo sapiens.*

Hypothesis 6: *Homo sapiens* are two-natured creatures, a symbiosis of genes and culture.

Hypothesis 7: Culture is a system of information that humans must construct so as to adequately serve the three tasks of interpreting the world in which humans live, guiding human behaviour, and interfacing with the physic-biogenetic cultural systems that constitute the environment in which we live.

Hypothesis 8: We now live in a condition that may be termed technological civilization. This condition is characterized by the fact that human decision has conditioned virtually all of the planetary physic-biogenetic system so that human decision is the critical factor in the continued functioning of the planets' system.

Hypothesis 9: Myth and ritual are the critical components of the cultural system of information and guidance. They are marked in linguistic form by declarative or imperative discourse, and their concepts are vastly undermined by the data of evidence. In the light of human evolutionary history, these marks were necessary if culture was to serve its evolutionary function.

As we see above, according to Hefner, humans are not only created creators but created co-creators. The *co* - is, in some ways, the most important, intriguing, and troublesome term. It is also the most theological, for it implies not simply that we are creating in and of our own right but that our creative acts are in cooperation with God's creative acts in a way that suggests partnership rather than subordination.[22] However, the implication of co-creator is radically different, for it suggests that we are as much in control or responsible for creation as God is. It implies that there is no blueprint for the future. The future is open, not determined. This sort of openness, radically shaped as it is by human freedom, is as thrilling and terrifying as the rocky course of human history, with considerable significance for thinking through issues of theodicy. The *co* - is suggestive of not only the role of humanity but also the nature of God, for it implies a God who radically values freedom over control. The deceitfully diminutive *co* - is in some ways the most radical and least appreciated part of Hefner's project.[23]

---

22 Gregory R. Peterson, "The Created Co-creator: What it is and is Not", *Zygon*, (Vol. 39, No. 4 December 2004), p. 829.

23 *Ibid.*

Concluding Remarks

Theology is a human product and, as such limited. The various theological insights provided above are not only meant to reduce tension between science and religion but also intended to bring mutual interaction and fruitful enrichment between the two so that there may be a creative and positive interface between science and religion. Natural theology uses scientific discovery as the source of theology, but it stresses too much on science and neglects or pays no attention to religious experience. While depending on religious sources for doing theology, theology of nature takes into consideration scientific theories and does not shy away from reformulating certain doctrines to take along these new scientific discoveries. Though sprung from radical and liberal process philosophy, Christian Process theology tries to strike a balance between religious experience and scientific thought. Hefner's anthropological theology of created co-creators seems to be quite significant for bringing harmony between science and religion. This theology entrusts human beings with high responsibility for the future of creation where they are in partnership with God, who values freedom in shaping and moulding the future.

Bibliography

1. Books

Aleaz, K. P., *Dimensions of Indian Religion: Study, Experience and Interaction*, Calcutta: Punthi Pustak, 1995.

Arthur, W. Brian, *The Nature of Technology: What It Is and How It Evolves*, London: Allen Lane, an Imprint of Penguin Books, 2009.

Artigas, Mariano, et al., *Negotiating Darwin: The Vatican Confronts Evolution 1877-1902,* Baltimore: The Johns Hopkins University Press, 2006.

Barbour, Ian G., *Religion and Science: Historical and Contemporary Issues*, San Francisco: HarperSanFrancisco, 1990.

Barlow, Nora (ed.), *The Autobiography of Charles Darwin, 1809-1882*, London: Collins, 1958.

Barrett, Peter, *Science and Theology since Copernicus: The Search for Understanding*, London: T&T Clark International, 2004.

Barrow, John D. and Frank J. Tipler, *The Anthropic Cosmological Principle*, Oxford: Oxford University Press, 1996, first published in 1986.

Bechtel, William, *Philosophy of Science: An Overview for Cognitive Science*, Hillsdale: Lawrence Erlbaum Associates, 1988.

Bennett, Gaymon, "Introduction" in *Bridging Science and Religion*, edited by Ted Peters and Gaymon Bennett, (Minneapolis: Fortress Press, 2003), pp. 1-15.

Blackwell, Richard J., "Galileo Galilei" in *Science and Religion: A Historical Introduction*, Baltimore: The Johns Hopkins University Press, 2002, pp. 105-115.

Bowler, Peter J., "Evolution" in *The History of Science and Religion in the Western Tradition: An Encyclopedia*, edited by Gary B. Ferngren, (New York: Garland Publishing, Inc., 2000), pp. 524-532.

Breuer, Reinhard, *The Anthropic Principle: Man as the Focal Point of Nature*, translated by Harry Newman and Mark Lowery, New York: Springer Science+Business Medis, 1991.

Brooke, John Hedley, *Science and Religion: Some Historical Perspectives*, Cambridge: Cambridge University Press, 2014, first published in 1991.

Collins, Francis S., *The language of God: A Scientist Presents Evidence for Belief*, New York: Free Press, 2006.

Copan, Paul and William Lane Craig. "Craftsman or Creator? An Examination of the Mormon Doctrine of Creation and a Defense of *Creatio ex nihilo*" in *The New Mormon Challenge: Responding to the Latest Defenses of a Fast-Growing Movement*, ed. Francis J. Beckwith, Carl Mosser, and Paul Owen, Grand Rapids, MI: Zondervan, 2002, pp. 95–152.

Copernicus, Nicholaus, *On the Revolutions of Heavenly Spheres*, Amherst, New York: Prometheus, 1995.

Craig, Willian Lane, *The Kalām Cosmological Argument*, Eugene, Oregon: Wipf and Stock Publishers, 1979.

Darwin, Charles, *On the Origin of Species by Means of Natural Selection*, London: Elec Book, 1997; first published in 1859.

Davies, P. C. W., *The Accidental Universe*, Cambridge: Cambridge University Press, 1982.

Deane-Drummond, Celia, "Biotechnology: A New Challenge to Theology and Ethics," in Christopher Southgate, et al., *God, Humanity and the Cosmos: S Companion to the Science-Religion Debate*, (London: T&T Clark International, 2005), pp. 361-390.

Dembski, W. A ., "Signs of intelligence: A primer on the Discernment of Intelligent Design," in W. A. Dembski & J. M. Kusiner (Eds.), *Signs of intelligence: Understanding intelligent design*, Grand Rapids, Michigan: Brazos Press, 2001.

________, *Intelligent Design: The Bridge between Science and Theology*, Downers Grove, Illinois: InterVarsity Press, 1999.

Dessain, Charles Stephan and Thomas Gornall (ed.), *The Letters and Diaries of John Henry Newman*, Vol. 24 (Oxford: Claredon Press), 1973.

DeWitt, Richard, "Philosophy of Science," *Philosophies of Science: A Guide*, edited by Fritz Allhoff, Chichester: Wiley-Blackwell, 2007, pp. 9-36.

Dodd, C. H., *The Bible and the Greeks*, London: Hodder &. Stoughton, 1935.

Dowe, Phil, *Galileo, Darwin and Hawking: The Interplay of Science, Reason, and Religion*, Grand Rapids: William B. Eerdmans Publishing Company, 2005.

Eckerman, Ingrid, *The Bhopal Saga: Causes and Consequences of the World's Largest Industrial Disaster*, Hyderabad: Universities Press, 2005.

Efron, Noah J., "Myth 9: That Christianity Gave Birth to Modern Science," in *Galileo Goes to Jail and Other Myths about Science and Religion*, edited by Ronald L. Numbers, Cambridge: Harvard University Press, 2009, pp. 79-89.

Enginer, Asghar Ali, *Rational Approach to Islam*, New Delhi: Gyn Publishing House, 2001.

Environmental Consequences of the Chernobyl Accident and their Remediation: Twenty Years of Experience: Report of the Chernobyl Forum Expert Group 'Environment', Vienna: International Atomic Energy Agency, 2006.

Francis, Keith A., *Charles Darwin and the Origin of Species*, London: Greenwood Press, 2007.

Fritjof Capra, *The Tao of Physics: An Exploration of the Parallel between Modern Physics and Eastern Mysticism*, London: HarperCollins Publishers, 1982, first published in 1975.

Gingerich, Owen, "The Copernican Revolution," in *Science and Religion: A Historical Introduction*, Baltimore: The Johna Hopkins University Press, 2002, pp. 95-107.

Grant, Edward, *Science and Religion 400 BC-AD 1550: From Aristotle to Copernicus*, Westport, Connecticut: Greenwood Press, 2004.

Griffin, David Ray, "Process Philosophy and Theology" in *The History of Science and Religion in the Western Tradition: An Encyclopedia*, edited by Gary B. Ferngren (New York: Garland Publishing, 2000), pp. 245-251.

Harding, Sandra, *The Science Question in Feminism,* Ithaca: Cornell University Press, 1986.

Harding, Sandra and Hintikka, "Introduction," in *Discovering Reality: Feminist Perspectives on Epistemology, Metaphysics, Methodology, and Philosophy of Science* Edited by Sandra Harding and Merrill B. Hintikka, Dordrecht, Holland: D. Reidel Publishing Company, 1983.

Harrison, Peter, *The Bible, Protestantism, and the Rise of Natural Science*, Cambridge: Cambridge University Press, 1998.

Hawking, Stephen, *A Brief History of Time: From the Big Bang to Black Holes*, (London: Bantam Books), 1989.

Hefner, Philip, *The Human Factor: Evolution, Culture and Religion*, Minneapolis: Fortress Press, 1993.

Henry, Sarojini, *The Encounter of Faith and Science in Inter-Religious Dialogue*, (Pune/Delhi; Indian Institute of Science and Religion/ISPCK, 2005.

Herschel, John Frederick William, *A Preliminary Discourse on the Study of Natural Philosophy*, Cambridge: Cambridge University Press, first published in 1830, digitally printed version in 2009.

Isaacson, Walter, *Einstein: His Life and Universe, London: Pocket Books, 2008.*

Jastrow, Robert, *God and the Astronomers*, New York: W. W. Norton & Company, 1978.

Karahalil, Bensu, "Pharmacogenomics and Toxicogenomics in Food Chemicals," in, *Advances in Food Biochemistry* edited by Fatih Yildiz, London: CRC Press, Taylor & Francis Group, 2010.

Keller, Evelyn Fox, "Feminism and Science" in *Feminism and Science* edited by Evelyn Fox Keller and Helen E. Longino, (Oxford: Oxford University Press, 1996, pp. 28-40.

Kuhn, Thomas S, *The Structure of Scientific Revolutions*, Chicago: The University of Chicago Press, 1996, first published in 1962.

Lee, Thomas F., *The Human Genome Project: Cracking the Genetic Code of Life*, New York: Springer Science + Business Media, LLC, 1991.

Losee, John, *A Historical Introduction to the Philosophy of Science*, Oxford: Oxford University Press, 2001, first published in 1972.

Lott, Eric J., "Approching a Religious Tradition," in *Religious Traditions of India*, edited by P. S. Daniel, David C. Scott and G. R. Singh, (Delhi: ISPCK, 2002), pp. 1-44.

Martin, Emily, "The Egg and the Sperm: How Science has Contributed a Romance Based on Stereotypical Male-Female Roles", in *Feminism and Science* edited by Evelyn Fox Keller and Helen E. Longino, Oxford: Oxford University Press, 1996.

McConnell, Craig Sean, "Twentieth-Century Cosmologies" in Cary B. Ferngren (ed), *Science and Religion: A Historical Introduction*, Baltimore: The Johns Hopkins University Press, 2002.

McGrath, Alister E., *Science and Religion: An Introduction*, Oxford: Blackwell Publishers, 1999.

McMullin, Ernan, *The Church and Galileo*, Notre Dame: University of Notre Dame Press, 2005.

Miller, Roxanne Greitz, "Cloning: A Critical Analysis of Myths and Media," *Science Scope*, Vol. 29, No. 6, Genetics (MARCH 2006), pp. 70-74.

Morvillo, Nancy, *Science and Religion: Understanding the Issues*, Chichester, West Sussex: Willey-Blackwell, 2010.

N. A. *Exploring the Nature of Science*, n.a. The American Association for the Advancement of Science (AAAS), Project 2061, 2010.

Nanda, Meera, *Prophets Facing Backward: Postmodernism, Science, and Hindu Nationalism*, Delhi: Permanent Black, 2006.

Neffe, Jürgen, *Einstein: A Biography, Trans. by Shelley Frisch, New York: Farra, Straus and Giroux*, 2007.

Northcott, Michael S., "Sociological Approaches" in *Approaches to the Study of Religion*, Edited by Peter Connolly, New York: Continuum, 2001.

Pandikattu, Kuruvilla, "Science-Religion Dialogue in India; Creative Challenges and Enabling Possibilities," *Together Towards Tomorrow: Interfacing Science and Religion in India*, edited by Kuruvilla Pandikattu, Pune: Association of Science, Society and Religion, 2006, pp. 407-425.

Peters, Ted, "Theology and Natural Science", in *The Modern Theologians: An Introduction to Christian Theology in the Twentieth Century*, Cambridge, Massachusetts: Blackwell Publishers Inc., 1997, pp. 649-666.

__________, *Playing God? Genetic Determinism and Human Freedom*, New York: Routledge, 2003.

Phy-Olsen, Allene, *Evolution, Creationism, and Intelligent Design*, Santa Barbara, California: Greenwood, 2010.

Polanyi, Michael, *Personal Knowledge: Towards a Post-Critical Philosophy*, London: Routledge & Kegan Paul Ltd., p. 1962, first published in 1958.

Poole, Verla, *A Comprehensive Introduction to Intelligent Design: Concepts and Theory*, Delhi: White Word Publications, 2012.

Post, Stephen G., "Introduction" in *Encyclopedia of Ethics*, Stephen G. Post (ed.), (New York: Macmillan Reference USA).

Ratzsch, Del, *Philosophy of Science: The Natural Sciences in Christian Perspective*, (Downers Grove: Intervarsity Press), 1986.

Rosser, Sue V., "Feminist Scholarship in the Sciences: Where Are We Now and When Can We Expect a Theoretical Breakthrough?" in *Feminism and Science*, edited by Nancy Tuana, (Bloomington. Indiana University Press, 1089), pp. 3-11.

Russell, Colin A., *Cross-Currents: Interactions between Science and Faiths*, Grand Rapids: William B. Eerdmans Publishing Company, 1985.

___________, *The Conflict of Science and Religion*, Cary B. Ferngren (ed), *Science and Religion: A Historical Introduction*, Baltimore: The Johns Hopkins University Press, 2002.

Salmon, Merrilee H., *et al., Introduction to the Philosophy of Science*, Englewood Cliffs: Prentice Hall, 1992.

Samir Okasha, *Philosophy of Science: A Very Short Introduction*, Oxford: Oxford University, 2002.

Science for All Americans: Project 2061, n.a. American Association for the Advancement of Science, New York: Oxford University Press, 1990.

Shank, Michael H., "Myth 2: That the Medieval Christian Church Supressed the Growth of Science," *Galileo Goes to jail and Other Myths about Science and*

Religion, edited by Ronald L. Numbers, (Ed.) Cambridge: Harvard University Press, 2009, pp. 19-27.

Shastri, Shakuntala Rao, *Aspirations From a Fresh World*, Bombay: Bharatiya Vidya Bhavan, 1954.

Shiva, Vandana, *Biopiracy: The Plunder of Nature and Knowledge*, New Delhi: Natraj Publishers, 2012.

__________, *The Vandana Shiva Reader*, Kentucky: The University Press of Kentucky, 2014.

__________, *The Violence of the Green Revolution: Third World Agriculture, Ecology, and Politics*, London: Zed Books Ltd., 1993.

Smart, Ninian, *The Religious Experience of Mankind*, Second Edition, (New York: Charles Scribner's Sons, 1973.

Smethurst, Arthur F., *Modern Science and Christian Beliefs*, New York: Abingdon Press, 1955.

Southgate, Christopher, *et.al*, *God, Humanity and the Cosmos: A Companion to the Science-Religion Debate*, London: T&T Clark International, 2005.

Steinbock, Bonnie (ed.), *The Oxford Handbook of Bioethics*, Oxford: Oxford University Press, 2007.

Stenmark, Mikael, *How to Relate Science and Religion: Multidimensional Model*, (Grand Rapids, Michigan: William B. Eerdmans Publishing Company), 2004.

_________, "Ways of Relating Science and Religion" *The Cambridge Companion to Science and Religion* edited by Peter Harrison, Cambridge: Cambridge University Press 2010.

_________, "Religion and Science", in Chad Meister and Paul Copan (eds.), *The Routledge Companion to Philosophy of Religion,* London: Routledge, 2007, pp. 692–701.

Thanzauva, K., *Transforming Theology: A Theological Basis for Social Transformation*, Bangalore: Asian Trading Corporations, 2002.

Voelkel, James R., *Johannes Kepler and the New Astronomy*, Oxford: Oxford University Press, 1999.

Watt, W. Mongtgomery, *Islamic Surveys I: Islamic Philosophy and Theology,* Edinburgh: Edinburgh University Press, 1962.

Wilson, David B., "The Historiography of Science and Religion," Cary B. Ferngren (ed), *Science and Religion: A Historical Introduction*, Baltimore: The Johns Hopkins University Press, 2002.

2. Journals

Abetti, Giorgio, "Galileo Galilei as a Pioneer in the Physical Sciences," *Publications of the Astronomical Society of the Pacific*, Vol. 43, No. 252, April, 1931, pp. 130-144.

Abraham, Itty, "The Contradictory Spaces of Postcolonial Techno-Science," *Economic and Political Weekly*, Vol. 41, No. 3, Jan. 21-27, 2006, pp. 210-217.

Alters, Brian J., "What Is Creationism?" in *The American Biology Teacher*, Vol. 61, No. 2 Feb., 1999, pp. 103-106.

Anderson, Warwick, "Introduction: Postcolonial Technoscience," *Social Studies of Science*, Vol. 32, No. 5/6, Oct. - Dec., 2002, pp. 643-658.

Arora, Vibha and Ngamjahao Kipgen, "'We Can Live Without Power, But We Can't Live Without Our Land': Indigenous Hmar Opposethe Tipaimukh Dam in Manipur", *Sociological Bulletin*, Vol. 61, No. 1, January-April 2012, pp. 109-128.

Ball, W. W. Rouse, "Newton", *The Mathematical Gazette*, Vol. 7, No. 112, July, 1914, pp. 349-360.

Begelman, Mitchell C., "Evidence for Black Holes," *Science, New Series*, Vol. 300, No. 5627, Jun. 20, 2003, pp. 1898-1903.

Ben-David, Joseph and Teresa A. Sullivan, "Sociology of Science," *Annual Review of Sociology*, Vol. 1, 975, pp. 203-222.

Bernat, James L., "The Human Genome Project Raises Ethical Issues that Deserve Our Attention", *Neurology Today*, Volume 1 - Issue 2, July/August 2001, p. 4.

Binder, Amy, "Gathering Intelligence on Intelligent Design: Where Did It Come From, Where Is It Going, and How Should Progressives Manage It?" *American Journal of Education*, Vol. 113, No. 4, August 2007, pp. 549-576.

Brill, Winston J., "Genetic Engineering Applied to Agriculture: Opportunities and Concerns", *American Journal of Agricultural Economics*, Vol. 68, No. 5, Proceedings Issue, Dec., 1986, pp. 1081-1087.

Brügmann, B., *et al.*, "Black Holes", *Proceedings of the National Academy of Sciences of the United States of America*, Vol. 98, No. 19, Sept. 11, 2001, pp. 10525-10526.

Bube, Richard H., "Man Come of Age: Bonhoeffer's Response to the God-of-the-gaps," *Journal of the Evangelical Theological Society*, 14 No. 4 Fall 1971, pp. 203-220.

Clark, Brett, *et al.*, "The Critique of Intelligent Design: Epicurus, Marx, Darwin, and Freud and the Materialist Defense of Science," *Theory and Society*, Vol. 36, No. 6, Dec., 2007, pp. 515-546.

Clayton, Philip, "Philosophy of Science: What one Needs to Know," *Zygon*, Vol. 32, No. 1, March 1997, pp. 95-104.

Cobb Jr., John B., with David J. Lull and Barry A. Woodbridge, "Introduction: Process Thought and New Testament Exegesis", *Journal of the American Academy of Religion*, Vol. 47, No. 1, Thematic Issue: New Testament Interpretation from a Process Perspective, Mar., 1979, pp. 21-30.

Cohen, I. Bernard, "The Progress of Science: The Heritage of Galileo," *The Scientific Monthly*, Vol. 54, No. 3, March, 1942, pp. 282-287.

Collins, John, "Science and the Denial of the Miraculous: Another Look" in *Perspectives in Religious Studies*, Vol. 10, No. 1983, pp. 123-133.

Collins, Randall and Sal Restivo, "Development, Diversity, and Conflict in the Sociology of Science," *The Sociological Quarterly*, Vol. 24, No. 2, Spring, 1983, pp. 185-200.

Colp Jr., Ralph, "Charles Darwin: Man and Scientist," *The Centennial Review*, Vol. 27, No. 2 Spring 1983, pp. 96-110.

Commoner, Barry, "Nuclear Power for the Third World: Bane or Blessing?", *World Policy Journal*, Vol. 4, No. 2, Spring, 1987, pp. 231-255.

Cowen, R., "New View of Quasars Sheds Light on Origin," *Science News*, Vol. 150, No. 21, Nov. 23, 1996, p. 326.

Craig, William Lane, "Professor Mackie and the Kalām Cosmological Argument," *Religious Studies*, Vol. 20, No. 3, Sept., 1984, pp. 367-375.

Cruz, Eduardo Rodrigues da, "It Started with Galileo," *Zygon*, Vol. 42, No. 3, September 2007, pp. 591-594.

CTNS Team, "Bridging the Gap between Science and Religion - The Center for Theology and the Natural Sciences," *Revista Portuguesa de Filosofia*, T. 57, Fasc. 3, Jul. - Sep., 2001.

Daley, George O., *et al.*, "The ISSCR Guidelines for Human Embryonic Stem Cell Research," *Science, New Series*, Vol. 315, No. 5812, Feb. 2, 2007, pp. 603-604.

Daly, Gabriel, "Science, Religion and Scientism," *The Irish Review*, Summer, 2001, No. 27, pp. 48-54.

Dasgupta, Biplab, "Patent Lies and Latent Danger: A Study of the Political Economy of Patent in India," *Economic and Political Weekly*, Vol. 34, No. 16/17, Apr. 17-30, 1999, pp. 979-993.

Davis, Bernard D., "Evolution, Human Diversity, and Society," *Zygon*, Vol. 11, No. 2, June 1976, pp. 80-95.

Duflo, Esther and Rohini Pande, "Dams," *The Quarterly Journal of Economics*, Vol. 122, No. 2, May, 2007, pp. 601-646.

Dwyer, Christopher, "Two Paths to Truth: A Tribute to Georges Lemaitre" *New Blackfriars*, Vol. 75, No. 886, October 1994, pp. 472-476.

Eastwell, Peter, "The Nature of Science," in *The Science Education Review*, Vol. 1, No. 2, 2002, pp. 43-48.

Eflin, See Juli T., Stuart Glennan and George Reisch, "The Nature of Science: A Perspective from the Philosophy of Science" in *Journal of Research in Science Teaching*, Vol. 36, No. 1, 1999, pp.

Egerton, Frank N., "A History of the Ecological Sciences, Part 18: John Ray and His associates Francis Willughby and William Derham," in *Bulletin of the Ecological Society of America*, Vol. 86, No. 4, October 2005, pp. 301-313.

Eldridge, John J., "Massive Stars in Their Death Throes," *Philosophical Transactions: Mathematical, Physical and Engineering Sciences*, Vol. 366, No. 1884, Astronomy, Dec. 13, 2008, pp. 4441-4452.

Feyerabend, Paul, "Imre Lakatos," *The British Journal for the Philosophy of Science*, Vol. 26, No. 1, Mar., 1975, pp. 1-18.

Filippenko, Alexei V., "Black Holes in the Milky Way Galaxy", *Proceedings of the National Academy of Sciences of the United States of America*, Vol. 96, No. 18, Aug. 31, 1999, pp. 9993-9994.

Finochiaro, Maurice A., "The Church and Galileo," *The Catholic Historical Review*, Volume 94, Number 2, April 2008, pp. 260-282.

Førland, Tor Egil, "Acts of God? Miracles and Scientific Explanation," *History and Theory*, Vol. 47, No. 4, Dec., 2008, pp. 483-494.

Forman, Paul, "Einstein and Newton: Two Legacies," *The Wilson Quarterly*, Vol. 3, No. 1, Winter, 1979, pp. 107-114.

Frankenberry, Nancy, "Some Problems in Process," *Religious Studies*, Vol. 17, No. 2; Jun., 1981, pp. 179-197.

Girela, Luis, "Many Simple Universes or Only a Very Complex One?" *Theoria: An International Journal for Theory, History and Foundations of Science*, Vol. 14, No. 2(35), Mayo 1999, pp. 331-337.

Glannon, Walter, "The Ethics of Human Cloning", *Public Affairs Quarterly*, Vol. 12, No. 3, Jul., 1998, pp. 287-305.

Greene, John C., "Darwin and Religion," in *Proceedings of the American Philosophical Society*, Vol. 103, No. 5, Oct. 15, 1959, pp. 716-725.

Gulick, Addison, "Charles Darwin, the Man," *The Scientific Monthly*, Vol. 15, No. 2 Aug., 1922, pp. 132-143.

Harding, Sandra, "After Eurocentrism: Challenges for the Philosophy of Science," *PSA: Proceedings of the Biennial Meeting of the Philosophy of Science Association*, Vol. 1992, Volume Two: Symposia and Invited Papers, 1992, pp. 311-319.

Harris, John, "'Goodbye Dolly?' The Ethics of Human Cloning," *Journal of Medical Ethics*, Vol. 23, No. 6, Dec., 1997, pp. 353-360.

Harrison, Peter, "Miracles, Early Modern Science, and Rational Religion," *Church History*, Vol. 75, No. 3, Sep., 2006, pp. 493-510.

Healey, Richard A., "How Many Worlds?" *Noûs*, Vol. 18, No. 4, Special Issue on the Foundations of Quantum Mechanics, Nov., 1984, pp. 591-616.

Hoffleit, Dorrit, "Observations of Supernovae," *Proceedings of the American Philosophical Society*, Vol. 81, No. 2, Jun. 30, 1939, pp. 265-276.

Högberg, Lars, "Root Causes and Impacts of Severe Accidents at Large Nuclear Power Plants," *Ambio*, Vol. 42, No. 3, April 2013, pp. 267-284.

Horst, Steven, "Miracles and Two Accounts of Scientific Laws," *Zygon,* Vol. 49, No. 2 June 2014, pp. 323-347.

Hoyle, Fred, "The Steady-state Universe," *Scientific American*, Vol. 195, No. 3, September 1956, pp. 157-169.

Hubble, Edwin, "Supernovae", *Publications of the Astronomical Society of the Pacific,* Vol. 53, No. 313, June 1941, pp. 141-154.

Hutchinson, Ian H., "The Genius and Faith of Faraday and Maxwell," *The New Atlantis*, Winter 2014, No. 41, Winter 2014, pp. 81-99.

International Stem Cell Forum Ethics Working Party, "Ethics Issues in Stem Cell Research" in *Science, New Series*, Vol. 312, No. 5772, Apr. 21, 2006, pp. 366-367.

Irons, William, "An Evolutionary Critique of the Created Co-Creator Concept," *Zygon,* Vol. 39, No. 4, December 2004, pp. 773-790.

Jayawardhana, Ray, "Could Quasars Get Their Shine From Stars?" *Science, New Series*, Vol. 259, No. 5102, Mar. 19, 1993, pp. 1692-1693.

Jefferson Davis, John, "The Design Argument, Cosmic 'Fine Tuning,' and the Anthropic Principle," *International Journal for Philosophy of Religion*, Vol. 22, No. 3, 1987, pp. 139-150.

Jerome, Lawrence E., "On Astrology and Modern Science: A Critical Analysis," *Leonardo*, Vol. 6, No. 2 Spring, 1973, pp. 187-188

Junankar, P. N., "Green Revolution and Inequality", *Economic and Political Weekly*, Vol. 10, No. 13, Mar. 29, 1975, pp. A15-A18.

Karimi, Mirsaeid Mousam, "Adolf Grünbaum on the Steady-State Theory and Creatio Continua of Matter Out of Nothing", *Zygon*, Vol. 46, No. 4, December 2011, pp. 857-871.

Kennel, Maxwell, "Technology in the Life of Faith: A Call for Critical Engagement," in *Vision*, Fall 2015, pp. 6-11.

Kourany, Janet A., "Towards a Female-Friendly Philosophy of Science", *PSA: Proceedings of the Biennial Meeting of the Philosophy of Science Association,* Vol. 1992, Volume Two: Symposia and Invited Papers, 1992, pp. 320-332.

Kozhamthadam, Job, "Science and Religion; Contenders or Collaborators?" in *Vidyajoyti Journal of Theological Reflection*, Vol. 52, No. 8, August, 1988, pp. 362-377.

_________, "The Genome Revolution and the Science-Religion Dialogue", in *Vidyajoti Journal of Theological Reflection*, Vol. 65, No. 2, February, 2001, pp. 85-97.

_________, "Towards a Constructive Interaction between Science and Religion," in *Vidyajoti Journal of Theological Reflection*, Vol. 54, No. 12, December, 1990, pp. 617-627.

Kranakis, Eda, "Patents and Power: European Patent-System Integration in the Context of Globalization," *Technology and Culture*, Vol. 48, No. 4, Oct., 2007, pp. 689-728.

Kulkarni, Harshada, *et al.*, "Genetic Engineering: A Question of Ethics," *Research Journal of Chemical and Environmental Sciences*, Vol. 2, No. 6, December 2014, pp. 1-5.

Kutrovátz, Gábor, "Lakatos' Philosophical Work in Hungary," *Studies in East European Thought,* Vol. 60, No. 1/2, *The Sociological Tradition of Hungarian Philosophy*, Jun., 2008, pp. 113-133.

Larmer, Robert A., "Miracles, Physicalism, and the Laws of Nature," *Religious Studies* 44, 2008, pp. 149-159.

Longino, Helen E., "Can There Be A Feminist Science?" *Hypatia*, Vol. 2, No. 3, Feminism & Science, 1, Autumn, 1987, pp. 51-64.

Lovering, Joseph, "Michael Faraday," *Scientific American*, Vol. 22, No. 4, January 22, 1870, pp.

Maathai, Wangari, "The Link between Patenting of Life Forms, Genetic Engineering & Food Insecurity", *Review of African Political Economy*, Vol. 25, No. 77, September, 1998, pp. 526-528.

Mayor, Susan, "UN Committee Approves Declaration On Human Cloning," *BMJ: British Medical Journal,* Vol. 330, No. 7490, Mar. 5, 2005, p. 496.

McCann, Joseph, "Georges Lemaître: The Priest Who Proposed the 'Big Bang,'" *Studies: An Irish Quarterly Review*, Vol. 105, No. 418, Summer 2016, pp. 212-224.

Missner, Marshall, "Why Einstein Became Famous in America", *Social Studies of Science*, Vol. 15, No. 2, May, 1985, pp. 267-291.

Montmorency, J. E. G. de, "Francis Bacon," *Journal of the Society of Comparative Legislation*, 1905, Vol. 6, No. 2, 1905, pp. 263-283.

Mudur, Ganapati, "India To Tighten Rules On Human Embryonic Stem Cells Research," in *BMJ: British Medical Journal,* Vol. 323, No. 7312, Sep. 8, 2001, p. 530.

Mullins, Phil, "The Spectrum of Meaning - Polanyian Perspectives on Science and Religion" in *Zygon*, Vol. 17, No. 1, March 1982, pp. 2-8.

Murphy, Raymond, "The Sociological Construction of Science without Nature", *Sociology*, Vol. 28, No. 4, November 1994, pp. 957-974.

Murray, Thomas H., "Ethical Issues in Genetic Engineering," *Social Research*, Vol. 52, No. 3, Bioethics, Autumn 1985, pp. 471-489.

Murrell, John N. and Nicole Grobert, "The Centenary of Einstein's First Scientific Paper, " *Notes and Records of the Royal Society of London*, Vol. 56, No. 1, Jan., 2002, pp. 89-94.

N. A., "Charles Darwin," *Proceedings of the American Academy of Arts and Sciences,* Vol. 17, June, 1881- June, 1882, pp. 449-458.

N. A. "Efforts to Ban Human Cloning Source," *The American Journal of International Law*, Vol. 99, No. 1, Jan., 2005, p. 266.

N. A. "Michael Faraday" *Scientific American*, Vol. 17, No. 11, September 14, 1867, p. 169

N. A. "Michael Faraday" *Scientific American*, Vol. 22, No. 15, April 9, 1870, p. 240.

N. A., *The Mathematics Teacher*, Vol. 24, No. 2, February, 1931, pp. 118-120.

Narayan, Ramesh and Eliot Quátaert, "Black Hole Accretion," *Science, New Series*, Vol. 307, No. 5706, Jan. 7, 2005, pp. 77-80.

Norman, Keith, "Ex Nihilo: The Development of the Doctrines of God and Creation in Early Christianity," *Brigham Young University Studies* , Vol. 17, No. 3, Spring 1977, pp. 291-318.

Numbers, Ronald L., "Clarifying Creationism: Five Common Myths," *History and Philosophy of the Life Sciences*, Vol. 33, No. 1, 2011, pp. 129-139.

O'Connor, Karen and Gregg Ivers, "Creationism, Evolution and the Courts," *PS: Political Science and Politics,* Vol. 21, No. 1, Winter, 1988, pp. 10-17.

Ostler, Blake T., "Out of Nothing: A History of Creation *ex Nihilo* in Early Christian Thought," *Review of Books on the Book of Mormon 1989–2011*: Vol. 17, No. 2, 2005, Article 9, pp. 253–320.

Peterson, Gregory R., "The Created Co-creator: What it is and is Not," *Zygon*, Vol. 39, No. 4 December 2004, pp. 827-840.

_________, "The Intelligent-design Movement: Science or Ideology?" *Zygon*, Vol. 37, No. 1 March 2002, pp. 7-23.

Pingali, Prabhu L., "Green Revolution: Impacts, Limits, and the Path Ahead," *Proceedings of the National Academy of Sciences of the United States of America,* Vol. 109, No. 31, July 31, 2012, pp. 12302-12308.

Rabino, Isaac, "Ethical Debates in Genetic Engineering: U.S. Scientists' Attitudes on Patenting, Germ-Line Research, Food Labeling, and Agri-Biotech Issues," *Politics and the Life Sciences*, Vol. 17, No. 2, Sep., 1998, pp. 147-163.

Reid, John, "Biopiracy: The Struggle for Traditional Knowledge Rights", *American Indian Law Review*, Vol. 34, No. 1, 2009-2010, pp. 77-98.

Schekman, Randy and Marjorie Shultz, "Stem Cell Research: Opportunities and Challenges," in *Bulletin of the American Academy of Arts and Sciences*, Vol. 59, No. 3, Spring, 2006, pp. 17-22.

Shanks, Niall and Keith Green, "Intelligent Design in Theological Perspective," *Synthese*, Vol. 178, No. 2, January 2011, pp. 307-330.

Shrivastava, Rashmi, "Environmental Stewardship and Sustainable Development: A Study of the Role of Government in Rehabilitation of Persons Affected by Sardar Sarovar Dam in India," *The Indian Journal of Political Science*, Vol. 68, No. 3, July - Sept., 2007, pp. 497-508.

Singh, Satyajit K., "Evaluating Large Dams in India", *Economic and Political Weekly*, Vol. 25, No. 11, Mar. 17, 1990, pp. 561-574.

Slocum, Frederick, "Galileo Galilei, A Pioneer in Scientific Research", *Publications of the Astronomical Society of the Pacific*, Vol. XLV, No. 265, June, 1933, pp. 103-126.

Stenmark, Mikael, "What Is Scientism?" in *Religious Studies*, Vol. 33, No. 1, 1997, pp. 15-32.

Stevenson, Ian P., "John Ray and his Contributions to Plant and Animal Classification," *Journal of the History of Medicine and Allied Sciences*, Vol. 2, No. 2, Spring 1947), pp. 250-261.

Storr, Anthony, "Isaac Newton," *British Medical Journal (Clinical Research Edition)*, Vol. 291, No. 6511, Dec. 21 - 28, 1985, pp. 1779-1784.

Team, CTNS, "Bridging the Gap between Science and Religion - The Center for Theology and the Natural Sciences", *Revista Portuguesa de Filosofia*, T. 57, Fasc. 3, Jul. - Sep., 2001, pp. 603-606.

Thagard, Paul R., "Why Astrology is a Pseudoscience," *PSA: Proceedings of the Biennial Meeting of the Philosophy of Science Association*, Vol. 1978, Volume One: Contributed Papers, 1978, pp.

Theckedath, K. K., "Dialectics and Cosmology: The Big Bang and the Steady State Theories" *Social Scientist*, Vol. 31, No. ½, Jan. - Feb., 2003, pp. 57-84.

Thorndike, Lynn, "The True Place of Astrology in the History of Science," *Isis* , Sep., 1955, Vol. 46, No. 3 (Sep., 1955), pp.

Turek Józef, "Georges Lemaître's Contribution to the Formation of the Dynamic View of the Universe," *Roczniki Filozoficzne/Annales de Philosophie/Annals of Philosophy*, Vol. 33, No. 3, 1985, pp. 59-74.

Voegelin, Eric, "The Origins of Scientism," Social Research, Vol. 15, No. 4, December 1948, pp. 462-494.

Wallace, R. W., "Charles Darwin," *The Journal of Education*, Vol. 69, No. 6, February 11, 1909, pp. 146-147.

Weinberger, Lael, "Reading the Bible and Understanding Nature," in *Journal of Creation*, Vol. 23, No. 3, 2009.

Weisskopf, Victor F., "What Is Quantum Mechanics?" in *Bulletin of the American Academy of Arts and Sciences,* Vol. 33, No. 7, Apr., 1980, pp. 27-39.

Whelan, Emma, "Politics by Other Means: Feminism and Mainstream Science Studies," *The Canadian Journal of Sociology*, Vol. 26, No. 4 Autumn, 2001, pp. 535-581.

Whitney, Barry, "Divine Persuasion and the Anthropic Argument," *The Personalist Forum*, Vol. 14, No. 2, The Hartshorne Centennial Conference, Fall 1998, pp. 141-169.

Wilson, Patrick A., "What Is the Explanandum of the Anthropic Principle?" *American Philosophical Quarterly,* Vol. 28, No. 2, Apr., 1991, pp. 167-173.

Wiser, James L., "Michael Polanyi: Personal Knowledge and the Promise of Autonomy", *Political Theory*, Vol. 2, No. 1 Feb., 1974, pp. 77-87.

Worrall, John, "Nachruf auf Imre Lakatos: Imre Lakatos (1922-1974): Philosopher of Mathematics and Philosopher of Science," *Zeitschrift für allgemeine Wissenschaftstheorie/Journal for General Philosophy of Science*, Vol. 5, No. 2, 1974, pp. 211-217.

Wright, Peter, "Astrology and Science in Seventeenth-Century England," *Social Studies of Science*, Vol. 5, No. 4, Nov., 1975, pp. 399-422.

Young, Frances, 'Creatio Ex Nihilo': A Context for the Emergence of the Christian Doctrine of Creation," *Scottish Journal of Theology*, Vol. 44, 1991, pp. 139-151.

3. Electronic Sources

"Cause of the Bhopal Tragedy" published by Union Carbide Corporation, in *http://www.bhopal.com/Cause-of-Bhopal-Tragedy* (18.02.2017).

"Environmental Impacts of Dams," in *https://www.internationalrivers.org/environmental-impacts-of-dams* (06.02.2017).

"Things a Computer Scientist Rarely Talks About" in *https://www-cs-faculty.stanford.edu/~knuth/things.html* (04.01.2021).

"What are Stem Cells?" in *http://www.medicalnewstoday.com/info/stem_cell* (accessed 30.01.2017).

"What Is Natural Theology?," in *http://www.giffordlectures.org/overview/natural-theology* (18.03.2017).

Bourdieu, Pierre, "The Specificity of the Scientific Field and the Social Conditions of the Progress of Reason," in *http://www.soc.ucsb.edu/ct/pages/JWM/Syllabi/Bourdieu/SpecificitySField.pdf* (accessed 06.01.2017).

Carroll, Marion L. and Jay Ciaffa, "The Human Genome Project: A Scientific and Ethical Overview," in *http://www.actionbioscience.org/genomics/carroll_ciaffa.html* (accessed 03.02.2017).

Christine V. McLelland, *The Nature of Science and Scientific Method*, in *https://www.geosociety.org/documents/gsa/geoteachers/NatureScience.pdf* (23.11.2020).

Clark, Josh, "Do parallel universes really exist?" in *http://science.howstuffworks.com/science-vs-myth/everyday-myths/parallel-universe2.htm* (accessed 07.01.2017).

Denny Casey, "The Nature of Science," Virgina Science Standard Institute, 2012, in *https://docplayer.net/14447685-The-nature-of-science-2012-virginia-science-standards-institute-denny-casey-ph-d.html* (17.12.2020).

Donald DeMarco, "The Christian roots of modern science" in *http://www.churchinhistory.org/pages/science/roots-of-science.htm* (12.12.2020).

Exploring the Nature of Science, The American Association for the Advancement of Science (AAAS), Project 2061, 2010), in *https://www.aaas.org/sites/default/files/reports/p2061-guide-science.pdf* (05.112.2010).

Francis Collins in an interview with him, in *https://www.pbs.org/wgbh/questionofgod/voices/collins.html.*

Francis Collins in an interview with him, in *https://www.pbs.org/wgbh/questionofgod/voices/collins.html* (20.05.2021).

Gary A. Anderson, "*Creatio Ex Nihilo* and the Bible" in *https://www3.nd.edu/~undpress/excerpts/P03385-ex.pdf* (10.09.2021).

Gough, Annette Greenall, "Beyond Eurocentrism in Science Education Research," in *http://www.aare.edu.au/data/publications/1994/gouga94282.pdf* (03.03.2017).

Harrison, Peter, "Christianity and the Rise of Western Science," in *https://www.abc.net.au/religion/christianity-and-the-rise-of-western-science/10100570* (16.12.2020).

http://www.bbc.co.uk/history/historic_figures/bacon_francis.shtml (26.12.2020).

http://www.bbc.co.uk/history/historic_figures/bacon_francis.shtml (27.01.2021).

http://www.bbc.co.uk/history/historic_figures/faraday_michael.shtml (01.01.2021).

http://www.bbc.co.uk/history/historic_figures/faraday_michael.shtml (01.01.2021).

http://www.bbc.co.uk/history/historic_figures/faraday_michael.shtml (01.01.2021).

http://www.bbc.co.uk/history/historic_figures/faraday_michael.shtml (01.01.2021).

http://www.bioethics.org.au/Resources/Resource%20Topics/Bioethics%20Default.html (29.01.2017).

http://www.biography.com/people/albert-einstein-9285408 (22.11.2016).

http://www.biography.com/people/albert-einstein-9285408 (22.11.2016).

http://www.biography.com/people/nicolaus-copernicus-9256984 (14.05.2016).

http://www.countercurrents.org/bhargava140709.htm (11.02.2017).

http://www.nobelprize.org/nobel_prizes/physics/laureates/1921/einstein-bio.html (22.11.2016).

https://aaac.cs.nott.ac.uk/members/138/rosalind-wright-picard (12.01.2021).

https://physicstoday.scitation.org/doi/full/10.1063/1.1480790 (04.01.2021).

https://sites.google.com/a/jdv.edu.in/assr-india/ (22.11.2016)

https://ucmp.berkeley.edu/history/ray.html (01.01.2021).

https://ucmp.berkeley.edu/history/ray.html (01.01.2021).

https://web.archive.org/web/20131029233107/http://www.consejoculturalmundial.org/winners-science-sirjohnhoughton.php (03.01.2021).

https://www.amnh.org/learn-teach/curriculum-collections/cosmic-horizons-book/georges-lemaitre-big-bang (02.01.2021).

https://www.britannica.com/biography/Albert-Einstein (accessed 23.11.2016).

https://www.britannica.com/biography/Francis-Bacon-Viscount-Saint-Alban/Thought-and-writings (27.01.2021).

https://www.britannica.com/biography/Francis-Collins (11.01.2021).

https://www.britannica.com/biography/Georges-Lemaitre (02.01.2021).

https://www.britannica.com/biography/John-Ray-English-naturalist (01.01.2021).

https://www.britannica.com/biography/John-Ray-English-naturalist (01.01.2021).

https://www.britannica.com/biography/Michael-Faraday (01.01..2021).

https://www.britannica.com/biography/William-D-Phillips (04.01.2021).

https://www.britannica.com/science/quantum-mechanics-physics (accessed 29.11.2016).

https://www.christianitytoday.com/history/people/scholarsandscientists/francis-bacon.html (27.01.2021).

https://www.encyclopedia.com/earth-and-environment/ecology-and-environmentalism/environmental-studies/modern-synthesis (19.04.2021).

https://www.encyclopedia.com/earth-and-environment/ecology-and-environmentalism/environmental-studies/modern-synthesis (19.04.2021).

https://www.encyclopedia.com/education/encyclopedias-almanacs-transcripts-and-maps/god-gaps (17.08.2021).

https://www.ewtn.com/library/HUMANITY/EVOLUTN.TXT (accessed 26.11.2016).

https://www.genome.gov/12011238/an-overview-of-the-human-genome-project/ (30.01.2017).

https://www.mediatheque.lindau-nobel.org/laureates/phillips (04.01.2021).

https://www.newworldencyclopedia.org/entry/Neo-Darwinism (19.04.2021).

https://www.nobelprize.org/prizes/physics/1997/phillips/biographical/ (11.01.2021).

https://www.nobelprize.org/prizes/physics/1997/phillips/biographical/ (11.01.2021).

https://www.pbs.org/moyers/faithandreason/portraits_houghton.html (03.01.2021).

https://www.pbs.org/moyers/faithandreason/portraits_houghton.html (03.01.2021).

https://www.pbs.org/moyers/faithandreason/portraits_houghton.html (03.01.2021).

https://www.pbs.org/wgbh/questionofgod/voices/collins.html (11.01.2021).

https://www.pbs.org/wgbh/questionofgod/voices/collins.html (11.01.2021).

https://www.quantumdiaries.org/2011/09/16/there-is-no-need-for-god-as-a-hypothesis/ (17.08.2021).

https://www.sciencemag.org/news/2020/05/francis-collins-honored-work-bridge-science-and-religion (11.01.2021).

James Hannam, "Science Owes Much to Both Christianity and the Middle Ages" in *http://blogs.nature.com/soapboxscience/2011/05/18/science-owes-much-to-both-christianity-and-the-middle-ages* (13.11.202).

Jonathan Sarfati, "The Biblical Roots of Modern Science" *in https://creation.com/biblical-roots-of-modern-science* (13.11.202).

Jonathan Sarfati, "The Biblical Roots of Modern Science" in *https://creation.com/biblical-roots-of-modern-science* (13.11.202).

Marcelo Gleiser, "What The 'God of The Gaps' Teaches Us About Science?" in *https://www.npr.org/sections/13.7/2015/04/08/398227737/what-the-god-of-the-gaps-teaches-us-about-science* (17.08.2021).

Megan Brandsrud, "Living Lutheran: I'm a Lutheran: Don Knuth" in *https://www.livinglutheran.org/2018/12/im-a-lutheran-don-knuth/* (04.01.2021).

Megan Brandsrud, "Living Lutheran: I'm a Lutheran: Don Knuth" in *https://www.livinglutheran.org/2018/12/im-a-lutheran-don-knuth/* (04.01.2021).

Megan Brandsrud, "Living Lutheran: I'm a Lutheran: Don Knuth" in *https://www.livinglutheran.org/2018/12/im-a-lutheran-don-knuth/* (03.04.2021)

Morris, Henry M., "The Tenets of Creationism" in *https://www.icr.org/article/168/* - An Official Website of Institute for Creation Research (19.12.2016).

N. A. "What is Genetic Engineering and How Does it Work" in *http://agbiosafety.unl.edu/basic_genetics.shtml* (23.01.2017).

Pandey, Suvarna, "Biopiracy Related to Traditional Knowledge & Patenting Issues", in *http://birac.nic.in/webcontent/dib.pdf* (11.02.2017).

Peters, Ted, "Science and Religion," in *http://www.academicroom.com/topics/science-and-religion* (accessed 27.7.2015).

Russell, Robert, "Feminist Critiques of Science and Religion," in *http://www.counterbalance.org/rjr/femin1-body.html* (21.02.2017).

Shiva, Vandana, "Vandana Shiva: Controversy over Biopiracy in India & Developing World" in *https://www.organicconsumers.org/news/vandana-shiva-controversy-over-biopiracy-india-developing-world* (11.02.2017).

Shuttleworth, Martyn, "Philosophy of Science History" *in https://explorable.com/history-of-the-philosophy-of-science* (18.09.2014).

Stenson, James B., "Evolution: a Catholic Perspective," in Jason Chu, "Parallel Universes and the Many-Worlds Theory," in *http://www.universetoday.com/113900/parallel-universes-and-the-many-worlds-theory/* (07.01.2017).

Susan D'Agostino, "The Computer Scientist Who Can't Stop Telling Stories" in *https://www.quantamagazine.org/computer-scientist-donald-knuth-cant-stop-telling-stories-20200416/* (3.01.2021).

The Atlantic, April 29, 1998 in *https://www.theatlantic.com/past/docs/unbound/digicult/dc980429.htm* (12.01.2021).

The Search for God: Can Science Help? Written by John Houghton and reviewed by Ernest Lucas in *https://www.thegospelcoalition.org/themelios/review/the-search-for-god-can-science-help/* (03.01.2021).

Times of India report in *http://timesofindia.indiatimes.com/event/Bhopal-gas-tragedy/articleshow/55053059.cms* (18.02.2017).

Wofford, Taylor, "Pope Francis's Remarks on Evolution are not that Controversial Among Roman Catholics," in *http://www.newsweek.com/pope-franciss-remarks-evolution-are-not-controversial-among-roman-catholics-281115* (accessed 25.11.2016).

Index

A

D

H

I

J

K

L

M

N

O

P

Q

R

X

Y

Z